The Nature of God

In *The Nature of God*, Gerard Hughes takes five central attributes – Existence, Simplicity, Omniscience, Omnipotence and Goodness – which are central to the classical concept of God.

Incorporating texts by Aquinas, Ockham, Molina, Descartes, Hume and Kant, he aims to give the reader first-hand acquaintance with these classical writers, and then to discuss their arguments in the light of contemporary debate. While the focus of *The Nature of God* is on the philosophy of religion, Hughes widens his scope to consider its implications in epistemology, metaphysics and moral philosophy. The issues he considers include necessity and possibility, the relation of logic to epistemology and the connections between causation and moral philosophy.

This book will interest senior undergraduates with some grounding in philosophy as well as those working in the philosophy of religion. Hughes' non-technical approach will encourage and enable the reader to understand the arguments about the nature of God from both a classical and a contemporary perspective.

Gerard J. Hughes is a Jesuit, and Chair of the Department of Philosophy at Heythrop College, University of London.

The Problems of Philosophy

Founding editor: Ted Honderich
Editors: Tim Crane and Jonathan Wolff, *University College London*

This series addresses the central problems of philosophy. Each book gives a fresh account of a particular philosophical theme by offering two perspectives on the subject: the historical context and the author's own distinctive and original contribution.

The books are written to be accessible to students of philosophy and related disciplines, while taking the debate to a new level.

* Also available in paperback

The Nature of God

Gerard J. Hughes

London and New York

First published 1995
by Routledge
11 New Fetter Lane, London EC4P 4EE

Simultaneously published in the USA and Canada
by Routledge
29 West 35th Street, New York, NY 10001

© 1995 Gerard J. Hughes

Typeset in Times by
Ponting–Green Publishing Services, Chesham, Bucks
Printed and bound in Great Britain by
TJ Press (Padstow) Ltd, Padstow, Cornwall

British Library Cataloguing in Publication Data
A catalogue record for this book is available from the British Library

Library of Congress Cataloging in Publication Data
Hughes, Gerard J.
The nature of God / Gerard J. Hughes.
p.   cm. – (Problems of philosophy)
Includes bibliographical references and index.
1. God–Attributes.   2. God–Attributes–History of doctrines.
I. Title.   II. Series: Problems of philosophy (Routledge (Firm))
BT130.H76   1994
212–dc20   94–32685

ISBN 0–415–10950–7 (hbk)
ISBN 0–415–12075–6 (pbk)

Contents

Contents

Acknowledgements

I would like to thank my colleagues, Philip Endean, Janice Thomas and Peter Vardy for the many helpful comments they offered on earlier drafts of this book. I would especially like to express my gratitude to the Philosophy Department of Santa Clara University for inviting me to be the Austin Fagothey Visiting Professor during the autumn of 1992. Their warm welcome and stimulating company provided a most congenial environment in which to work. Particular thanks are due to Linda Zagzebski and the other anonymous reader whom the publishers invited to comment on the manuscript, and whose many helpful comments were extremely valuable.

I would also wish to acknowledge several permissions from other publishers to reproduce translations of classical texts: to Cornell University Press for extracts from Alfred J. Freddoso's *De Molina: On Divine Foreknowledge*; to the University of Notre Dame Press for extracts from Marilyn McCord Adams's *William Ockham*; to Cambridge University Press for extracts from John Cottingham *et al.*, *Descartes: Select Philosophical Writings*; and to The Hackett Publishing Company for permission to reprint extracts from Marilyn McCord Adams and Norman Kretzmann's *William Ockham: Predestination, God's Foreknowledge, and Future Contingents*, to whom all rights are reserved.

A Note on References

Most references are given by author and year to works which are fully described in the Bibliography. Below is given a list of those works of the major classical authors which are discussed in the text, together with their titles, and any abbreviations used.

THOMAS AQUINAS

Unless otherwise noted, all references to Aquinas are to the First Part of his *Summa Theologiae*. Thus, I, 14, 5, reply 2 is to the *Summa*, Part I, question 14, article 5, reply to the second objection. I have made my own translations.

Quodl.   *Quaestiones Quodlibetales*. A set of brief works containing Aquinas's replies to various questions submitted by others.

WILLIAM OF OCKHAM

Ord.   *Ordinatio*. The introduction to his commentary on what was a standard theology textbook in the University of Paris at that time, Peter Lombard's *Liber Sententiarum* ('Book of the Sentences').

PFC   *Predestination. God's Foreknowledge and Future Contingents*. Marilyn McCord Adams and Norman Kretzmann (1969).

Quod.   *Quodlibeta Septem*.

Report.   *Reportatio*. Commentary on Books II–IV of Lombard's *Sentences*.

Since most of these works are difficult to obtain in translation, I have where possible given references to Marilyn McCord Adams (1987), in the form of 'A' (for Adams) followed by a page reference such as (A1242), where a translation is to be found, and which will guide the reader to many other relevant passages which give the context for those I have quoted.

LUIS DE MOLINA

Disp.   *Disputatio*, a disputation on free-will and foreknowledge, which forms part IV of his *Concordia*, in which he tries to reconcile free-will with the effectiveness of the grace of God, translated with commentary in Alfred J. Freddoso (1988).

RENÉ DESCARTES

I have referred to the *Meditations*, the *Replies*, and to various letters in which Descartes discussed his opinions with friends and critics. The best place to find all of these is in *The Philosophical Writings of Descartes*, edited by J. Cottingham and others (1985) Cambridge: Cambridge University Press.

DAVID HUME

Dialogues   *Dialogues concerning Natural Religion.*
Enquiry   *An Enquiry concerning Human Understanding.*
Treatise   *A Treatise of Human Nature.*

IMMANUEL KANT

All references to Kant, unless otherwise noted, are to the A text of his *Critique of Pure Reason*.

Introduction

Philosophers have always acknowledged that to embark on a philosophical discussion of the nature of God is to push philosophy to its
limits, if not to transgress those limits entirely. Even those who were
most confident that philosophy could and should throw light on the
nature of God have usually been comparatively modest about how
bright we should expect the light to be. Many other philosophers
have simply denied that the nature of God is a topic that can even be
meaningfully discussed in philosophical terms.

To ask what are the proper limits of philosophy and what are the
limitations of philosophical method is to raise issues which are
themselves philosophical issues, too large in scope to be tackled
directly in this book. Perhaps the proof of the pudding is in the
eating. To form a view on whether, in the past, or the present, or in
this book itself, the proper limits of philosophical discussion have
been transgressed, one needs to consider how these discussions in
fact proceed, what assumptions they make, which types of argument
are recognised as being useful and which not. I hope it will become
clear that discussion of the nature of God has consistently raised just
those fundamental issues in epistemology and metaphysics which are
at the heart of all philosophical endeavour.

In particular, three topics will be seen to recur throughout this
book. They are non-contradiction, possibility and necessity, and
cause. Indeed, it would perhaps not be too much of an exaggeration
to say that almost the entire discussion of the nature of God has been
shaped by the positions which philosophers have taken up on these
three issues, and on the relationships between them. To what extent
can we use the principle of non-contradiction to give an account of
what is and is not possible, or of what is necessarily the case? What
is the connection between what is possible or necessary and the

notion of 'cause'? What are causes, and to what extent if at all can we know about causes? These issues are just as alive in contemporary discussion among analytic philosophers as they were in the days of Aquinas, Ockham, Hume, or Kant, and they are apt to surface in a particularly provocative way when they are considered in their application to the nature of God.

I have chosen to discuss the nature of God in terms of five features which have traditionally been considered the most central: existence, simplicity, omniscience, omnipotence, and goodness. Chapter I on existence is primarily concerned with the *sense* of existential statements, and hence with the sense in which existence might be attributed to God, rather than with the question whether or not God exists. In so far as this latter question is considered, it is in Chapter II, for reasons which will be explained there. Chapter II considers the implications of the claim that in God existence and essence are identical, and the difficulties to which it gives rise. In particular, the identification of essence and existence, which is allegedly the defining characteristic of a necessary being, requires some detailed discussion of the notions of necessity, possibility, and potentiality. The content of the remaining three chapters is fairly self-explanatory. The problems connected with omniscience and omnipotence are familiar enough; and the final chapter, on God's goodness, offers a slightly different angle of approach to the traditional problem of evil.

Other volumes in this series have arranged the discussion more strictly in chronological order, concluding with an assessment of the history of the issues in the light of contemporary discussion. I have thought it better to proceed by topic rather than chronology, since the most interesting historical discussions are given by different writers on different topics. Aquinas has much to say on most topics; but Ockham is at his most interesting on omniscience and omnipotence, Descartes on omnipotence, Hume and Kant on existence and simplicity. Accordingly, the focus in each chapter is on different writers, and I have offered my own assessment of the topic at the end of each chapter, rather than at the end of the book as a whole.

I have also tried to discuss the historical texts in considerable detail, for two main reasons. The first is that many of these texts are less well known. Both because of their philosophical terminology, and because of the unfamiliarity of the background against which they were written, they are difficult to understand accurately unless they are read with some care and in some detail. The second reason is that the classical writers are all too often inaccurately represented by popular summaries of their positions. My hope is that by presenting the texts rather fully, I will make it easier for readers to assess not only the accuracy of my own interpretations, but, more importantly, the value of the arguments which the original authors have to offer. The requirements of space meant that the discussion of contemporary views 'has therefore had to be less detailed. Where I have not offered extended accounts myself, I have tried in the text and the notes to give pointers to where more detailed treatments are to be found, together with some indications of the line taken by philosophers today.

CHAPTER I

Existence

To begin a discussion of the attributes of God with existence might appear to be a very unwise choice. Existence, it will commonly be said, is not an attribute at all, whether of God or of anything else.[1] Indeed, it has often been argued that one of the cardinal errors of the classical tradition in philosophy of religion has precisely been its assumption that existence was an attribute.

Perhaps for that very reason, though, this is a good place to start. The classical tradition did nail its colours very firmly to the view that existence is an attribute of things. It further held that existence was pre-eminently an attribute of God, and even a defining attribute of God. Hume and Kant, two of the most influential critics of the traditional position, fastened on just this claim as the one which was most open to criticism. Critics from Hume and Kant to Russell, Flew and Findlay have believed that once it has been shown that existence is not an attribute, and that talk of a necessarily existent being embodies an elementary logical mistake, the classical position on the existence and nature of God is undermined almost in its entirety. In this they are quite correct. It was a central tenet of the classical position that existence is an attribute, that perfect existence is a perfect attribute, and that other attributes which are ascribable to God are so because perfect existence is ascribable to God. If these claims cannot be sustained, then discussion of the other attributes of God is largely a waste of time, at best. At worst, it simply adds to the confusions already inherent in a position which is logically vitiated from the outset. So the unpromising starting-point is unavoidable.

This chapter will primarily be concerned with the question whether existence might in any sense be said to be an attribute of things. This issue is often treated in the tradition alongside questions about necessary existence, and about whether necessary existence might be a defining attribute of God. In this chapter we shall examine some classical and modern arguments about whether existence is an attribute, and whether it makes sense to speak of necessary existence. The question about the defining attribute of God will be dealt with more in detail in Chapter II, though it will not be possible to steer entirely clear of it here. As will appear, though, the issues are separate, and it is important not to run them together too closely.

THE HISTORY OF THE PROBLEM

Is existence an attribute?

HUME

Does Hume believe that existence is an attribute? In the *Treatise of Human Nature*, he asks whether we have an idea of existence. He points out that some such idea might appear to be produced by all our experiences. However,

> So far from there being any distinct impression, attending every impression and idea, . . . I do not think there are any two impressions which are inseparably conjoined. Though certain sensations may at one time be united, we quickly find that they admit of a separation and may be presented apart. And thus, though every impression and idea we remember may be considered as existent, the idea of existence is not derived from any particular impression. The idea of existence is the very same with the idea of what we conceive to be existent.
>
> (I, ii, 6)

Hume here is perhaps not at his clearest. But the argument appears to run as follows: no impressions which are genuinely two are ever inseparable; hence the ideas to which they give rise can never be inseparable; but since the idea of existence is inseparable from every idea, it cannot after all be really different from any of the ideas it accompanies. One possible way of understanding what it is that Hume denies might be put in Aristotelian terms as follows: all our conceptions or impressions are of necessity subsumed under one or other of the categories of being.[2] But, just as Aristotle denies that Being is a genus, which would imply that there is one common feature which is shared by all beings and hence is distinguishable from any given being, so Hume denies that there is one common idea of existence shared by all things, and hence separable as a concept from that of any given thing. Elsewhere he says 'whatever the mind clearly conceives includes the idea of possible existence' (*Treatise*, I, ii, 1). To be a being just is to be a possible existent. The concept of colour just is the concept of being-a-possibly-existent-colour, and the concept of horse just is the concept of being-a-possibly-existent-horse. There is no concept simply of being, which is separate from being-a-possibly-existent-X.

This could be used as the basis of an argument that existence is not to be thought of as an attribute, if by 'attribute' one understands something *separate* which might be said to belong to something *else*. Hume's contention would be that 'horse' and 'being-a-possibly-existent-horse' are identical. Existence is therefore quite unlike largeness, or blackness, or ill-temperedness, in that each of these ideas derives from a separate impression; so horses can properly be said to have, or to lose, the properties of being large, black and ill-tempered. A well-tempered horse is just as much a horse as an ill-tempered one; but a not-possibly-existent horse is simply not a horse at all, and is strictly inconceivable. Moreover, existence is not something which a horse can have, or lose. 'The idea of existence is *the very same* with the idea of what we conceive to be existent.'

Which would all be fairly straightforward, did it not turn out that Hume thinks that we can think of absolutely everything as non-existent just as easily as think of it as existent. In the *Dialogues*, Cleanthes offers an argument against the more or less traditionalist Demea which, he claims, is 'so entirely decisive' that he is 'willing to rest the whole controversy upon it.' The target of the argument is the notion of a necessarily existent being, which Cleanthes explains as 'asserting that if we knew his whole essence or nature, we should perceive it to be as impossible for him not to exist as for twice two not to be four.' The supposedly fatal objection is this:

> There is an evident absurdity in pretending to demonstrate a matter of fact, or to prove it by arguments a priori. Nothing is demonstrable, unless the contrary implies a contradiction. Nothing, that is directly conceivable, implies a contradiction. Whatever we conceive of as existent, we can also conceive as non-existent. There is no being, therefore, whose non-existence

implies a contradiction. Consequently, there is no being, whose existence is demonstrable.

(*Dialogues*, IX)

We have here the standard Humean contrast between experience, in which things are either given or not, and where the notion of proof is simply inapplicable; and the work of reason, which is to discover the connections between ideas. The contrast is applied in such a way as to make the question 'Does X exist?' answerable to experience; reason itself can provide no necessary connection between the idea of existence and any other idea whatsoever. Unless we are to accuse Hume of blatant inconsistency between the *Enquiry* and the *Dialogues*, 'existence' in the first passage cannot have the same sense as it does in the second. In commenting on the first passage, I did in fact use the term 'being' rather than the term 'existence' to explain what Hume might have had in mind. Part of the justification for this is that it makes sense of the inseparability claim in the *Treatise*; there is some support also in the *Dialogues* for this reading, for Hume here says that there is no *being* (my italics) whose *existence* is demonstrable. Two different notions are involved in the *Dialogues* then, 'being' (or 'possible existent') and 'actual existent'.

Further support for this interpretation can be sought from a passage in the *Treatise* in which Hume endeavours to distinguish between fictions and really existing things. The belief that there exists an X involves more than having the concept of an X. It is having that concept plus an otherwise indefinable sense or feeling about X. This sense or feeling is not a concept of real existence, since it is not a concept at all. To believe that something exists is to have a particular kind of feeling. Hume might have gone on to say that despite the fact that this belief is expressed in words, it does not consist in relating the idea of existence to the idea of the thing in question; for the idea of existence, as Hume understands it, is already there in that we are thinking of some thing, hence of some being.[3] What is involved in believing that there really exists such a thing is quite different. So the reason why we can without contradiction conceive of anything whatsoever as non-existent is that for there to be a contradiction there would have to be two incompatible ideas, whereas here there is only one, the idea of the thing. To conceive of something as non-existent is, necessarily, to conceive of a being; but it is to conceive of entertaining this concept without having the peculiar sentiment which betokens that that being really exists (*Enquiry*, V, ii).

If this reconstruction is correct, Hume's view that existence is not an attribute involves two assertions. Firstly, that existence is not a separate idea which can be added to the idea of some being; and secondly, that believing that something really exists involves not attribution, but sentiment; it is a work not of reason, but of feeling. Those who believe that existence is an attribute might, as we shall see, accept the first of Hume's contentions; but they would simply deny the second, for which Hume does not offer any very effective argument. In particular, the first of his two points does not offer any support whatever for the second. In favour of the second, Hume offers simply the argument that reasoning about matters of fact depends upon the relationship of cause and effect, which is not given to us in our experience at all (*Enquiry*, IV, ii). But while (if one accepts Hume's account of causation) this argument might indeed tell against the possibility of reasoning from one matter of fact to another, it does not serve to establish that all knowledge of the existence of things involves this kind of reasoning. Hume nevertheless claims that knowledge of, as distinct from beliefs about, things outside our direct experience would have to involve cause and effect in just this way.

> We can, in our conception, join the head of a man to the body of a horse; but it is not in our power to believe that such an animal has ever really existed.
>
> It *follows, therefore*, [my italics] that the difference between *fiction* and *belief* lies in some sentiment or feeling, which is annexed to the latter, not to the former, and which depends not on the will, nor can be commanded at pleasure. It must be excited by nature, like all other sentiments, and must arise from the particular situation, in which the mind is placed at any particular juncture. Whenever any object is presented to the memory or senses, it immediately, by the force of custom, carries the imagination to conceive that object, which is usually conjoined to it. And this conception is attended with a feeling or sentiment, different from the loose reveries of the fancy. In this consists the whole nature of belief.
>
> (*Enquiry*, V, ii)

Even the sentiment in which belief wholly consists will amount to knowledge only to the extent that the force of custom provides a justification; but justification is just what constant conjunction, in Hume's view, cannot provide. In short, belief that something really exists is a sentiment, not an assertion that the thing has an attribute; and knowledge cannot include the reasoned attribution of existence to something, because knowledge of existence is not to be had. The adequacy of Hume's case against existence being an attribute therefore depends largely on whether his view of causation is defensible. To this I shall return later. Moreover, Hume's only way of showing that something is or is not a possible existent is to ask whether or not it can be distinctly conceived. He offers no reason why we should suppose that what is in fact possible or impossible should be limited in this way by our present concepts, or our present abilities to believe that such a thing might exist.

KANT

Kant also gives reasons for supposing that existence is not an attribute. His principal argument for the incoherence of the concept of an absolutely necessary being turns on the 'confusion of a logical with a real predicate (that is, with a predicate which determines a thing)' (A598).[4] He explains the distinction in this way:

> Anything we please can be made to serve as a logical predicate;[5] for logic abstracts from all content. But a determining predicate is a predicate which is added to the concept of a subject and enlarges it. Consequently, it must not already be contained in the concept.
>   '*Being*' is obviously not a real predicate: that is, it is not a concept of something which could be added to the concept of a thing. It is merely the positing of a thing, or of certain determinations, as existing in themselves. Logically, it is merely the copula of a judgment.
>
> (*Ibid.*)

What is meant by a 'real' predicate? Kant excludes not merely 'exists' in 'John exists', but also 'John' in its second occurrence in 'John is John', on the grounds that nothing is added to the subject in either case.[6] Given that Kant maintains that all existential statements are synthetic, one might be tempted to think that even in the case of existential propositions the predicate must add something to the subject, otherwise the proposition would be analytic. This would be

9

a mistake, however. In saying that existential propositions are synthetic, Kant means no more than that existence is not part of the definition of any term; an existential proposition is synthetic not because it adds some further content ('determination') to what is already contained in the subject, but because it 'posits' the subject.

Kant goes on to explain. The copula of any judgment serves one of two similar functions, either to relate one concept to another (as for example, 'John is tired'), for which his expression is 'posits the predicate *in its relation* to the subject': or it serves to 'posit it as being an *object* that stands in relation to my *concept*' (as in 'There is such a person as John'). Since the same word 'is' occurs each time, he wants to say that its function is likewise the same, to introduce a relation. The different uses correspond to the different relations involved. The modern equivalent of this distinction is to distinguish one sense of 'is' which is properly predicative, and another which is not predicative but existential.

So far, Kant's position is merely asserted rather than argued for. He does in fact go on to produce an argument for it, but perhaps not a very good one:

> By whatever and by however many predicates we may think a thing – even if we completely determine it – we do not make the least addition to the thing when we further declare that this thing *is*. Otherwise, it would not be exactly the same thing that exists, but something more than we had thought in the concept; and we could not, therefore, say that the exact object of my concept exists.
>
> (*A600*)

Similarly, Kant explains his assertion that 'the real contains no more than the merely possible.'

> A hundred real thalers do not contain the least coin more than a hundred possible thalers. For as the latter signify the concept, and the former the object and the positing of the object, should the former contain more than the latter, my concept would not, in that case, express the whole object, and would not therefore be an adequate concept of it.
>
> (A599)

The argument will hardly do as it stands. If the reason that 'the hundred thalers exist' cannot add anything to the concept of a hundred thalers is because if it did I would no longer be talking about 'the same object I had thought in the concept' it would apparently follow that when I say 'Socrates is tired', it could not be exactly Socrates who is tired, but something more than Socrates (for instance, tired-Socrates). In short, the argument would exclude all but analytic statements, which is absurd. To say that Socrates is tired is indeed to talk about Socrates, but also to say something new about him. To say that those hundred thalers are not simply a thought but exist in my pocket is to talk about them, and to say something new about them. It is not to add *more thalers* to what I am talking about, nor is it to give a fuller description of them, but it is to say more about them, namely that they exist.

So might it not simply be that they have the further attribute of existence? Kant's position is that existence is not a 'real' attribute; but he does speak of 'the positing of something, or of certain determinations, as existing in themselves.' The phrase 'as existing in themselves' must in some sense be an addition to the subject, despite Kant's apparent denial that it does at A600 (quoted above), otherwise the sentence would not be synthetic, as Kant says it is. What it is not is an additional 'determination'. But are only determinations attributes?

It is striking that Kant, like Hume, is forced to reintroduce talk of existence at some later point, having carefully minimised its importance in the earlier part of his discussion. He appeals simply to what he takes to be an intuitive difference between various senses of 'is', expressing identity, predication, and existence. It remains to be seen how well founded this intuition is, and whether it is sufficient to establish the view that in no sense is existence an attribute of things.

AQUINAS

Aquinas is often thought to have straightforwardly asserted that existence is an attribute of things – for he holds that existence is not merely an attribute of God, but is the essential attribute of God. His position, however, is not so simple. He distinguishes three cases: *i)* existence is predicated of a substance (as in asserting that a lion exists); *ii)* essential properties are predicated of substances (as in asserting that lions are mammals); *iii)* accidental properties are predicated of substances (as in assertions such as that lions live in Africa).[7] His claim is then twofold: firstly,

11

Existence is not part of the definition of any created thing, since it is neither a genus nor a differentia; and hence the questions 'Does it exist?' and 'What is it?' are different. Now, since whatever is not part of the essence can be called an accident, the 'is' which responds to the question 'Is there an X' is an accident. So the commentator on Aristotle's *Metaphysics* Book V states that 'Socrates exists' involves accidental predication, since it concerns the existence of the thing, or the truth of the proposition. On the other hand the word 'being' in so far as it means the thing to which existence belongs refers to the essence of the thing, and is divided by the ten Categories.

(Quodl. II, 3c)

The statement that Socrates exists is said to be an instance of accidental predication, since Socrates need not exist. But, Aquinas claims, it is still to be distinguished from accidental predications such as the assertion that Socrates is pale:

The substantial being of a thing is not an accident, but rather the actuality of some existing form. . . . Thus properly speaking, it is not an accident. Following Hilary, I claim that there is a broad sense of the term 'accident' which includes whatever is not part of the essence of something; and it is in this [broad] sense that existence is an accident of created things.

(Quodl., XII, 5)

We here have a distinction between two senses of 'accident', one Aristotelian, the other 'broader'. Given this distinction, Aquinas distinguishes existential predications from both accidental and essential predications in the strict sense of these terms. 'Socrates exists' is not like 'Socrates is human', nor like 'Socrates is pale'. 'God exists' in this respect is like 'Socrates is human' and unlike 'Socrates exists', in that, as Aquinas hopes later to demonstrate, existence is of the essence of God, whereas it is not of the essence of Socrates.

Leave aside the special case of God, for the moment. In distinguishing as he does between existential predications and straightforward predications like 'Socrates is human' and 'Socrates is tired', Aquinas takes a view which is, arguably, very close to Kant's claim that 'existence' is not a 'determination'. As Aquinas would put it, 'existent' is not an answer to the question 'What is X?' since it does not give either an accidental or an essential attribute of X. Only the kind of concept which could function as a genus or a differentia could possibly be a 'determination'. Aquinas would also, I believe, accept Hume's view that there is a sense of 'exists' in which existence is inseparable from the concept of anything whatsoever. The final sentence of the first passage quoted above says just this. The concept of anything is necessarily the concept of a substance, or of an accident, or of a relation, or of something in one of the other Aristotelian Categories of being. In the broad Aristotelian sense in which it is permissible to speak of the essence even of accidental attributes,[8] accidental-being is their essence, and hence inseparable from them, just as Hume says that the idea of existence is inseparable from the idea of the thing in question.

Like both Kant and Hume, therefore, Aquinas talks of existence on two levels. Where he differs from them is in the way the levels are to be distinguished. When he says that existence is, in the broad sense, an accident of all created things, he is echoing what both Hume and Kant say (and indeed, it is obvious enough) that we can conceive of any created thing whatever as non-existent. But whereas Hume thereafter goes on to speak of the sentiment associated with the belief that something exists, and Kant goes on to speak of 'positing the thing as existing in itself', which is an act of intellectual judgment, Aquinas says that existence is the actuality of a form (whether a substantial, or an accidental form). It is this notion of actuality which is the basis of Aquinas's view that existence is properly an attribute of things, rather than the content of a psychological state, as in Hume, or related in an undefined way to judgment, as in Kant.

The differences between the three philosophers is best seen in their treatment of the concept of necessary existence, to which we may now turn.

Is necessary existence an attribute?

AQUINAS

As we have seen, Aquinas accepts the tradition, stemming from Aristotle, that 'What is X?' and 'Is there an X?' are quite different questions, and that we look for the answers to them in different ways. What is initially puzzling, however, is his further statement that we cannot answer the 'What is X?' question until we have already assured ourselves that there is an X in the first place. One might perhaps have thought that the question 'What is X?' could readily be answered by giving a definition of the term 'X', and that this could be done quite independently of whether there are X's or not. To give a definition of 'mermaid' or 'dodo' or 'lion' is something that can be done by anyone who has a proper understanding of how these terms are related to other terms in the English language. Defining these terms does not commit us to any particular view on whether there are mermaids or dodos or lions, still less to establishing that there are these things before we attempt to give definitions. Moreover, if it is possible to produce definitions before we have established that there are things which satisfy those definitions, it would seem to follow that existence at least cannot be a defining property of anything at all. But this too is puzzling, since Aquinas certainly holds that existence is a defining property of God.

Puzzlement over Aquinas's view is increased by his approach to the question whether 'God exists' is evident. He provides some examples of statements which he does take to be evident: 'The whole is greater than one of its parts', 'Man is a rational animal', 'Spiritual beings do not occupy space' (I, 2, 1). While he points out that some of these (the last one for instance) are evident only to those who have sufficient training to see that they are evident, nevertheless he claims that all of these are 'evident in themselves'. Since he gives as his reason that 'the predicate is contained in the definition of the subject', it might seem natural to conclude that by 'evident' Aquinas means 'analytic'. Not all analytic statements are obviously so; hence, when Aquinas states that there are statements which are 'evident in themselves but not evident to everyone', one might conclude that the reason why this is so is that not everyone has a sufficient grasp of all the terms of our language, and especially not of the more technical terms of our language, so as to be able to see which statements are analytic and which are not. Nevertheless, statements which are true by definition are analytically true, and can be known to be so by those who have a sufficient grasp of the terms involved. However, this can be only a partial account of what Aquinas has in mind. For he is willing to state that 'There is a God' is 'evident in itself, *but not to us.*' And by this he means 'not to *any* of us' – including believers, and, importantly, even theologians like himself or Anselm. Aquinas explicitly considers in this context Anselm's definition of God as 'that than which nothing greater can be conceived'. He nowhere attempts to criticise the suggestion that 'X is a being than which nothing greater can be conceived' entails 'X exists', which is a crucial step in the Anselmian ontological argument. Aquinas is therefore willing to accept that 'If X is that greater than which nothing can be conceived, then X exists' could be analytically true. What he denies is that it is evident to us, while claiming that it is 'evident in itself'.

The clue is to be found in the source from which Aquinas derived his examples of statements which are evident. Aquinas repeatedly refers to Aristotle's first principles. These are of two kinds: there are principles like non-contradiction (and perhaps others, as we shall see), and there are statements which express the essences of things. The Aristotelian origin of Aquinas's examples explains the ease with which he, like Aristotle before him, moves from talking about words to talking about the things those words are used to denote, and from talk about defining terms to talk about defining things. Secondly, it ties his use of 'evident' to a particular view of necessity and possibility.

Aquinas shares Aristotle's (rather optimistic) view that we can readily discover the essences of many things, from eclipses to humans, and that these discoveries are reflected in the usage of our language. He regularly moves from talking about the definitions of terms to talking about the essences of things not because he believes that to speak about the essences of things simply is to speak about the conventions we have adopted in describing them, but for precisely the opposite reason. Our conventions about describing things standardly are as they are because we have discovered their real essences, and tailored our language accordingly. 'The whole is greater than one of its parts' is analytic, indeed, true because of the meanings we have given to the terms 'whole', 'part' and 'greater than'; but we have given the terms those meanings only because of the natures of wholes and parts which we have correctly discovered. The same is true, Aquinas believes, of 'Man is a rational animal' and 'Spiritual beings do not occupy space.'

The important point is that to discover the essence of something, one has to be able somehow to study that thing, or things of that kind. Aquinas here is quite faithful to Aristotle's view that discovery of what something essentially is is based on an inductive inquiry, culminating in an act of insight, which can then be expressed in a definition. It is for this reason that Aquinas says that one cannot know what something is unless one already knows that it exists. One has to have actual instances for the induction to get going. There is therefore all the difference in the world between mermaids, dodos and lions. Assuming that there are no such things as mermaids, there is no real essence to be discovered; and since there is nothing in the world to inhibit us, we may use the term 'mermaid' as we please, defining it as we like. And though there are no dodos, there once were, and (given that we still have the remains of some of them, and given our increasing genetic technology) there might once more be some, there is something whose essence we can in principle discover, just as we can discover the essence of actual lions. The question 'What is X' is usually understood by Aquinas to be concerned with real definitions – definitions of things – and not with nominal definitions – definitions of terms.[9]

So, a statement is 'evident in itself' if it correctly expresses an essence, whether we know that essence or not. The use of 'in itself' reflects the Aristotelian view that there is no *deductive* proof that E is the essence of X. The claim that many statements about essences are also evident to us reflects what Aquinas takes to be the standard situation in which the essences of things are simply seen once one has studied them sufficiently carefully.

The argument then is that Anselm may define the *term* 'God' in whatever way he pleases; given his definition, 'God exists' is what we might call analytic; but it would not be evident in itself, as Aquinas uses that phrase, because there is as yet no reason to suppose that that definition reflects the real essence of anything in the actual world. As Aquinas points out, there are plenty of other definitions of 'God' on offer besides Anselm's; and on some of these it might be analytically false that God is a spirit, or that God is eternal. If that is correct, then 'evident' is only indirectly related to 'analytic', to the extent that it is true that our language will be adapted to reflect whatever we discover about the essences of things; and it goes well beyond the modern use of 'analytic' in its commitment to a theory of real essences and hence to a theory of *de re* necessity of which analyticity is, at best, only a linguistic representation.[10] In line with this, 'predicate' and 'subject' are to be taken primarily as ontological terms, as in Aristotle, and only derivatively as logical or grammatical terms. Aquinas is non-committal on the proper logical form of assertions of existence.[11]

Aquinas's view is therefore that things differ from one another in their real natures. Those natures determine what is and is not *de re* possible. The *de re* capacities of things are truly attributes of those things. For that reason, Aquinas can hold that one of God's attributes

16

is that he cannot cease to exist. Once this has been shown, but only then, are we justified in re-arranging our language to reflect that situation in terms of *de dicto* necessity. Anselm's mistake is not in claiming that 'That than which nothing greater can be thought exists' is analytic, but in making that claim simply *a priori*.

What Aquinas does not show is on what grounds one might establish that there is such a thing as *de re* necessity at all. He takes over from Aristotle the assumption that there is, but this assumption, central to his entire position, is simply taken as evident. More importantly, if he is to make his view of God coherent Aquinas needs to establish that it is reasonable to claim that *de re* necessary existence as an attribute of something. It is just this that Hume and Kant would deny.

HUME

Hume's proof that the concept of a necessary being is incoherent is, as we have seen, extremely simple:

> Nothing, that is directly conceivable, implies a contradiction. Whatever we conceive of as existent, we can also conceive as non-existent. There is no being, therefore, whose non-existence implies a contradiction. Consequently, there is no being, whose existence is demonstrable.
>
> (*Dialogues*, IX)

Plainly, the argument immediately turns on non-contradiction. But if it is put simply in these terms, it relies purely on necessity *de dicto*, and hence reflects little more than our customary linguistic usage. Hume, of course, freely admits that in our use of terms like 'power' and 'cause' we import a different sense of 'necessary'. But it is a major part of his enterprise to exhibit the limitations of what we habitually say in these ways. His crucial claim is not that there is nothing of which it is contradictory to say that it does not exist. The key assertion is that *de dicto* necessity is the only kind of necessity which can be spoken of with proper philosophical justification. The attribution of any kind of necessity to *things*, as for instance in our talk about the necessary connection between cause and effect, is a projection on our part. Hence he can say

> When any natural object or event is presented, it is impossible for us, by any sagacity or penetration, to discover, or even

conjecture, without experience, what event will result from it, or to carry our foresight beyond that object which is immediately present to the memory and senses. Even after one instance or experiment when we have observed a particular event to follow upon another, we are not entitled to form a general rule, or foretell what will happen in like cases.

(Enquiry, VII, ii)

Hume's commonest way of establishing this startling conclusion is once again to insist that

> It implies no contradiction that the course of nature may change, and that an object, seemingly like those which we have experienced, may be attended with different or contrary effects. May I not clearly and distinctly conceive that a body, falling from the clouds, and which, in all other respects, resembles snow, has yet the taste of salt or the feeling of fire?
>
> *(Enquiry,* IV, i)

But that argument is insufficient. One cannot prove that there is no such thing as *de re* necessity in things by arguing that it is *de dicto* possible that there should be none. On the other hand, neither will it do to argue against Hume simply by saying that his conclusion is startling. He is well aware that it is, though he is also at pains to show that his conclusions are not wholly sceptical in their import, since our natural propensity to read necessity into the perceived regularities of nature works well. It is no part of his brief to stop us from thinking in these ways. He is arguing against philosophical pretensions:

> It is universally allowed that nothing exists without a cause, and that chance, when strictly examined, is a mere negative word, and means not any real power which has anywhere a being in nature. But it is pretended that some causes are necessary, some not necessary. Here then is the advantage of definitions. Let anyone *define* a cause, without comprehending, as a part of the definition, a *necessary connection* with its effect; and let him show distinctly the origin of the idea, expressed by the definition; and I shall readily give up the whole controversy. But if the foregoing explication of the matter be received, this must be absolutely impracticable. Had not objects a regular conjunction with each other, we should never have entertained any notion of cause and effect; and this

regular conjunction produces that inference of the understanding, which is the only connection, that we can have any
comprehension of.

(Enquiry, VIII, i)

The challenge depends on his empiricist assumptions about the origin
and justification of the ideas we employ in thinking about the world.
The opponent is required to show where any further idea of necessity
can originate, and what kind of proof can be given that it is being
correctly employed. This challenge is directly applicable to all
notions of *de re* necessity, as well as to the notions of real essence
and real powers which go along with *de re* necessity. I have suggested
that Hume's argument from non-contradiction is inadequate to
support his view. But he was surely right to be unconvinced by the
mere assumption of the contrary as he might have found it in the
tradition from Aristotle to Aquinas. Unless Hume's challenge is met,
there is no justification for arguing that any such natures, powers, or
necessity are truly attributes of things.

KANT

From the earlier discussion, it will be evident that Kant's discussion
of the incoherence of the concept of a necessary being owes a great
deal to Hume.

> If, in an identical proposition, I reject the predicate while
> retaining the subject, contradiction results; and I therefore say
> that the former belongs necessarily to the latter. But if we reject
> subject and predicate alike, there is no contradiction; for
> nothing is left that can be contradicted. . . . The same holds true
> of the concept of a necessary being. If its existence is rejected,
> we reject the thing itself with all its predicates, and no question
> of contradiction can then arise.

(A594–5)

Kant also asks that, even if one were to waive the difficulty that
existence is not a real predicate,

> We must ask: Is the proposition that *this* or *that thing* (which,
> whatever it may be, is allowed as possible) *exists*, an analytic
> or a synthetic proposition? If it is analytic, the assertion of the
> existence of the thing adds nothing to the thought of the thing;

19

but in that case either the thought, which is in us, is the thing itself, or we have presupposed an existence as belonging to the realm of the possible, and have then, on that pretext, inferred its existence from its internal possibility – which is nothing but a miserable tautology.

(A597)

With these remarks of Kant we may compare a very similar passage from Aquinas:

> Even if the meaning of the word 'God' were generally recognized to be 'that than which nothing greater can be thought', nothing thus defined would thereby be granted existence in the world of fact, but merely as thought about. Unless one is given that something in fact exists than which nothing greater can be conceived – and this nobody denying the existence of God would grant – the conclusion that God in fact exists does not follow.

(I, 2, 1, reply to 2nd objection)

If the 'realm of the possible' is to be constructed *a priori* merely by combining (or trying to combine) the concepts we already have, we are speaking in terms of *de dicto* possibility. In that case, the only check on what is and is not possible is non-contradiction. But equally, the only product is 'miserable tautology' and nothing follows about the world of fact. This is the agreed view of Hume, Kant, and Aquinas. What is in dispute is not that; it is whether this is the only kind of possibility and necessity to which we have access. Hume holds that it is. Kant and Aquinas hold that it is not. But Kant's willingness to extend his conception of what is possible and necessary is much more limited than Aquinas's.

Principles such as that there are substances with fixed natures, and that every event has a cause, are held by Kant to be both necessary and synthetic, and form an essential part of his criticism of Hume. It therefore looks as if Kant is committed to a form of necessity which cannot be reduced to logical necessity, and which, he would maintain, is a condition of the possibility both of our common sense and of our scientific knowledge of the empirical world. To that extent Aquinas would be in agreement.[12]

Kant's objections to extending necessity to cover the *de re* necessary existence of God are two.[13] Firstly, he maintains that any cosmological argument will invoke the ontological argument which he has just refuted. The reason is that any cosmological argument will in the end be forced to move from the concept of an absolutely unconditioned being to one whose existence is absolutely necessary: and this is the central, false, step of the ontological argument. However, it is not clear that Kant is right about this. He supports his view by giving an analysis of any proposed cosmological argument, which on the basis of A608 might be set out as follows:

i)   If I exist, an absolutely necessary being must exist.
ii)   I exist.
iii) Therefore an absolutely necessary being must exist.
iv)   An absolutely necessary being must be the most real being.
v)   There is only one absolutely necessary being.
vi)   Therefore, the most real being must be absolutely necessary.
vii) vi) must be true *a priori*, in virtue of its concepts alone.

He points out that vii), which follows from the conjunction of iv)–vi), is simply the ontological argument all over again, stating that necessary existence can be deduced from the concept of the most perfect being.

But suppose that vii) is true. That fact alone does nothing to show that iii) does not follow from i)–ii), which is what the cosmological argument sets out to prove. iv) is not used as a premiss at any stage in the cosmological argument; and vi) only follows given the truth of iv) and v). Hence, that the ontological argument is presupposed by the cosmological argument will be true only if iii) cannot be shown to be true independently of iv)–vi), and hence independently of vii). Did Kant simply fail to see this?

Well, perhaps he was thinking along the following lines. He might (for the moment – his second type of objection is directed at this step) concede for the sake of argument that it is a synthetic *a priori* truth that if anything exists, there must be a ground for its existence, and hence concede *some* version of i)–iii). So Kant might invite us to look again at i). i) contains *two* modal concepts, 'absolutely necessary' and 'must'. The 'must' expresses whatever necessity is involved in the principle of causation. But whence comes the 'absolutely necessary'? It is worth recalling at this point a remark Kant has made earlier, and which throws considerable light on his position. In outlining in a general way the motives for which people develop arguments for the existence of God, he outlines what the concept of an *ens realissimum* (a 'supremely real being') might be. It is, he suggests, something like this:

> that which in its concept contains a therefore for every where-fore, that which is in no respect defective, that which is in every way sufficient as a condition, seems to be precisely the being to which absolute necessity can fittingly be attributed.
>
> (A585)

But, he goes on, such a concept is 'very far from sufficing to show whether I am still thinking anything in the concept of the un-conditionally necessary, or perhaps rather nothing at all' (A593). For all we know, a much more limited, worldly being might contain the 'therefore for every wherefore' (A588) .

So it is to i) that he is really objecting. At most, he believes, one might argue for

i)*   If I exist, then an *ens realissimum* must exist.

There is no way of going from *ens realissimum* to 'absolutely necessary' unless one invokes vi), the fatal step of the ontological argument.

But is this correct? If the *ens realissimum* contains a 'therefore for every wherefore', it must, so the classical argument goes, not be accidental in any respect of its being, using 'accidental' in the broad sense. If it were, one could sensibly ask why it *happens* to be as it is, and this question must include why it happens to exist, even given that it does. To this, Kant says no more than that existence is not a real predicate; since there is no contradiction involved in its non-existence, even unconditioned existence cannot entail necessary existence; an argument which, as we have seen, is inadequate in itself.

I therefore think that the truly central difficulty which Kant raises is not this one, but the more fundamental objection to *any* argument of the form i)–iii). This is that the notion of *de re* necessity cannot be invoked beyond the realm of experience. A crucial assumption of the classical argument, says Kant, is

> the transcendental principle whereby from the contingent we infer a cause. This principle is applicable only in the sensible world; outside that world, it has no meaning whatsoever. For

the mere intellectual concept of the contingent cannot give rise to any synthetic proposition such as that of causality. The principle of causality has no meaning and no criterion for its application save only in the sensible world. But in the cosmological proof it is precisely in order to enable us to advance beyond the sensible world that it is employed.

(A610)

Kant claims to have shown that the principle of causality is a condition of the possibility of our experience being as it is. But that, he believes, is all that can be shown. The necessity involved is that of being a necessary condition of experience. It might be urged against this that merely because he has established only a limited application for the principle of causation and the notion of *de re* necessity which is bound up with that principle, it does not follow that a wider application might not also be possible, as the classical position claims it is. But what he certainly has shown is that it will not do simply to *assume*, as the classical tradition exemplified by Aquinas does assume, that such a wide application is possible.

To sum up. That existence, and even necessary existence, is an attribute of things has not been shown to be false, even if it is accepted, as all our authors do accept, that existence is not an attribute like tiredness or redness. But if it is a correct view, it is so only because to speak of causation, real essences, actuality and potentiality, is to speak of *de re* necessity; and to speak of a being that exists *de re* necessarily requires that this notion can be shown to have application across the whole range of the Aristotelian Categories, despite the limitations of our experience. Hume denies that there is any such feature of the world as *de re* necessity. Kant denies that we can justify talk of such necessity beyond the realm of experience. Aquinas claims that we can. On what grounds, then, can this issue be determined?

SOME ANSWERS

Existence

To some extent, the debate about whether existence should or should not be considered as a predicate of things might seem to be simply a matter of terminology. Of course, by definition, quantifiers are not predicates. So in $(\exists x)(Fx)$, 'There exists something which is fat', 'F' is a predicate, and $(\exists x)$ is a quantifier. The two have quite different logical roles, and that is really all that there is to it.

There is, however, more to be said. We need not uncritically adopt the half-explicit ontology presupposed by our logical conventions. The x's, featureless bearers of properties, over which we quantify, and of which properties are predicated, suggest some quasi-Humean I-know-not-what, a convenient logical peg and nothing more. Such a notion may not at all correspond to whatever ontology of substance we might wish to adopt. Moreover to content oneself with reading $(\exists x)(Fx)$ as 'The property F is instantiated' is to say little or nothing of what it is for a property to be instantiated. In speaking of 'instantiation', it already presupposes some notion of an individual. Quine (1961: 1–19), in saying that 'to be is to be the value of a bound variable', is hospitable enough, in that he places no restrictions on the domain of the individual variables over which we quantify – the kinds of individual things which we are prepared to say that there are. But he is inhospitable in that we can quantify only over variables. As a result, there is no direct or intuitively obvious way of expressing in logical form such everyday sentences as 'King Arthur really existed' or 'Bertram is no more'. $(\exists a)$ and $\neg(\exists b)$ are simply not well-formed sentences at all. We are reduced to circumlocutions such as $(\exists x)(Ax)$ ('There exists something which arthurises') or $(\exists x)(x = a)$ ('There exists some individual which is identical with Arthur'). It might just be acceptable to suppose that 'arthurising' or 'being arthurish' is a property; but it is much odder to suppose that for Arthur to exist is for a property-less *individual* to have arthurising predicated of it, and odder still to suppose that for Arthur to exist is for some individual to exist which is identical with *him*. On the face of it, it is surely much simpler to say that the individual Arthur has existence as an attribute.

My point is not to dispute the value of the logical notation which we have adopted, and the systematic advantages which it brings with it. I wish simply to question the move which would readily assume that logic is a good guide to ontology. What kinds of things a person is willing to quantify over may indeed reveal what that person takes there to be, but it provides no *justification* for that person's ontology, and offers no answer at all to the question 'What is there?' or to the questions 'What is it for something to exist?' or 'Is existence an attribute of things?'

Neither is it a good argument to suggest that 'existent' cannot be a predicate since, if it were, 'non-existent' would equally have to be one (see Miller 1992: ch. 4). Of course it is true that 'non-existence' cannot be a real property which something has. So 'This tiger is non-existent' is misleading, and quite unlike 'This tiger is tame'. But if 'King Arthur existed' ascribes some property to King Arthur, namely, the property of being existent, it does not follow that 'King Arthur never existed' involves the bizarre view that *he* has the property of non-existence instead. To say that King Arthur never existed is simply to deny that any existing individual has ever fitted the description of King Arthur. Similarly, to say that unicorns do not exist is not to ascribe non-existence to unicorns, nor to any individual unicorn. We can, of course, *describe* unicorns; but in so doing we are not attributing properties to *them*; we are saying what properties they would have if they existed. We are describing a *type* of thing, and such an exercise in conceptual analysis need not commit one to any particular ontology. It is also important that it is not strictly possible to describe a non-existent *individual* if by that is meant an individual who does not and never did exist. The most that can be done, once again, is to construct a concept, a series of predicates, which together specify a type, but do not specify an individual as such.

To attribute existence to something typically involves a more complex commitment than might at first sight appear. For existing things are not 'bare' *x*'s, to which we can 'then' attribute some other, more interesting, properties. An existing thing is a thing of some kind, necessarily possessing the set of properties which are essential to that kind, as well as possessing other properties which are not essential properties.[14] Existence is not properly thought of as something which a thing might have or lack; rather, it is the thing itself. In that sense it is not an attribute at all, even though to say that the last dodo is no more is to say something true about it.

How, then, is one to interpret such a statement as 'King Arthur really existed', if not as attributing existence to King Arthur? I suggest something along the following lines. Common to all the many uses of 'to exist' is some notion of actuality, which needs to be spelled out. What is it, then, for King Arthur to be actual? In speaking of King Arthur at all, we must have in mind a complex description; and in saying that King Arthur really existed we claim that an individual satisfying that description was capable of entering into causal relations with other things. The pattern of causal relationships in which that individual was involved had just the characteristics appropriate to the kind of thing which Arthur was. Arthur came to be because of the actions of his parents; he breathed air, digested food, and so on. To exist, or to be actual, just is to be involved in causal relationships of the relevant kind.[15] We can, if we wish, think of that involvement as an attribute of the existing thing; but if we do, it is not an attribute somehow alongside all its other attributes; the possession of a particular set of causal powers just is the nature of the thing. It is perhaps better to think of that ability simply as the thing itself. An existing thing just is an actual set of causal powers.

Anselm seems to me to have been fundamentally wrong in speaking of 'existence in the mind' as somehow a less perfect kind of existence than 'existence outside the mind'. Whatever view one might take of the mind/body problem, what exist in the mind are such things as beliefs, concepts, doubts, and so on. To be sure, the intentional content of those mental states is somehow a feature of those states. But for God to be the intentional content of one of those states is not at all for God to have a somewhat shadowy existence, less perfect than existing in the world of things; it is not for God to exist at all, but for a mental state to exist which has God as its content. That mental state is doubtless part of a network of causal relationships; but its content is not an additional existent, not an additional somehow imperfect node in a causal network. Suppose two mental states are each, say, the thought of a number. It may well be that, for all we know, their having that characteristic alters the causal relationship between them. But the causal relationship between mental states is not thereby a causal relationship between their intentional contents.[16] The relationship between the numbers which those mental states have as their intentional contents is a logical, not a causal, relationship. We should not commit ourselves to the view that numbers are actual existents, since they simply are not the kinds of things which can have causal interactions. If we wish to say that, in some sense of 'exist' weaker than 'being actual', numbers, or the Equator, or mermaids exist, well and good. But such usage needs care if it is not to mislead.

To exist, then, in its fundamental sense of 'to be actual', is to be capable of causal activity. To say that John exists is to say something about John, that he is capable of causal activity. To say that King Arthur does not exist is not to deny that Arthur has that ability; it is to deny that anything with that ability fits a certain description.

Necessity, possibility and potentiality

Actuality, both in Aristotle and in the medieval tradition which followed Aristotle in this respect, was regarded as the correlative of potentiality. Perhaps unfortunately, the notion of potentiality became closely linked to that of possibility, whose correlative is not actuality, but necessity. Once possibility and necessity came to be interpreted in logical terms, 'actuality' came to have a much weaker sense,[17] and potentiality lost its original *de re* sense.

It has become fashionable to try to analyse the notion of potentiality in terms of possible worlds. Thus, 'Jemima is a potential philosopher' is explained by saying that there is a possible world in which Jemima exists and is a philosopher. This move is, in itself, harmless enough as a pedagogical device. But it is apt to confuse if it is taken to be an *explanation* of potentiality. For it relies on the notion of a *possible* world, and 'possible' here is not defined. If it is taken to mean 'logically possible', it is plainly too weak to capture what is meant by 'Jemima is a potential philosopher'. For while it is logically possible that Jemima be a philosopher, it might also be that she has no such potential. On the other hand, if by 'possible world' is meant a causally possible world, then we need some account of how we are to distinguish causally possible worlds from causally impossible worlds. Since logical possibility is often thought to depend on our current usage of terms, what we take to be logically possible and impossible will reveal nothing more than that usage. If, as is no doubt quite often the case, our current usage adequately reflects the causal features of our world, then of course we could with at least some confidence suppose that that usage is a good guide to what is causally possible. But since a perfect match cannot be guaranteed, logical possibility is neither a necessary nor a sufficient condition for causal possibility. It is therefore inadequate as an explanation of potentiality.

The same considerations apply to the attempt to explain what is *de re* necessary in terms of possible worlds. Some examples: suppose that humans are essentially animals, and that essential properties are taken to be properties which things *de re* necessarily have. 'Humans are essentially animal' clearly cannot mean simply that any human is animal in all the possible worlds in which humans exist. If 'possible' means no more than 'logically possible', we have managed to say no more than that humans are by definition animal. But what we wished to say was that it is *causally* impossible to bring it about that a human being, say Jemima, exists without being an animal. Again, it is frequently hoped that some satisfactory analysis of causal statements might be based on counterfactuals, or subjunctive conditionals, and that these, too, can be explained in terms of possible worlds. But there are intractable problems. It is by no means clear which possible worlds are the 'closest' to the actual world in such cases; and in any event a satisfactory analysis of causal statements in terms of counterfactuals has not as yet been forthcoming. The reason again seems to me to be that 'possibility' and 'closeness', if they are to be of any assistance in all this, must themselves be causal, not logical, terms. And if they are, then the proposed explanation is going to be narrowly circular.

Again, the attempt to explain the difference between *de re* and *de dicto* necessity by calling attention to a change in scope of the modal operator seems to me doomed to failure. For instance, it is said, 'Necessarily, all bachelors are unmarried' is a case of *de dicto* necessity, since the modal operator 'necessarily' applies to the whole sentence; whereas 'John is necessarily-human' will, if true, be an instance of *de re* necessity, since the modal operator has for its scope simply the predicate of the sentence. But this leaves it still unclear what might be meant by 'necessarily-human', and what sense of 'necessary' is involved here. It cannot be the same sense as in the first case. And it will not, I think, do to say that John is human in all the possible worlds in which John exists, unless one can in advance spell out what is to count as a possible world, and hence explain what sense of 'possibility' is involved. Supporters of a notion of *de re* necessity are not going to admit that it simply *happens* to be true that John is human in any world in which John exists. They wish to claim that any world in which John is not human is not a possible world at all, and it is this sense of 'possible' which is crucial to the distinction.

The root problem, as I see it, is that mere alteration of the *scope* of the modal operator is in principle insufficient to explain the *de re/ de dicto* distinction. The distinction is between two different *kinds* of necessity/possibility, and hence between two different senses which the modal operator must have. A difference in sense is not simply to be spelt out in terms of a difference in scope, unless one offers a further explanation of why it is that an operator on sentences can, without more ado, be treated as an operator on predicate terms.[18] The important distinction is surely to be drawn in terms of the grounds on which different claims about possibility/necessity are made. 'Bachelors are unmarried' is of necessity true because of the way in which the terms are defined, and the necessity is logical. John is necessarily human is true because of the kinds of alteration which are compatible with John remaining the same individual, as distinct from simply being *counted as* the same individual, or being recognisable as the same individual. The notions of 'compatible with' and 'same individual' are not primarily to be understood in a logical sense, but as reflecting the fixity of natural kinds, with the powers and limitations inherent in those kinds.

To maintain that 'John is human' expresses a *de re* necessity is therefore not necessarily to say that that statement is analytic, nor that it can be reduced to some other statement which is analytic, such as, for example, 'The child of Jemima and James who are both human beings is human.' Even if being the child of Jemima and James were a sufficient criterion for us to pick out John, and even if it were agreed that the child of two humans is by definition human (two conditions which are far from obvious, be it noted), the necessity of John's being human is not captured by the analyticity of 'The child of two humans, Jemima and James, is human.'

Unfortunately, though, I have no better insight to offer on precisely what causal powers are, or precisely what it is for something to be causally necessitated; and, since I have defined the actuality-sense of 'exist' in terms of the possession of causal powers, it might seem that I have wasted a good deal of ink to little purpose. Not quite, though. To be forewarned is to be somewhat forearmed. Firstly, we can refuse to equate what causation is with the evidence we have for saying that there are causes. To be sure, our evidence for which causal powers various things in our world possess is drawn from the regular patterns of interaction in which they engage. We can gradually approximate to an exact account of how things with natures of a certain kind interact with other things which also have natures, and hence formulate progressively more accurate causal laws. But to interact according to these laws is not a *definition* of causation, nor of what it is to have a causal power. Secondly, we can insist that causal agents are individual, existing, things, not types of thing, even though it is true that we can express the patterns of their interactions only in universal terms, because those individuals are indeed individuals of a kind. Thirdly, a stress on the possession of causal powers perhaps makes it easier to speak of causation in cases where there is no particular event which can be said to be the cause of some other event, as we should, for instance, in speaking about gravitational attraction, or force-fields quite generally. I therefore incline to think that the possession of causal powers, like existence, should be treated as a primitive notion, unanalysable into other more basic terms. It is a basic fact that causal agents exist, and that, at least for the most part, to exist is to be part of a network of causal interaction. We can *describe* such interactions in terms of the natures which things have, and hence perhaps construct causal laws which, reflecting our understanding of those natures, may then, but only then, be taken to be logically necessary truths. But causal necessity is not thereby defined, nor explained.

We may return, then, to consider the relation of existence to actuality, and to the sense in which it might be said that God exists of necessity. Necessity in this context is the correlative of *de re* potentiality. The claim that God exists necessarily is therefore twofold: *i)* it says that God is an actual being, hence a being in a causal network; *ii)* it says that it is not causally possible that God should not exist. Both of these, if they are true at all, say something about God, and in that sense express an attribute of God; and the second asserts that God has that attribute *de re* necessarily. This latter expression is still intolerably obscure. But it might be possible to clarify it if we can achieve a better grasp of its correlative, *de re* potentiality.

De re potentiality

Quite generally, existing things can both produce changes in other things, and can be changed by other things; more specifically, the following would be commonly believed:

1 Some things are able to change without being caused to change – for instance, the atoms of some radioactive substances.
2 Some things are able to act without being caused to act; and to do so either randomly, or for a reason.
3 Some individuals can cease to exist.
4 Energy in our universe is conserved.

None of these is unproblematic. 1 and 2 would not be acceptable to determinists, and 1 especially runs counter to what we take to be the case at least in the macroscopic world of our everyday experience, where we suppose that all events do have causes and not just statistical explanations. In addition, 2 is vulnerable to two suggestions; firstly, that people never truly act in a random fashion, not even when asked to call 'Heads' or 'Tails', for instance; and secondly, that perhaps reasons for acting will after all turn out to be causes. These are at least in part empirical disputes, as it seems to me, rather than differences of purely philosophical opinion, and it is not my purpose here to pursue them in any detail. I wish to point out only that if there are things which have the powers mentioned in 1 and 2, then it does not seem that being an unmoved mover, or an uncaused cause, could be even close to what is required in an account of what it is to be God. Radioactive atoms and beings with undetermined choices might both be thought to be in some sense unmoved movers.

3 is philosophically, and not merely empirically, problematic. It presupposes a clear account of what it is to be and to remain the same individual, and there are enough borderline cases, even undecidable cases, to make it unclear just what this presupposition involves. We may leave it an open question whether Mt Everest, or this desk, or the oft-repaired M1 Motorway are individuals at all. It is sufficient for my present purposes that there are at least some cases which we might accept as clear cases of individuals ceasing to exist. Most of these are higher organisms – such individuals as Queen Anne, notoriously dead,[19] or the elm at the bottom of my garden, alas a prey to Dutch elm disease, or the wasps in the nest which has just been destroyed under the roof. That an individual can cease to exist is a feature of the kind of thing it is, and hence of the ways in which it can enter into causal relationships. Animals can die because of the ways in which their parts causally interact with one another; and organisms can be killed by the causal action of other things. Moreover, individual atoms (if atoms are individuals) can be destroyed, either spontaneously in radioactive decay, or by causal intervention. We can often, though doubtless not always, give an account of the causal interactions which bring it about that individuals cease to exist, and hence say what it was about them that made their non-existence possible.

So far as I know, however, all the cases in which individuals cease to exist are cases in which the materials in which they consist are re-arranged; and the causal powers which are capable of bring about their non-existence are powers to re-arrange those constituent materials.

We do not have evidence to suggest that there are in the world any causal powers to *annihilate* anything – to bring it about that both the individual as such and its material constituents should cease to exist. 4 is one of the most fundamental physical laws which we take to delimit what is and what it not causally possible in our universe. The denial of 4 would totally undermine just about everything we believe that we know about the causal powers of existing things. Energy cannot be annihilated, and hence neither can the matter which constitutes the things which we can cause to disintegrate.

If then we ask whether it is *de re* possible that the energy/matter of which our universe is composed should not exist, we are asking a question to which the scientific answer is quite simply 'No'. It is axiomatic that there is no causal power in the universe which could bring about such a state of affairs. Hence, in that sense, the non-existence of energy/matter of the universe is not causally possible, and the energy/matter of the universe could therefore be described as existing by causal necessity. Kant is, I believe, quite right to say that the kinds of causal arguments which might lead us to conclude that something exists of necessity are quite inadequate to establish the existence of anything remotely resembling the traditional God. We cannot simply assume that an *ens necessarium* is also an *ens realissimum*, endowed with the perfect attributes of God. Aquinas, correctly insisting that our experience shows us many individuals which need not exist and whose existence therefore requires causal explanation, has not thereby shown that no individuals need exist, still less that the material which constitutes those individuals need not exist. It is at the very least not at all evident that the energy/matter of the universe is 'by nature' (to use Aquinas's term) capable of annihilation. If it is not, then its existence is *de re* necessary. But if God is defined as a being whose annihilation is *de re* impossible, then there is no reason so far to reject an identification of God with the energy/matter of the universe.

Suppose that in reply to this point it is argued that it is still possible that the entire universe should not have existed, or should cease to exist, and hence that its actual existence requires explanation. If 'possible' here means 'logically possible', then the reply has no force at all, in my view. What is logically possible, I have already argued, is neither a sufficient nor a necessary condition for being causally possible; and this point is surely especially strong when the causal possibility under discussion is so utterly global in its scope. We have no experiential grip whatever on what it would take to annihilate a universe, if indeed it could be done at all. That we can imagine such a state of affairs (if we can) is quite irrelevant; on the other hand, that we cannot imagine such a state of affairs, or have no scientific need even to consider such a state of affairs, is equally beside the point. What is clear, though, is that if this question is to be taken seriously at all, it cannot be understood in terms of the causal powers of anything in the universe, and hence it is not a question which can be posed, or answered, in terms of the laws of physics and the natures of physical things. If, with Kant, we refuse to allow that the question can be meaningfully put in any other terms, then to say that God is a being which *de re* cannot be causally annihilated is false unless we pantheistically identify universe and God. I conclude that there is *a* clear enough sense in which we can speak of the universe both as having the attribute of existence, and indeed of *de re* necessary existence, as Kant quite properly urges against Hume. The terms, then, are not meaningless or incoherent. But in *this* sense, of course, they are of little service to the would-be theist. And it is Kant's contention that no broader sense can be shown to have any application, and that the attempt to go further produces insoluble problems.

What would be required for the traditional view of God, and for that matter the traditional versions of the cosmological argument, to meet this kind of criticism? The traditional reply would be that the mere fact that the Law of the Conservation of Energy states that no physical process can alter the overall amount of matter/energy in the universe does not of itself establish that the annihilation of all the matter in the universe cannot be brought about by some other causal power.[20] What is required is that we identify the feature which differentiates God, whose non-existence is *de re* impossible, from everything else, whose uncaused existence is likewise *de re* impossible.[21] The feature which, it is claimed, God has, and the universe does not have, is simplicity.

In the classical tradition, to say that God is simple is to say that God is such that there is in God no *de re* potentiality; it was also claimed that this feature is one which only God can have. So whether it makes sense to talk about the attribute of *de re* necessary existence in anything more than the Kantian sense in the end depends on whether the problems with simplicity can be resolved. As will presently be seen, the traditional attempts to speak of a simple God encountered just those difficulties to which Kant called attention.

CHAPTER II

Simplicity

Most of the medieval philosophers believed that it could be shown that an absolutely necessary being was totally simple. 'Simplicity' is a highly metaphysical notion, and, as it was traditionally understood, it seems to have such utterly counter-intuitive implications as hardly to merit serious discussion. For it appears to require the denial of all distinctions in God; God's omnipotence is supposed to be the same as his mercy, or his justice; God is identical with each of his actions, and hence each of his actions seems to be identical with each of the others. Perhaps most difficult of all, simplicity, involving as it does the identity of essence and existence in God, seems to involve the view that no descriptive predicates can possibly be true of God – not even the traditional ones such as 'omniscient', 'omnipotent' or 'creator'. For all these terms are obviously intended as descriptions of God, however inadequate they might be; but if God's essence simply is to exist, and 'exist' is not a descriptive term at all, then it would appear that no description can be of the essence of God. Kant, as we have already discussed in Chapter I, saw no prospect of proving any link between the notions of absolute necessity and transcendent simplicity; and Hume believed that any attempt to describe a totally simple God was both gratuitous and vacuous. As a result, simplicity has until recently been perhaps the least discussed, as well as one of the most fundamental, of the attributes of God proposed by the classical tradition.[1] This chapter will attempt to chart the course of the debate.

Since the notion of simplicity is intimately related to that of an absolutely necessary being, which in turn is closely bound up with the cosmological arguments for the existence of God, a consideration of how those arguments were supposed to work is a good place to begin to consider what was meant by the claim that God is in all respects simple.

THE HISTORY OF THE PROBLEM

Aquinas

THE BACKGROUND ASSUMPTIONS

Aquinas distinguishes between two kinds of *demonstratio*, or scientific proof.[2] The first (doubtless highly idealised) consists in an explanation why something must happen as it does. The explanation takes the form of a deduction. The statement that an event happens, or that some particular state of affairs obtains, is shown to follow deductively from statements giving the essences of the various items involved in bringing about that event or state of affairs and from whatever further first principles are required. Since the first principles are *de re* necessarily true, and the deduction is valid, the conclusion is thereby shown to be necessary, and hence to be an instance of scientific knowledge.

To provide this kind of explanation of worldly events, by exhibiting their connection with the essential attributes not merely of worldly causes but also of God, is not possible, Aquinas believed. The essence of God cannot be known in the way required for the explanation to get off the ground.[3] What is possible is another kind of *apodeixis* which Aquinas terms *demonstratio quod*, a 'proof that something is the case'. Since it is a *demonstratio*, it does claim to establish a necessary conclusion, and hence to start with premises which are similarly necessary. But, as Aquinas puts it, 'when proving something to exist, the middle term is not what the thing is (since we cannot even ask what it is until it has we know it exists), but rather what we are using the name of the thing to mean' (I, 2, 2, reply 2). That is to say, instead of using an expression giving the real essence of something as a middle term, we have to use a nominal definition instead. The nominal definition of 'God' would be something like 'the ultimate causal explanation of the existence of whatever we experience'.

Two examples to illustrate this. Suppose that we do not know what epilepsy is. That is to say, we do not know in what the illness itself essentially consists. What we do know are the effects it has on sufferers. We can offer a nominal definition of the *word* 'epilepsy' in terms of those symptoms; and using that definition we can correctly prove that a particular patient is suffering from epilepsy. Similarly, for centuries scientists worked with a nominal definition of copper, in terms of its being a metal with a set of observed properties – malleability, conductivity, colour, chemical powers, and so on. It was possible to show that copper was present; what was not possible was an explanation of its properties in terms of its atomic structure. That type of explanation became available only when the essential structure of copper was discovered (for the example, see Harré and Madden 1975: 21–5).

A diagnosis of epilepsy, even when correct, amounts to saying no more than that the patient must have whatever it is that produces these symptoms, which we call 'epilepsy'. The conclusion of the cosmological arguments in Aquinas is similarly modest: that there must exist whatever it is that causally explains the existence of the things we experience, which we call 'God'. It is from this very jejune conclusion that Aquinas deduces the characteristics of the attribute of simplicity. To see how this is supposed to work, it is important to notice the points at which necessity enters into the argument.

The argument has the following form:[4]

i)   If anything exists which need-not exist, there must exist an adequate causal explanation for its existence.
ii)   An adequate causal explanation of existence must involve some entity which exists-of-necessity.
iii) There are things which need-not exist.
iv)   Hence there must exist something which exists-of-necessity.

The 'must' in iv) is the 'must' of logical necessity, since the form of the argument is a valid form. But what of the occurrences of 'must' in i) and ii)? Aquinas would claim that both i) and ii) were evident 'first principles' in the Aristotelian sense; and he takes these principles to express a *de re* necessity. As I have already remarked, i) and ii) are not simply claims about what we would regard as satisfactory explanations, or what we would regard as making the universe *intelligible*. They are to be taken as claims about what is *de re* possible. Things whose non-existence is merely *de re* possible, it is claimed, could not exist at all unless there existed something whose non-existence is *de re* impossible. Similarly, the modal expressions which I have hyphenated distinguish between those things which have existence as (in the broad sense) an accidental attribute, and whatever (in fact just one thing, as he subsequently undertakes to prove) has existence as an essential attribute. The proof therefore depends upon *a)* whether it is correct to speak of existence as being an attribute which can belong to things accidentally or essentially, and *b)* whether it can be shown that i) and ii) express *de re* necessary truths. I have already discussed *a)* in the preceding chapter. To discuss *b)* it will be helpful to spell out somewhat more in detail what Aquinas took to be the implications of saying that something was such that its non-existence was *de re* impossible, since these considerations are also relevant to whether or not i) and ii) can be shown to be true.

The entire discussion hinges on the actuality/potentiality distinction, interpreted in a *de re* sense. I have already argued that *de re* potentialities are actual features of actual things. Thus Socrates's ability to learn a language consists in his having an actual brain of the relevant kind; his ability to speak a language consists (we may suppose) in features of that brain's organisation produced by the learning-process. That it is a real possibility that Socrates should die, or be killed, is an actual feature of the way in which his body is organised, and of the capabilities of those things which can interfere with that organisation. It is at least relatively easy to understand what is meant by the potentialities or powers of actual things. What is needed is a general account of which features of things entail that the things possess *de re* potentialities; a totally simple being will then be one which has none of those features. Aquinas endeavours to provide just such an account.

SIMPLICITY AS THE ABSENCE OF *DE RE* POTENTIALITY

Aquinas believes that a being which exists-of-necessity cannot be a material individual; cannot have any intrinsic accidental properties; cannot, therefore, change in any way; and cannot be an individual of any given species or genus. Hence, an absolutely necessary being does not have a nature in any straightforward sense at all. In short, a being which exists-of-necessity cannot be something whose existence actualises a real potentiality, and each of the features in this list entails the possession of such a potentiality.[5]

The first item in the list, that a necessary being cannot be a material individual, he takes to be assured by the fact that any material being can be caused to cease to exist by re-arranging its constituents. This, I think, is not in dispute. The difficulties begin as soon as one tries to spell out more in detail the remaining claims. Apart from doubts about the whole notion of *de re* necessity and potentiality, and the status of principles i) and ii) in the overall argument, this detailed account of simplicity seems to entail such strange conclusions that it might be thought in itself to constitute a *reductio ad absurdum* of the assumptions from which it is derived, even if one had no other grounds for questioning those assumptions. Nevertheless, there is a case to be made for the view that the further conclusions are not as indefensible as they at first sight might appear, and that at least the *reductio* argument against them does not succeed, whatever one might think of the other problems which they present. We shall consider the various consequences of simplicity one at a time, and examine the problems they each present.

a) The absence of intrinsic accidental properties

Theoretically, the distinction between intrinsic and extrinsic accidental properties is clear enough. Those properties are intrinsically accidental the gaining or losing of which involves an accidental change in the subject of the properties. Thus, walking is an intrinsic accidental property of Socrates, as is knowing Greek, or talking Greek. My being taller than my brother is an intrinsic accidental property of both of us, since it depends on the sizes which we both happen to have. Such intrinsic properties are distinct from those involved in what Geach (1969) has termed Cambridge changes, in which something comes to be true of a subject without that subject changing in itself. So, being the last surviving member of one's family is not an intrinsic accidental property. Neither is it an intrinsic accidental property of Socrates that he is being thought about by Callias, though it is an intrinsic accidental property of Callias that he is thinking of Socrates. Aquinas holds that X's extrinsic properties are relational properties of X to some Y which do not depend on X's possessing any non-relational property.[6]

What is denied of a being which exists-of-necessity is that it has any intrinsic accidental properties, but not that it has extrinsic accidental properties. Comparatively unproblematically, then, it can be accidentally true that God is believed in by Abraham, and forgives Israel her sins, since, although neither of these need be true, neither, according to Aquinas, involves any alteration in God. The relationships between Abraham or Israel and God, such as believing, or being forgiven, depend on actual dispositions in Abraham and Israel which they need not have had, but do not involve any change in God. So there are many things which could be truly predicated of God, without any of them being necessarily true. To hold that God is simple is therefore not to say that whatever can truly be said of God must be a necessary truth. Truths about God are necessary only if their truth conditions consist solely in an intrinsic attribute of God himself.

But this can hardly be a sufficient account. Take for example the truth that God created this universe. Aquinas does not believe that God of necessity created this universe, or indeed that of necessity he created any universe at all. It is a contingent truth that God created this universe. But is not God's decision to do so an intrinsic attribute of God? Aquinas seeks to explain this, too, along the lines suggested by the notion of a Cambridge change, by saying that it is the universe that comes to be, while God does not change at all. Being related to God is, as it happens, a property of this universe, not of some other possible universe, just as thinking of Socrates was, as it happens, a property of Callias not of Socrates.

> So it is that when we speak of his relation to creatures we can apply words implying temporal sequence and change, not because of any change in him but because of a change in the creatures; just as we can say that the pillar has changed from being on my left to being on my right, not through any change in the pillar but simply because I have turned round.
>
> (I, 13, 7)

But the parallel does not work. For if God could have created a universe other than the one which as it happens he did create, must this not imply *a)* that God has the potential to do other than in fact he did, and *b)* that he is different from he would otherwise have been had he never created at all? To create is, after all, an activity in God, whereas to be thought about by Plato is not. The logical contingency of 'God created this universe' seems clearly to depend upon a real potentiality in God, which is precisely what simplicity excludes.

One might try to avoid *b)* by arguing that if God has the attribute of simplicity, he is unchangeable, and hence eternal. If God is eternal, then there never was a time before which God decided to create this universe rather than some other. There never was a time at which God was other than he is, namely, creator of this universe. Though it is possible that things could have been different, in fact this possibility is eternally unactualised: so God never in fact *changes*.

39

Even if this is accepted, point *b)* can still be pressed, by asking whether God would not have been really different had he chosen differently? Aquinas would answer that although of course God would have been different, this is not a real difference, since a real difference is a relationship only between actual things.[7] Although God would be different had he chosen differently, 'different' here does not denote real difference in God, since a real difference involves a real change, and not simply change which is never actual though it might have been.

But the argument is insufficient. Even if we grant that God never was different from the way he is, difficulty *a)* remains. It is not just *logical* possibilities and 'real' differences which simplicity is supposed to exclude, but *de re* potentiality. Invoking the idea of eternity leaves this problem quite untouched. God is still eternally able to do other than he does. To meet *a)*, Aquinas perhaps takes a rather different line. What simplicity in God excludes is only the *de re* potentiality of *being changed* by something else. That God could have created other than he did, or not have created at all, does not lead to problems about dependency. He is not caused to create. Even though Aquinas believes that there is an explanation for his creating, in terms of the goodness of the created world, this explanation of his choice is not a causal explanation. To be free is to be able to present several objects of choice as good, and hence to be able to explain any given choice in those terms. So God's choice between good possible universes is not brought about by any external factor,[8] though it can be explained in terms of the features of whichever universe he chooses to create. Aquinas perhaps believes that free decisions to do this rather than that do not, once the information about the choices is given, involve any further actualisation of a potentiality; he does say that 'acts of will are not alterations, but operations', where the word for 'alterations', *motus*, suggests a being acted upon, and 'operations' does not.[9] However this may be, Aquinas clearly admits that God could have chosen otherwise than he (eternally) does; and that therefore some things which can be truly said of God are contingent truths *about God*, and not merely about other things which are related to God. What remains puzzling is how Aquinas believes this can be true without God having any intrinsic accidental properties; and the puzzle is not solved simply by saying that these properties are in fact unchangeable.[10] We shall come across a parallel problem about God's knowledge later.

b) Simplicity excludes membership of a species or genus

In anti-Platonic vein, Aquinas rejects the view that a species is an actual entity; there actually exists no such thing as Humankind. What is meant by saying that a species exists is that the actual world is such that it is *de re* possible for there to exist individuals of that species. So, had he been asked now why is it that 'Dodo' is a genuine species term, whereas 'Mermaid' (we may suppose) is not, he might reply that it is in fact possible, given the way the world is, for there to exist a dodo, and not possible for there to exist a mermaid.[11] Genus terms, such as 'animal', are similarly potentiality-terms, which we use to refer to the fact that it is possible for there to be species such as Horse, Man, and Dodo. This level of potentiality is yet more removed from individuals, however, in that it is not possible to have an individual which is simply an actual animal without also being an animal of some species. Since 'nature' is equivalent, in Aquinas as in Aristotle, to 'real definition', and hence to 'species-of-a-genus', it follows that 'nature' too is a potentiality term. For an individual to 'have' a nature is for that real potentiality to be actual in this individual. To be an individual is to be a member of a natural kind.[12]

The most obviously difficult implication of this position is that it seems to imply that God cannot be properly described by any sortal term. God is not a thing of any particular kind. It is clear enough why Aquinas says something like this; he believes that to be of a certain kind (whether a generic or a specific kind) is to be only in a limited way which is just one of the ways in which it is possible to be. For that reason, Aquinas argues, if some member of a kind actually exists, it must be because that real potentiality has been actualised. The consequence is that none of the terms which denote kinds of things can be truly used to describe God. All that can be properly said of God is that he is bare existence. And that seems tantamount to saying that he barely exists; for what could it be to exist, but not to exist in any kind of way? To put the matter in terms of our earlier discussion, Aquinas is in agreement with Kant that to say that something exists is not to add any further 'determination' to the concept of a thing; here it seems further to be true that in the case of God there is no determinate concept of God's nature either. Hence talk about God seems wholly 'indeterminate'.

Despite this, Aquinas does believe that several other predicates can be properly used of God; God knows, has a will, and hence is personal; God is omnipotent, merciful, just, and good. But this apparent prodigality with real descriptions of God immediately loses its attractiveness when it is pointed out that all these attributes are identical with God's existence. Problems at once arise: if they are each identical with God's existence, are they not then identical with each other? But how can such diverse attributes be identical with one another? Moreover, if they are all identical with 'bare existence', the multiplication of apparently interesting descriptions seems to be no more than an illusion. The radical indeterminacy remains. Even Aquinas, at least sometimes, is willing to say that 'we cannot know what God is like, but rather what he is not like',[13] a position which derives from his view that none of our terms can adequately represent God at all.

> The words we use of God are indeed derived from his causal activities: for just as creatures, according to the variety of ways in which their perfections are derived, represent God albeit imperfectly, so the human mind knows God in the causal process by which creatures derive from him, and describes him accordingly. Still, these processes do not constitute the sense of the words we apply to God (as if to say 'God is living' were simply to say 'Life comes from God'); rather, we use these words to refer to the origin of all things insofar as life pre-exists in him, although it does so in a way which transcends both our powers of understanding and our way of referring.[14]
>
> (I, 13, 2)

To speak of God as 'transcending our powers of understanding' is all the more disquieting if all God's attributes are identical with his simple existence. Although Aquinas is aware of these difficulties, and tries to deal with them, quite how he does so is not always easy to determine. Part of the problem lies in deciding what Aquinas might mean by 'identical' or 'same as'. One, albeit negative, clue, is to be found in a remark he makes in asking whether any words can possibly be used of God. In considering abstract and concrete nouns, such as 'goodness', or 'John', he says:

> Now God is both simple like a form, and subsistent, like a concrete thing, and so we sometimes refer to him by abstract nouns to indicate his simplicity and sometimes by concrete nouns to indicate his subsistence and completeness;

though neither way of speaking measures up to his way of being, for in this life we do not know him as he is in himself.

(I, 13, 1)

The natural reply to the question 'What is it for two forms to be identical?' (for instance, whiteness and goodness) is to suggest that they are identical if they have the same definition; that is to say, if what it is to be F_1 is the same as what it is to be F_2. On this view, the property of being the Morning Star is not the same property as being the Evening Star. On the other hand, to ask whether two individuals are identical is normally to ask whether they have the same spatio-temporal location.[15] Now in saying that it is inadequate to think of God either as an abstract entity such as Goodness (since Aquinas is sufficiently anti-Platonist to deny that the Form of the Good itself exists), or as an individual such as John, it seems unavoidable that neither of our normal criteria for identity will be applicable to God. God is not a kind, and hence issues about identity in God cannot be settled by appeal to our criteria for identifying kinds; but neither is God an individual, since to be an individual is to be one of a kind; and so whatever tests for identity we might devise for deciding about individuals will for that very reason be inapplicable to God. Aquinas does indeed say that we cannot avoid speaking of God, however inaccurately, in both ways; and the suggestion perhaps is that each way serves to correct the other. But it does not do so in the way that we might correct something by modifying it. In the case of God, we say incompatible things, each of them in different ways helpful, while recognising that neither can be properly accurate. It is as though we were to describe light both as a wave-form and as a particle, without having any higher-level theory from which both types of equation could be derived. Wave-forms are universal, and particles are individuals; and we have (let us suppose for the sake of the parallel) no direct insight into the fundamental nature of light. To ask, therefore, whether any two attributes of God are identical one with the other is to ask a question which might be answered in two different ways, neither of which is adequate to the reality with which we are trying to deal. Both our notions of identity are strictly inapplicable.

Well, then, are God's mercy and his justice the same attribute or not? An obvious first-shot answer would be to say that they cannot be the same, since they are differently defined. The definition of mercy is in terms of, let us say, forgiveness and generosity; the definition of justice is in terms of giving people what is fair, or what they have a right to. The normal consequence of this, in Aquinas's view, would be that if an individual has both properties, there will be two numerically distinct property-instances, just because they are properties of different kinds. If they are of incompatible kinds, it will not be possible for one and the same individual to have both properties simultaneously. If there were (which he does not believe) a quasi-Platonic immaterial individual identical with Mercy Itself, that individual could not be identical with Justice Itself. Aquinas would fully accept Aristotle's views about the differences between Platonic Forms, if such there were. Moreover, he would fully accept Aristotle's criticism of Plato, that nothing can simultaneously be both a universal and an individual. On the other hand, and supposing that mercy and justice are not incompossible properties, it is quite possible that a merciful individual should be the same individual as a just individual; but her mercy would not be the same property as her justice, for all that, any more than being the Evening Star is the same property as being the Morning Star.

But this approach to the question cannot properly be applied to God. In the case of God, both types of answer are strictly inapplicable. God's mercy is not an instance of mercifulness, since instances are individual instances, and neither God nor God's mercy are individuals; yet neither is God's mercy a universal, and thereby a different universal from God's justice.[16] Hence Aquinas tries, as his preliminary remarks suggest he would, to make two claims which are strictly incompatible with one another, and yet which, as it were by making opposite mistakes, serve as mutually corrective:

> The perfections which pre-exist in God in a simple and unified way are in creatures received as many and divided. Just as to the different perfections of creatures there corresponds one simple source represented by the different perfections of creatures in many and varied ways, so to the many and varied concepts of our intellect there corresponds something entirely simple, imperfectly understood through these concepts. And so the terms applied to God, although they refer to just one thing, are not synonymous, because they refer to it through many different concepts.

> (I, 13, 4)

Aquinas is not saying that the concepts we use for God's attributes refer to the same individual reality in God; for there is no 'individual' reality in God, and 'something entirely simple' certainly does not mean a numerically one, individual, thing. Not that we have any better expression to use than 'signify just one thing'; it is simply that 'one' gives, and inevitably gives, quite the wrong impression. Moreover, it is no use denying that the different perfections of creatures are really different, so that it is beyond our conceptual grasp to explain the 'simple and unified way' in which these perfections pre-exist in God. We can do no better than use different words, for Aquinas holds that it is true to say that God is just, and that God is merciful; and he believes we need to say both. It is just inevitably the case that in so saying, we think of it as though God had both attributes; and the 'both' is incorrect.

At the very least, then, it seems to me a mistake to try to explain this passage by invoking any of our more ordinary notions of 'same X as'. The root of the problem, as Aquinas sees it, is that we cannot formulate an adequate notion of identity for use in talking about God.[17] The model which he does offer, however, of a 'simple source represented in many different ways' depends on his overall view that created things are inherently limited expressions of an actuality which is not limited. At least part of the reason why, in Aquinas's view, even true descriptions of God are so inadequate is that, precisely in having different senses, they necessarily fail to exhibit the fact that justice, mercy and existence in God are all somehow 'one' attribute.

Perhaps the following analogy might help. Consider the relationship between a loving disposition towards some person, and the actions in which that disposition finds expression. Some we might correctly describe as forgiving, others as helpful, others as severe, others as sensitive, or as critical, or practical. Moreover, some situations are such they allow someone to give a fuller expression to being loving than it is possible to achieve in others. Now, the descriptions of these various loving actions refer to genuinely different characteristics which those actions have; to be severe is not the same as to be forgiving, to be practical is not the same as to be sensitive, and so on. If one then asks whether the action-producing virtues are all identical in the loving person, the answer might reasonably be both yes and no: no, because they are different dispositions, defined in different ways; and yes, because they are

45

expressions of one fundamental disposition, which is not itself exhaustively definable. There is no end to the list, 'To be loving is to be severe when . . ., and sensitive when . . ., etc'. To discuss whether each of these dispositions is identical with being loving, or identical with one another, is in a way to ask the wrong question. 'Express' rather than 'being identical with' is the category which is needed; and the mode of expression depends on the circumstances, and on what is possible in those circumstances.

Analogies are, it must be emphasised, no more than that. One might, for instance, very reasonably say that each of these dispositions is a part of what it is to be loving, and that there is nothing more to being loving than having all these dispositions. Being loving is not one disposition at all, but involves several, distinct, dispositions. Moreover, even in expounding the analogy, I used terms like 'one' disposition, which, as has already been said, is misleading. Nevertheless, I suggest that to speak of a fundamental attribute being expressed differently according to circumstances at least puts the problems in the right places. The differences are in the actions in which the attribute is expressed, and are genuine; the relationship of fundamental attribute to the actions expressing that attribute is that between a disposition and the behaviour-patterns which are limited by various external situations. Moreover, whether the person has the disposition or not does not depend on whether it is expressed. A final advantage of this model is that the weight of the analogy rests on the notion of 'expression' and 'fundamental attribute', and thus correctly locates the points at which Aquinas would find the nature of God and his relationship to creation least open to our scrutiny.

That being said, however, Aquinas's general approach to philosophical theology requires that some attempt be made to show that even fundamentally inscrutable aspects of God must at least not be contradictory. He adopts various manoeuvres to this end. One we have already seen: we derive our distinct concepts of God's attributes from the different effects we ascribe to God, since the effects themselves are really different. But the ground in God which is expressed in these different ways is one, and it is this one ground which is the common referent of all the attribute-words we apply to God. He further claims that though we can show that there exists such a ground, we cannot know what that ground in itself essentially is. The second move which he makes is much more difficult to understand. It derives from his general Aristotelian principle that effects must somehow resemble their causes, since causes must already actually be what the effect potentially is. The obviousness of Aquinas's customary example – that to produce heat in something else, a thing has itself to be hot already – hardly disguises the fact that the similarity in question is far from clear. It is not even so obvious that an electric wire has to be as hot as the fire which it causes to heat up; and, as Anthony Kenny (1979) crisply pointed out, a cattle breeder does not have to be fat in order to fatten cattle. This kind of problem can be minimised, however, if causal statements are expressed in those terms which indicate the kind of explanation which they are intended to provide. Aristotle had already noted that even if it is true that the builder produces health, it is not *qua* builder that he does so, but because, as it happens, he is also a doctor. Now Aquinas does say that the respect in which God most properly accounts for his effects is that those effects *exist* (I, 8, 1). Such a solution, though it does go some way to making things clearer, is still only of limited value. To say that God explains his merciful effects in creation in respect of their existence, and to offer the same explanation of his just effects, is to offer little or no explanation at all. Aquinas would doubtless wish to say that the different effects differ because of differences in the worldly circumstances in which God's action is experienced. But even if one accepts that, what still remains difficult is that the one ground resembles all these effects simply in virtue of their existence, and that is 'bare' resemblance indeed. This is perhaps a criticism that Aquinas would accept as unavoidable. He does not think it is possible to appeal to anything in God as an *explanation*,[18] since for him explanations require prior knowledge of the essence of the explanans, knowledge which is not available where the explanans is God. So the key notions of 'expression' and 'fundamental attribute' turn out not to be explanatory at all.

So the best Aquinas can do is to argue that, since he has already, as he believes, proved that there is such a ground, we know that it must be such as to be capable of being expressed in just these different ways. Since we correctly ascribe various attributes to a simple God, our attributions to God must, *a fortiori*, be consistent. But, just as our explanations appeal to the relevant kinds of features in a causal agent, so our normal test for consistency involves appeal to kinds of attributes which are, or are not, compatible. Still, if God is entirely simple, he has no attributes of a particular kind, generic or specific; and to say that God explains the existence of things because he is himself unlimited existence is completely vague once it is remembered that existence is not a kind of thing at all. Aquinas does not believe that the divine simplicity makes God completely indescribable; but he does believe that it places severe restrictions on our ability to grasp the sense of the descriptions which might justifiably be offered.

c) The identity of essence and existence in God

Aquinas frequently and unhesitatingly speaks of the essence of God. Such talk is liable to mislead, since the normal sense of essence, in Aquinas as in Aristotle, is an answer to the question 'What is X?'; the term 'essence' refers to the *de re* potentiality for there to be an individual of the kind specified in the essence, and essences in the full sense are species of a genus. None of these things is true of the essence of God. It is not an answer to the question 'What is it to be God?', since Aquinas holds that we do not know the answer to that question; it does not refer to any potentiality; and it cannot be defined in terms of genus and species. Perhaps his view of the matter involves an extended use of the term 'essence', just as to speak of existence as an accident of existing created things involves a broader, non-Aristotelian, sense of 'accident'. To say that existence is essential to God then amounts to saying no more than that God exists *de re* necessarily, without giving any account of what it is for something to exist *de re* necessarily. This leaves us with a notion of a necessary being which, as Kant says, 'is very far from sufficing to show whether I am still thinking anything in the concept of the unconditionally necessary, or rather nothing at all.' Or, as Christopher Hughes (1989: 57) puts it, 'a subsistent individual constituted of existence, and nothing but existence is too thin to be possible'.

d) Summary of classical definition of simplicity

Simplicity excludes *de re* potentiality, and hence is not an attribute of any being B if any of the following conditions are met:

i)   B can be caused to undergo some intrinsic accidental change.[19]

ii) B consists of material which could constitute some X which is not identical with B.[20]

iii)   B is a member of a kind.

The consequences of saying that there is a being which is potential in none of these ways are highly important: such a being is non-material, unchangeable, hence eternal, transcendent (that is to say, not such that it can be described adequately in any of the Aristotelian categories);[21] and since the reasons for supposing that there is such a being would be causal reasons, it might be thought reasonable to suppose that such a being is the causal explanation of everything else that there is. The notion of simplicity is quite central to Aquinas's attempts to identify the being whose existence he takes to be established by the Five Ways with the God of traditional Christian belief.

Everything therefore depends on whether i) – iii) can each be said to be a sufficient condition of the presence in something of a *de re* potentiality. In this connection, i) and ii) are uncontroversial. The main problems arise with iii), and with the very strong conclusions which Aquinas draws from it. For it is his contention that whatever is a member of a kind is such that, unless it is being caused to exist, it would simply cease to exist altogether. Why should one believe this at all? What feature of the members of kinds involves this totally radical existential instability?[22]

So put, the question might seem to Aquinas to be not too well phrased. Because he believes that in the strictest sense every *kind* of thing, if by that is meant an essence specifiable in terms of genus and species, is such that there need be no things of that kind, it simply seems obvious to him that if any member of that kind exists, it must be being caused to exist, since it actualises the potentiality expressed by the kind-term. There is no *further* feature of such things which explains their instability. Similarly, the only thing which exists of necessity is precisely one whose essence is not to be a kind of thing. In which case it follows that it is simply not possible to spell out what it is that renders some things contingent by nature, and God not. There just is no attribute F, other than the negative 'attribute' of not being a member of a kind, such that God has it, and all other things do not have it, which will function in an explanatory way to distinguish between the necessarily and the contingently existing. Nevertheless, he would claim, any structured thing – where 'structured' means 'being of some specifiable kind' – cannot exist without being caused to exist. As we have already seen in the previous chapter, it was just this claim that Kant sees no reason to accept, since Kant thinks that even the structured universe might well be unconditionally necessary, for all we know to the contrary.

So there are at least two major problems with Aquinas's view:

a) It is not obvious that kind-terms do refer to real potentialities in the world, whose actualisation requires a cause.

b) Even if a) is conceded, it still does not follow that *at every moment* beings which actualise that potentiality need a sustaining cause in order to exist. Once in existence, why can't they remain so of themselves, so to speak?

Hume

Hume's attack on the notion of simplicity begins with the difficulty of giving any coherent description of something which is simple in the traditional sense.

The down-to-earth Cleanthes has attacked Demea's denial that the Deity resembles ourselves, claiming that Demea retreats into a kind of unintelligible 'mysticism' of the ineffable. The following passage is Demea's reply, spelling out his traditionalist position, and protesting that 'mystic' need not be a term of abuse. To be a 'mystic' is better than crudely depicting God in all-too-human terms:

What is the soul of man? A composition of various faculties, passions, sentiments, ideas; united indeed into one self or person, but still distinct from each other. When it reasons, the ideas, which are the parts of its discourse, arrange themselves in a certain form or order; which is not preserved entire for a moment, but immediately, gives place to another arrangement. New opinions, new passions, new affections, new feelings arise, which continually diversify the mental scene, and produce in it the greatest variety, and the most rapid succession imaginable.

How is this compatible, with that perfect immutability and simplicity which all true Theists ascribe to the Deity? By the same act, say they, he sees past, present, and future: His love and his hatred, his mercy and his justice, are one individual operation; He is entire in every point of space; and complete in every instant of duration. No succession, no change, no

50

acquisition, no diminution. What he is implies not in it any shadow of distinction or diversity. And what he is, this moment, he ever has been, and ever will be, without any new judgement, sentiment or operation. He stands fixed in one simple, perfect state; nor can you ever say, with any propriety, that this act of his is different from that other, or that this judgment or idea has been lately formed, and will give place, by succession, to any different judgment or idea.

(*Dialogues*, IV)

Demea's account is a pretty fair summary of Aquinas's view. Cleanthes is quite unconvinced. He takes this defence as providing yet further evidence that Demea's position is unintelligible. Indeed, it is worse than that:

I can readily allow that those who maintain the perfect simplicity of the Supreme Being, to the extent in which you have explained it, are complete MYSTICS, and chargeable with all the consequences which I have drawn from their opinion. They are, in a word, ATHEISTS without knowing it. A mind . . . that is wholly simple, and totally immutable; is a mind, which has no thought, no reason, no will, no sentiment, no love, no hatred; or, in a word, is no mind at all. It is an abuse of terms to give it that appellation, and we may as well speak of limited extension without figure, or of number without composition.

(*Ibid.*)

In short, for God to be simple, as traditionally defined, would entail that God has no attributes at all, since all these attributes are differently, and hence distinctly, defined. Moreover, all the attributes which theists might regard as most important in a Deity presuppose that of being a Mind, since without that, to claim that something possesses attributes like justice, mercy, love, freedom, reason and knowledge simply make no sense; but God cannot be simple and have a mind in any intelligible sense of that term.

Hume's criticisms are two-pronged. For no sooner has Cleanthes accused mystics of being implicit atheists, than Philo (doubtless here speaking for Hume himself) criticises the anthropomorphism into which Cleanthes himself must retreat. Philo waives, for the moment, his own views about the inadequacy of causal arguments and objects in the following way:

i)   God has a mind like ours.

ii) The regularity of the operations of our minds needs an explanation in terms of God the all-wise designer (according to Cleanthes).

iii) But by parallel argument, the regularity of God's mind must also require a causal explanation.

iv) In both cases, the 'explanation' will simply be an appeal to an occult property of 'rationality'.

v)   But *either* this is no explanation at all

    or this, and no further, explanation will suffice in our case too, without bringing God in at all.

A useless explanation might just as well be brought in early as late in the argument. Cleanthes will be unwilling to deny iv) as it applies to God; if he persists in rejecting Demea's 'mysticism' he cannot deny i); Cleanthes is already committed to ii), and hence, given i), to iii). Cleanthes blusters, and tries to deny iv) by claiming simple ignorance of explanations in the case of God, a view which Philo dismisses out of hand as a simple evasion.

The dilemma is thereby posed. If simplicity is taken seriously, it is impossible to say anything whatsoever about God, and this is tantamount in practice to atheism; if it is not, then God provides no end to the need for causal explanation if there is such a need at all.

Though the argument is put in terms of attributes which Hume would accept as being genuine attributes, it could be adapted, I think, to take in the case of existence, which Hume does not believe to be an attribute in the proper sense at all. Consider:

i*)   God exists, as we do.

ii*) Our existence stands in need of explanation.

iii*) By parallel argument, so also does God's existence.

iv*) In both cases, the 'explanation' will take the form of an appeal to the occult property of 'necessity'.

v*)   But *either* that is no explanation at all

    or it might as well be invoked at the outset.

The theist, it might be said, would be unwise to deny i*) under threat of being an implicit atheist; and will be unwilling to deny ii*) and hence cannot escape iii*). But any cosmological argument to explain the existence of empirical things will invoke some notion of necessity, as iv*) states. Hence the unpalatable v*) remains. It might further be argued that if the theist attempts to deny i*) by appealing at *that* point to *de re* necessary existence, which distinguishes God's existence from ours, the first limb of v*) seems all the more pressing. If God's existence is so different, is it proper to describe it as 'existence' at all, and is not this once more a case of an 'abuse of terms', unless we can spell out in what respects necessary and contingent existence resemble one another? But, Hume pointedly remarks, 'when you go one step beyond the mundane system, you only excite an inquisitive humour, which it is impossible ever to satisfy.'

The force of the arguments (both Hume's, and the one I have reconstructed on Hume's behalf) rests on i) and iv) in each case. These premises therefore need more careful assessment. In support of i), Hume's suggestion is that the only way to deny it involves a relapse into such a version of 'mysticism' as to be altogether vacuous. It is to use terms like 'mind' or 'exists' in a fashion which deprives them of all the criteria by which we normally give meaning to those terms. Just as we cannot imagine a mind in which there is no reasoning, no set of changing ideas, no new opinions, so neither (Hume might say) can we imagine an existence which is not existence-as-an-X, where X is some readily comprehensible term like 'human being' or 'geranium' or 'instance of whiteness'. To say in the one case that what is central to being a mind (as distinct from our *concept* of what it is to be a mind) is distinct from the operations which some minds might perform is to appeal to an 'occult property', which is quite incapable of explaining the connection between the activities of the minds with which we are acquainted. Similarly, to say that what is central to existence itself (as contrasted with the finitely existing things with which we are acquainted) is distinct from any way of existing as-an-X is to invoke an occult notion which has no explanatory power at all. At least at the outset, this latter objection is quite separate, as Hume claims it is, from any further problems one might have with causal explanations generally, or with the particular problems about whether existence is properly considered as an attribute at all.

Hume's criticisms, then, come to this: he objects to using 'occult powers' as explanations, quite in general. 'Rationality' is one such alleged explanation of the regular workings of our minds; and (I suggest) 'necessary existence' is another pseudo-explanation of the existence of things. In either case, Hume might say, appeal to such powers might as well be made at the outset, without having to go all the way back to God. Our minds behave as they do, and things exist as they do, because of the way they are. If the theist attempts to avoid this, by saying that it is only these powers *as possessed by God* which will provide an adequate explanation, Hume will retort that if the divine version of these powers were so different from earthly versions as to avoid the need for further explanation, then the powers would be even more 'occult' than they are in the earthly cases. God's self-explaining mind, and his self-explaining existence would have to be so different from ours as to be beyond all our powers of expression. That, he argues, is a position which is tantamount to atheism. God fails as an explanation for the properties of the world, and for the existence of the world because no coherent sense of 'explanation' is available. Aquinas believes that he can give some sense both to the terms used of God, and to the sense of 'explanation' in which God explains the existence of the universe.

In short, the crucial point to emerge from Hume's criticisms of divine simplicity is that the meaningfulness of any of the terms which might be used to speak of a simple God will depend upon the explanatory framework within which those terms are employed. To the extent that we have a genuine explanation, the sense of the terms involved can then be examined. But if, as Hume claims, there is no genuine explanation at all, the diagnosis of the failure will be that the allegedly explanatory terms in fact carried no coherent sense. If this is a correct reading of Hume, his position will to this extent be not unlike that of Aquinas, who also maintains that the justification for saying that terms used of God have a sense will in the end depend on whether these terms can function in an adequate explanation of the things we experience and call by our ordinary names. Aquinas believed that he can spell out what is meant by 'adequate explanation', and can therefore give at least some sense to the terms which that explanation will contain. Hume does not believe that either of these claims can be defended.

Kant

Kant does not directly deal with the attribute of simplicity as it was classically conceived. But he deals at great (indeed repetitive) length with the concept of absolute necessity which, as we have seen, Aquinas links very closely to the notion of God's simplicity. And he offers a notion of the *ens realissimum* ('the supremely real being') which is not unlike that defended by Aquinas. The concept of an *ens realissimum*, says Kant, involves all the following claims:

i)   It is the sufficient condition of the existence of everything else.

ii)   It contains all reality.

iii) It is absolute unity.

Hence, says Kant, it is reasonable to suppose that it is the source of all created possibility (A587). The difficulty, as Kant sees it, is to demonstrate that the combination of these three concepts corresponds to an objective possibility. Moreover, he remarks, while it may be granted that i) – iii) would indeed provide a sufficient ground for all possibilities, what proof do we have that ii) and iii) are necessary conditions for something to be the unconditioned ground of all possibilities (A588)? Why should we think that if i) is true of something, ii) and iii) must also be true of it? Why should we assume that the ultimate reality is also the highest reality (A590)?

His answer is that there is no good reason why we should make that assumption:

> The transcendental object lying at the basis of appearances (and with it the reason why our sensibility is subject to certain supreme conditions rather than to others) is and remains to us inscrutable. The thing itself is given, but we have no insight into its nature.

Why? Because the only way we have of recognising whether a concept is a concept of what is really possible is by demonstrating that the object of that concept can be an object of experience. But this cannot be done in the case of an *ens realissimum*. At most we could show that the concept of such a being involves no contradiction; but that is quite insufficient to show that it is the concept of something really possible.

In some ways, Kant approaches the matter from the opposite direction to that taken by Aquinas. Whereas Aquinas tries to determine what simplicity is by excluding *de re* potentialities, Kant considers attempts to define it by determining the concept of *de re* necessity. Would he have found Aquinas's approach any more likely to succeed? Clearly, in a formal sense what is in no way *de re* potential will be equivalent to what is *de re* necessary. So the question then is, would Kant accept Aquinas's general view that, although we have no direct grasp of what it is to exist *de re* necessarily (which is Kant's point too), nevertheless we do have a grasp of what it is to be *de re* potential, since empirical things, though 'less knowable in themselves, are more knowable to us.' We could then use this knowledge at least to arrive at a notion of what 'God is not', as Aquinas puts it.

But this Kant would not accept. He argues firstly that there is no *a priori* way of knowing that a concept is a concept of something which could exist: this is implied by his willingness to distinguish between the necessity of judgments and the necessity of things (A593). We can establish *a priori* that of necessity triangles have three angles, but this says nothing about whether triangles exist-of-necessity. Nor does it establish more than what Kant terms 'internal possibility' (A597); he comments

> For though, in my concept, nothing may be lacking of the possible real content of a thing, something is still lacking in its relation to my whole state of thought, namely, that knowledge of this object is also possible *a posteriori*. And here we find the source of our present difficulty. Were we dealing with an object of the senses, we could not confound the existence of the thing with the mere concept of it. For through the concept the object is thought only as conforming to the *universal conditions* of possible empirical knowledge in general, whereas through its existence it is thought as belonging to the context of experience as a whole.
>
> (A600)

The first occurrence of 'possible' in this passage must be to 'internal' possibility, the criterion for which is simple non-contradiction. 'Possible *a posteriori*' will then refer to *de re* possibility. Whether something *de re* can exist cannot be discovered merely by showing that our concept of it contains no contradiction. It can be discovered only by experiencing that the thing is *de re* actual. That the concept of X contains no contradiction is a necessary, but not a sufficient, condition of X's being *de re* possible. One might, indeed, strengthen Kant's case, by saying that the non-contradictoriness of the concept is not even a necessary condition. Our concepts, as they happen to

56

be, need not reflect the natures of things accurately at all; and the conceptually contradictory might be *de re* possible for all we know to the contrary. Of course, were we to discover that it is possible to produce, say, a winged horse, we would thereby revise the concept 'horse'; but such revision would follow, not precede, the discovery. Well, then, how could we discover whether it is possible that the universe is contingent? Kant claims that, for all we know, it exists *de re* necessarily.

> It by no means follows that the concept of a limited being which does not have the highest reality is for that reason incompatible with absolute necessity. For although I do not find in its concept that unconditioned which is involved in the totality of conditions, we are not justified in concluding that its existence must for this reason be conditioned.[23]
>
>   (A588)

I take it that Kant believes that the conditionedness of many individual material things is given to us in experience, since we of necessity relate them by cause and effect. What he is here denying is that the *mere* fact that something is conceived of as limited precludes our conceiving of it as unconditioned. Thus one might ask whether the universe might not be unconditioned, and have no criterion on which to answer that question. Aquinas would argue that the fact that something is limited shows that it has existence in a limited way, and for that very reason shows that it need not exist, since the idea of limitation involves *de re* potentiality. It is for that reason that, in his view, we are justified in extending the principle of causation beyond the realm of possible experience. Kant believes this is illegitimate, precisely because he sees no conceptual connection between being limited and being *de re* contingent. 'On the contrary, we are entirely free to hold that any limited beings whatsoever, notwithstanding their being limited, may also be unconditionally necessary, although we cannot infer their necessity from the universal concepts we have of them' (A588). And, of course, we cannot, other than by an invalid use of the ontological argument, try to argue that the *ens realissimum* is unconditionally necessary.

In short, Kant's most basic problem with the notion of a totally simple and unconditioned being which is the sufficient condition for everything else is not directly with its simplicity; it is that there is no justification in our experience for linking the ideas of simplicity and being absolutely unconditioned. Of course he objects to 'existence' being part of the definition of anything, and would therefore object even more strongly to 'existence' being a complete definition of anything. But that objection is not really central; the basic point is that not even necessary existence can be the definition of anything. Existing-of-necessity is not an empirical feature of anything, nor can it be deduced from the concept of anything which we can experience. Aquinas's efforts to arrive at the divine simplicity through negation of *de re* conditionedness is therefore doomed to failure, unless one can demonstrate the link between the mere fact of being limited and being *de re* capable of non-existence.

SOME ANSWERS

The core of the doctrine of simplicity is the identity of essence and existence. But this core doctrine, at least in its classical formulation, involves two distinguishable claims. The first is that the non-existence of something in which existence and essence are identical is *de re* impossible; and the second is that something in which essence and existence are identical is not a member of any kind, that is to say, has no internal structure at all. It will be convenient to take these two points separately.

Simplicity and necessary existence

In one of the most recent studies of the nature and logic of God's existence, Barry Miller (1992) undertakes the ambitious task of showing not merely that the concept of a necessarily existent being is coherent, but in addition that it is logically contradictory to assert the existence of the universe while denying the existence of a necessarily existent being. To establish the point about coherence, he argues that there is no conclusive objection to the view that existence is genuinely an attribute of things; and he takes it as evident that, since some things need not exist, they do not exist of necessity. That is to say, their existence and their essence are distinct. He then argues that there is a logical contradiction involved in saying both that we can understand 'Fido exists' because we have a *prior* understanding of 'Fido' and '—— exists', and that Fido is conceivable only as existing (or having existed). He then argues that the contradiction can be removed only on the assumption that Fido's existence is caused.[24]

I have considerable sympathy with this argument. If I hesitate to endorse it entirely, it is because I am less confident than Miller that one can make the jump from logic to ontology in the way in which Miller does. But the general strategy seems to me sound. If it is possible to distinguish between something's capacity for existence and its existence, then it is not the case that it exists simply in virtue of the fact of its existence.

So let me come at the problem from a different angle, to reach somewhat the same place. I have already argued that to exist just is to be capable of entering into causal relationships. Taken in that way, existence is a property of all existing things, but, as Anthony Kenny points out (1979: 95), the property is so vague, so 'thin', as to be largely uninteresting. Not completely uninteresting, though, since it does serve to distinguish some things from others – for instance, it distinguishes between the Eiffel Tower and the Number Two.[25] Be that as it may, 'being such as to be able to cease to exist' and 'being such as to be unable to cease to exist' are by no means uninteresting properties, even if 'exists' itself fails to excite. And they are interesting precisely because they lead directly to a discussion of what something which has either of those properties would be like. To be able not to exist is a property which, as we might expect, is different in different cases. We know, and can spell out, what it is for my pain to cease to exist, or for my friendship with Jemima to cease to exist, or for me to cease to exist, or for an atom to cease to exist. We have to give somewhat different accounts in each case, and hence different accounts of what it is about these various existing qualities, or relationships, or substances, which makes their non-existence *de re* possible. What is not by any means so clear is whether we can give a *complete* list of the various ways in which existing things are able not to exist. In particular, we are at the very least unclear whether the energy/matter in the universe has this ability or not, and, if it does, what it is for it to have this ability. I take this to be the central point that Kant makes in his discussion of the notion of an *ens necessarium*. He rightly sees that the question cannot be answered in the terms which are provided by our everyday experience and the scientific accounts of that experience which we can develop.[26] The interesting question is whether there is any other account which is possible, and whether such an account in any way forces itself upon our attention.

Necessary existence and transcendence[27]

Aquinas maintained that there is a close connection between being an individual, being a member of a kind, and being capable of non-existence.[28] The link between the first two is Aristotelian, in that it was taken as clear that a substance is a 'this-such' – an individual of a kind. Since there is no kind of thing to which God belongs, God is not an individual either. To be an individual is to be *an* individual, one among possibly many individuals. But it is the second link which is more controversial. Were it to be shown that to be a member of a kind is to be capable of non-existence, a major step would have been taken towards showing that all empirical entities are capable of non-existence. For to be a member of a kind is to have some structural features which are essential features; and even the universe itself, or the energy in which it consists, is essentially structured. Were this not the case, the most fundamental laws of physics, including the Law of the Conservation of Energy, simply would not hold at all. They hold good in the nature of things. Everything in the universe, and the universe itself, is a thing of a kind whose essential properties account for the truth of the causal laws according to which it behaves. Once again, it has to be emphasised that whether the universe is capable of non-existence is not a question which can be resolved by appeal to the fact that there is no logical contradiction involved in supposing that the universe might not exist; nor is to be resolved by supposing that we can imagine that it does not, if indeed we can. The issue is whether it embodies such a *de re* possibility or not; and that is an empirical and not simply a conceptual or psychological matter, as I have argued in Chapter I.[29]

In contrast to Miller's appeal to logic at this point, the question is why should membership of a kind involve such a *de re* possibility? I suspect that Aquinas simply takes it as evident that kind-terms denote real possibilities, and that to be a member of a kind is therefore for that possibility to have been caused to be actual. He also takes it as evident that no possibility is actualised except by the action of a moving cause. But that assumption might simply be denied altogether, or at least it might be denied that it is evident, as Kant does by implication.

Perhaps an argument might be made along the following lines, in three main stages. The first step is this. To be a member of a kind is to satisfy the description by which that kind is defined. Since kind-terms are universals it is logically possible for there to be indefinitely many individuals which satisfy that description, and equally, that it is logically possible for there to be none. There is no logical necessity for there to be any individual satisfying any given predicate, and in any case logic is not a good guide to what is causally possible. Still, in general there is reason to believe that natural kind-terms describe not merely logically possible individuals, but causally possible individuals. Perhaps one can conclude that natural kind-terms are likely to describe *de re* possibilities, and where they do not there is still room for science to progress. If this is so, then the causal laws which are true of our universe describe what is causally possible. And this causal possibility is not merely logically, but also onto-logically prior to the existence of this individual universe in which that set of possibilities is actualised.

The second step goes like this. Unlike purely logical possibilities, *de re* possibilities must be grounded in something actual. For a *de re* possibility to exist just is for something to have the causal power to produce an individual instance of the kind in question. And if the *de re* possibility of this universe existing is ontologically prior to the existing universe, then that possibility must be grounded in something which is causally able to produce such a universe. Did such a ground not exist, then the universe would not be *de re* possible at all, and therefore could not exist.

The third step is to notice that, if the preceding steps are right, no existing thing is *de re* possible at all unless there exists something which is *de re* necessary; that is to say, something which is not a member of any kind, and hence is not an individual realisation of a prior *de re* possibility. Hence there must exist a being which is altogether simple and unstructured, or nothing else *de re* could exist.

The key moves in this argument are the two assertions that existing in a structured way is an actualisation of a *de re* possibility; and that the ground of such a possibility must lie in something actual. It is of course a matter of dispute whether these assertions are true, and, if they are, how we could know that they are. As with Aristotelian first principles, there is no further known truth from which these assertions can be logically derived. There is inductive evidence for both of them; but if it is questioned whether inductive evidence can produce *knowledge*, the question then becomes one about our criteria for applying the honorific term 'knowledge' quite generally. The very nature of that question is far from clear, at least to me. What

I think is clear is that the success or failure of anything like the classical doctrine of simplicity, and indeed of the classical proofs for the existence of God, depends on some argument of the kind I have just sketched.

Describing the transcendent

Supposing that God exists *de re* necessarily, and hence is simple in the sense elaborated in the preceding discussion, it is plain that attempts to describe God must either fail completely, or at best be very inadequate. Our language is developed precisely to deal with individuals and kinds of thing; with John or Jemima, with humans, colours, atoms and energy. It is under strain when we try to describe even this-worldly items which we are not equipped directly to experience, such as quarks, or Black Holes, or the *n*-dimensional universe. To grasp the significance even of the mathematical formulae with which we try to capture the behaviour of such things, we have to interpret them using metaphor and other similar devices, in an attempt to 'read' what we think we have discovered. We have to construct models to aid our understanding, and these models function for us only because they are constructed using the ordinary items of which we do have direct experience.[30]

Our language is surely even less well adapted to attempt to describe a being which is not an individual, nor classifiable under any univocal kind-term. We shall be much more clear in saying what such a being is not than in giving positive descriptions of what it is like. Since I have already discussed this point at some length elsewhere (G.J. Hughes 1987), I shall content myself here with saying that we need to be sufficiently modest to recognise that the deficiencies in our knowledge of God derive not from any incoherence in God, but from our own limited experience, and sense-bound cognitive apparatus. In particular, though, I think we should be wary of the view that to hold that God is simple makes it impossible for us to say anything useful about God in human terms. It is sometimes argued that unless God is at least in some respects much more like us, then we will be inevitably deprived of the rich metaphorical tradition which characterises the language of all religions. There is no need to suppose that a strong doctrine of God's transcendence has as an inevitable consequence that we must *think* of God in remote, impersonal terms which are religiously quite unhelpful. On the contrary, it seems to me that such terms are quite unavoidable, and not necessarily useless or uninformative, provided that they are not taken for more than they are.

CHAPTER III

Omniscience

The classical tradition in philosophy of religion was unanimous in saying that God knows everything. Such an all-encompassing knowledge was considered essential to belief in a God who was in all ways perfect, and whose providence guided all things for good. But the notion of an omniscient God was far from unproblematic. The tradition wrestled with the difficulties inherent in the attempt to assert simultaneously a series of apparently conflicting claims, each of which seemed to have solid reasons in its favour. These were:

A God has the attribute of simplicity.
B God cannot be changed.
C God knows all things.
D Human beings can make free choices.

The apparent conflicts are easy to see. A, which denies that there are any real distinctions in God, at least does not easily fit with C, which suggests that God has various pieces of knowledge, above all knowledge of each individual human being. B is difficult to reconcile with C; for how can God have knowledge which is both complete and unchanging of a world which is essentially time-bound and changing? And while D seems to involve the thought that things might turn out differently right up until a particular choice is made, B and C together strongly suggest that God unchangeably knew in advance what the person was about to choose, and that his knowledge is not altered by any choice that person might make. The long and complex history of the discussion consists of a series of attempts to interpret each of these four statements in such a way that they are both philosophically coherent, and at the same time consonant with what were taken to be essential elements of the Christian belief in a perfect, all-wise and all-provident God.

THE HISTORY OF THE PROBLEM

Three writers have been especially influential in discussions of omniscience. Aquinas provided a systematic and integrated version of the various views expressed in the Aristotelian and Platonist traditions as they came down to him through Augustine, Boethius, the Arab Commentators on Aristotle, and the Jewish philosopher Maimonides. William of Ockham, who taught at the University of Oxford fifty years later, found much to criticise both in Aquinas and in his own predecessor Duns Scotus. And the Jesuit theologian, Luis de Molina, writing in the sixteenth century, endeavoured to defend a roughly Thomist position against earlier critics, by supplementing Aquinas's treatment with some radically new ideas of his own. The views of all three men have recently aroused renewed interest. Aquinas, Ockham and Molina therefore provide the best historical introduction to the current state of the debate.

Aquinas

OMNISCIENCE AND SIMPLICITY

Aquinas's account of what it is to know something derives in most of its essentials from Aristotle.[1] Aristotle begins with an explanation of sensing and perceiving.[2] Perceiving involves an alteration in the perceiver. This alteration can be described both in physical terms, as a process of change brought about in a sense-organ, and in psychological terms as having a particular sensation. The sensation truly represents the sense-property of the object because, quite generally, causes produce effects which resemble those causes. So the alteration in the perceiver resembles that property of the object which enabled it to interact with the perceiver's sense-organ. In short, the perceiver becomes like the perceived object, at least in that the perceiver becomes, say, seeing-red when perceiving a red-object.[3]

Perhaps unwisely, Aristotle endeavours to adapt the general outlines of this account of sensation to provide an account of what it is to know something. In knowing, the mind comes to be like the object known. If what is known is a horse, the mind takes on the form of horse, without, of course, becoming a horse, and this mental state just is the state of knowing what a horse is. The object is known because the knower is aware of himself as related to the object

65

through his conscious mental state. It remains rather unclear quite how this mental state is further to be characterised. Aquinas is willing to use terms like 'representation' and even 'likeness' to describe the relationship between a concept and the object known through that concept. But it is not at all clear to what extent, if at all, either Aquinas or Aristotle take it to be the case that the mental state of the knower is a kind of image of the object. Their use of terms like 'likeness' might suggest that it is, whereas their general view that understanding is not a physical state might suggest that expressions such as 'likeness' and 'representation' are to be understood metaphorically.

Whatever the details of this account might be, Aquinas's general strategy for reconciling the statement that God knows things with the view that God is totally simple is clear. He suggests that the various elements in the Aristotelian analysis of knowing are all, in God, identical one with another. Thus the mind of God is identical with the essence of God, and the formal assimilation of mind to object – what Aquinas terms the *species intelligibilis* – is identical with the mind of God. The act of knowing is identically the same act by which God exists (I, 14, 4). God's knowledge in no way involves being affected by something else, since that would entail that it was incomplete prior to being so affected (I, 14, 2 reply 2). God knows all things in himself, in that he knows all the ways in which things can resemble him by participating in his perfections (I, 14, 5).

It is, of course, one thing to make these assertions, and quite another to make sense of them. It might help to recall what was argued in the previous chapter, that our normal criteria for identity are difficult to apply when one is talking about the attributes of God. From our human standpoint, we distinguish between different formal characteristics by defining them differently; and when we speak of the identity of different individuals (whether substances, or property-instances), we have in mind numerical identity. Aquinas reminds us that both of these ways of speaking, while unavoidable, are strictly inapplicable to God. But he takes it that they can serve as mutually corrective. Thus, we do have to distinguish between God's intellect and God's will, since, in our own understanding of these powers, intellect and will are differently defined and have different objects. The intellect is defined in terms of truth, the will in terms of goodness. But if God is simple, these two powers must be one – except that 'two' and 'one' cannot be taken in a numerical sense when applied to God.

Even if, given the difficulties in speaking about God, one is willing to accept that some such general account will do, it seems to be much more problematic when it comes to the claim that God's knowledge of any one thing is identical with his knowledge of any other. The difficulty is hardly lessened by Aquinas's insistence that God knows individual things not in general terms (for instance, simply as falling under the notion of 'existence') but as having all the properties they have,[4] and as being distinct individuals.[5] How is it possible that distinct individuals are known in all their individuality in one simple act of knowledge?

Aquinas was later to be criticised by Ockham for holding that being a knower and being an immaterial substance somehow go hand in hand.[6] Whatever the difficulties of this view, it is important in that it throws some light on what Aquinas takes perfect knowing to be like. It is something like 'perfect self-awareness', which includes an awareness of all the relationships in which one stands to other things. This awareness does not presuppose a piecemeal formulation of its content, but is given all at once. Human self-awareness, which is as it were spread out over time, and needs to be formulated in order to be appropriated, is a very imperfect kind of knowing. Some such picture of perfect knowledge underlies everything that Aquinas says in trying to reconcile God's knowledge with God's simplicity.

He makes several attempts to formulate this basic idea, in order to deal with the more general problems. The first, in I, 15, 1–3, follows the Christianised version of the Platonic tradition as exemplified in Augustine. Aquinas concedes that there are as many (as it were Platonic) ideas in the mind of God as there are things that God knows. This tradition seemed to be worth keeping because it fitted so well with the doctrine of a providential God who, unlike the Neo-Platonic One, is concerned with the fate of each individual creature. Still, in going along with this respected view, Aquinas tries, rather unsuccessfully, to reconcile it with his own doctrine of the divine simplicity. He offers a comparison. The architect knows all the details of the house he is designing by having its form completely in mind:

> It is not contrary to the simplicity of the divine intellect to understand many things; but it would be if God's mind were informed by several likenesses. . . . This can be seen in the following way. God knows his essence perfectly, and hence

knows it in every way in which it is knowable. Now, it can be known not only as it is in itself, but in so far as it is participable by creatures with some degree of resemblance. But every creature has its own specific way of somehow participating in the likeness of the divine essence. Therefore God, in knowing his essence as being imitable in this way by such and such a creature, knows it as the definition and idea which belongs to that creature, and so on.

(I, 15, 2)

The contrast is between the total prior grasp which an architect has of the house he will build, and the piecemeal way in which this knowledge is expressed in building the house, feature at a time. To know the house through and through as the architect does is thereby to know all its features, in one act of knowing. In an attempt to head off objections to this, Aquinas does comment that 'the relations which multiply Ideas are not in created things but in God. But they are not real relations . . . but relations understood by God' (*Ibid.*, reply 4). In so saying, he is trying to maintain the notion of simplicity. But why stress that God has several ideas, if they are not really distinct, rather than say straight out that it is *we* who have to think of God's knowledge in this way?

A more useful approach is offered in I, 14, 14, in which Aquinas, while arguing that God must know all propositions, also denies that God knows propositions as such:

Just as God knows material things in an immaterial way, and composite things in a simple way, so he knows propositions, but not in a propositional way, as though in his intellect there were a combining and separation [of terms] into propositions, but rather by knowing each thing by a simple intellectual act, understanding each thing's essence. In such a way we too, did we know what it is to be a man, would thereby know everything that could be predicated of a man.

Part of the difficulty in understanding a passage like the above lies in the term *enuntiabile*, which I have here translated as 'proposition'. The relationship between an *enuntiabile* and a state of affairs or an event is not immediately clear. Aquinas explicitly denies the 'Nominalist' position that 'Christ is being born', 'Christ was born' and 'Christ will be born' are one and the same *enuntiabile* just because they refer to one and the same event (I, 14, 6). He gives two reasons:

> A difference in the parts of what is said produces a difference in propositions;[7] further, it would follow that a proposition which is once true is always true, contrary to Aristotle who states that the saying 'Socrates is sitting' is true while he is sitting, and the same saying is false when he is getting up.

Aquinas defends the immutability of God's knowledge by agreeing that what God timelessly knows is the event of Christ's birth. But he also defends the view that God knows all three of these different statements, though not by formulating each of them one term at a time. I take the suggestion to be that in one simple act God knows not simply the event, but the event *as time-bound*. To know it as time-bound is to know that tensed propositions about it can be formulated, even though God does not need to formulate those propositions in order to have that knowledge.[8] As we might put it, God's knowledge of the birth of Christ as time-bound consists in God's knowing 'At t_1 Christ's birth lies in the future', 'At t_2 Christ's birth is present' and 'At t_3 Christ's birth is past'.[9]

OMNISCIENCE ABOUT A TIME-BOUND WORLD

Aquinas was firmly committed to the view, already formulated by Boethius, that God is eternal, though the detailed interpretation of his view is a matter of controversy.[10] On general grounds, Aquinas thinks that our attempts to speak about eternity in a language which is primarily adapted to express our time-bound experience are bound to be unsatisfactory. 'We can understand and speak of the simplicity of eternity only after the manner of time-bound things, since it is these composite and time-bound things that we ordinarily and naturally understand' (I, 13, 1). His general remarks about using language which is known to be inadequate, but which can be used in a self-correcting way, will apply here too. In that spirit, I think, Aquinas would wish to say the following things:

i)   Eternity is not an everlasting length of time, since it is not a length of time at all. In that sense, eternity has no duration.

ii) Eternity is not durationless in the sense in which a point in time is durationless. A point in time is an abstract entity, conceived of as the limit of an extended period of time. In so far as eternity is the most real form of existence, it is therefore not durationless.

iii) Nothing in eternity takes place at the same time as any event in time; firstly because nothing in eternity 'takes place' at all; and secondly, because nothing in eternity can be said to be 'at a time', let alone 'at the same time as' something else.

iv) Eternity 'includes the whole of time' in that no event in time is temporally prior to, or subsequent to, eternity. To that extent, as it were by exclusion, we are forced to say that the whole of time is 'present to' eternity. But 'present' here is to be understood as 'immediately accessible to God's knowledge and causal activity', and not in a temporal sense.[11]

Aquinas distinguishes among the things that God knows.

> We must pay attention to a difference between things which do not actually exist. Some of these, although they are not actual existents at present, either did actually exist, or will actually exist; all of these God is said to know by knowledge of vision. This is because God's understanding, which is his existence, is measured by eternity, and eternity, which exists without succession, takes in the whole of time. So God's 'present' gaze is directed to the whole of time and to everything that exists at whatever time, as to things which 'presently' lie before him.
>
> There are other things which God or a creature are able to produce, which nevertheless neither exist, nor once existed, nor ever will exist. God is not said to know these by knowledge of vision, but by knowledge of simple understanding. We speak in this way, since we use the word 'vision' in connection with objects which have an existence separate from that of the one who sees.
>
> (I, 14, 9)

God has knowledge ('knowledge of simple understanding') of everything which is merely possible but never actual. This knowledge does not at all depend on whether, or what, God might decide to create. But God also knows whatever is actual in causing its existence. It is this awareness of his own causal activity which Aquinas terms 'knowledge of vision', since this awareness involves the real existence of things which are other than God (I, 14, 8). In reply to the objection that since this knowledge of vision is eternal, the created things which are its object must likewise be eternal, Aquinas says,

> Knowledge causes things to be in the way in which they are known. But God does not know that [created] things are eternal existents. Hence from the fact that God's knowledge of them is eternal, it does not follow that they exist eternally.[12]
>
> (*Ibid.*, reply 2)

On this account, then, which propositions can we say that God knows about, say, the Battle of Hastings? I shall adopt the convention of using an uninflected, tenseless, form of the verb within angle-brackets to denote the eternal 'present' as explained above in iii) and iv). Aquinas, as I interpret him, would claim that God <know> all the following propositions:

a)   The date of the Battle of Hastings is AD 1066.
b)   The Battle of Hastings is earlier than the birth of Aquinas.
c)   The Battle of Hastings is later than the death of Julius Caesar, and contemporaneous with the death of King Harold.

On this view, God can properly be said to understand propositions about time, which include temporal expressions like 'before', 'later than', and 'at the same time as'. The sense of 'understand' here is that in which a man might be said to understand what childbirth is, although it is something which he is not capable of experiencing himself. In that sense, God <understand> what it is for events to succeed one another in time. On the other hand, God does not, and indeed cannot <know>

d)   The Battle of Hastings is taking place at this moment, now.
e)   Thomas Aquinas will be born in 1225.
f)   The death of Julius Caesar took place many centuries ago.

Tensed statements like d) – f) presuppose a claim about the relationship between the position in time of the speaker (or knower) and the event which the statements are about. Hence a necessary condition for such a statement to be true is a prior truth about which position in time the speaker in fact occupies. Since God does not occupy any position in time, no such proposition expressed by God could be true. For that reason, no such proposition could be known by God. It seems to me that Aquinas means by an *enuntiabile* a possible statement which could be made by someone saying something.[13] True *enuntiabilia* are therefore things which some particular person could truly say. The same sentence uttered by different speakers will express a different proposition if that sentence contains spatial or temporal indexicals like 'here', 'she', 'now', etc. It follows that God cannot <know> d) – f) as said by himself, since those sentences would express statements which *God* could not truly make, though each of them is a statement which might be truly made by some time-bound person. Nevertheless, God <know> that d) – f) would be true if said by some creature at the appropriate times. Similarly, God <know> of my speaking at 9.30 on 18th July 1993, which happens to be now, but it is not the case that God *knows* that I am speaking *now*, where the 'now' plus the tensed verb refers to God's location in time. And while it is true that my speaking now is 'eternally present' to God, it is not the case that *at the same time as* I am now speaking God <know> that I am speaking. And though at any given time I can say 'It is true now that God <know> of my speaking', the 'now' does not modify '<know>' but 'is true'. Created things are 'eternally present' only in that God eternally <create> things, not that he <create> eternal things.

It is not a consequence of this view that all time-bound events are simultaneously real to God; what is true is that they <are> real to God, since he <know> his atemporal act of creating them. But the <are> does not express simultaneity in God. Nor, obviously, does it suggest that time-bound events are simultaneous in time, or that they are equally actual at any moment in time. Time-bound events are truly time-bound, and we are not mistaken in our perception that some of them no longer exist, and others do not yet exist.[14] For Aquinas, that they truly are time-bound is a consequence of the fact that God <create> and hence <know> that they are such. When I say that my having completed this book is not yet an actual state of affairs, what I am saying is perfectly true, and God <know> that this is what I can truly say, even though God cannot say 'Gerry Hughes has not yet completed his book.' There is no divine equivalent of that time-bound proposition; for although God <know> that the state of affairs which is Gerry Hughes having completed his book is not an actual state of affairs in 1992, that truth is not the same truth as the truth uttered by me in saying that 1992 has come to an end and the book is still not finished. That is the point of Aquinas's rejection of the Nominalist claim that 'Christ will be born', 'Christ is being born' and 'Christ will be born' are one and the same *enuntiabile* simply because they are all about the same event. The existence and timing of that event is only one element in the truth conditions of those three *enuntiabilia*; the other element is the relation in time of the speaker's utterance to the time of that event.[15]

OMNISCIENCE AND CONTINGENT FUTURE EVENTS

The interpretation of Aquinas I have so far given is not beyond dispute; but I believe it fits well with his view of what he himself identifies as one of the most serious problems. How does God know things which will happen but need not happen, or which could happen in the future but in fact will not? I, 14, 13, where Aquinas deals with this issue, is an extremely difficult text, and one which was endlessly commented upon in subsequent controversy. He begins by summarising his position so far: God knows all things; those which he does create, those which are possible for him to create, and those which created things are capable of producing. God must therefore know contingent events. But how?

> To see this we must consider that a contingent thing can be looked at in two ways: *i)* In itself, in so far as it is actual; and in this way it is not being regarded as future, but as present, nor as something which might turn out either way, but as determinately the way it is. For that reason, it can be an object of certain and infallible knowledge, just as something can be an object of vision, as when I see that Socrates is sitting down. *ii)* As it is in its cause: from this point of view it is regarded as future, as something which could turn out either way, because a contingent cause is one which is compatible with opposite effects. From this point of view, a contingent thing is not an object of any certain knowledge. So whoever knows a contingent thing only in its cause has no more than a conjectural knowledge of it. God, on the other hand, knows all contingent things not merely as they are in their causes, but also as each of them actually is in itself.
>
> Although contingent things become actual one after another, God does not know them one after another in the way that they come about, as we do. He knows them all at once, since his knowledge is measured by eternity just as his existence is, and eternity, as we have said, includes the whole of time. So all the

things that are in time are eternally present to God, not simply in that he has their natures present to him, as some maintain, but because his gaze is eternally upon them as they are in their presence to him.

Once again, the comparison with my seeing that Socrates is sitting down could mislead. Aquinas is not maintaining that actual events can *have an effect* on the divine consciousness in a way that possible events cannot. The point is that events which are actual are determinate objects of knowledge in a way in which events which are simply possible are not. God <know> all contingent events as actual, through his awareness of his act of creating them. He does not <know> them as future, if by that is meant that his act of knowledge exists at a time prior to the events; nor does he <know> them as happening now, if by that is meant that he <know> them at the same time as they are happening. The futurity of future contingents, like the present-ness of an actually present event, are properties that they have only relative to a knower who is situated in time. Aquinas is not committed to the absurd view that an event 'already' exists in eternity 'before' it has come about in time. But he is committed to the view that God <know>, because God <create>, events which, from our point of view have not yet come about, need never come about at all, and can only be conjectured about.

Precisely here the really acute problems arise. If God infallibly <know> what will in fact come about, can it be true in any important sense that they need not come about? Is the uncertainty and indeterminateness of the future, as we see things, only an illusion? And if God <know> what will come about, because God <create> all events, is it likewise an illusion on our part to think that we can by our decisions make one possible future determinately come about rather than another?

Aquinas tries to deal with these problems in stages. First, he claims that a necessary first cause can nevertheless produce contingent effects.[16] This is part of his general view about the relationship between the way in which God's transcendent causal activity is related to the genuine causal activity of 'secondary' causes in this world. This relationship is not to be thought of as similar to that between several ordinary causes contributing to one earthly event, as when the lighting of a safety match is caused by friction, by the nature of the chemicals in the match, and by the chemicals in the impregnated strip on the matchbox. Nor is it like the relationship between two bullets simultaneously entering someone's head, either one of which would of itself be fatal. It is not like this latter, since without God's causal activity, the secondary cause would not exist at all. Nor is it like the former, since each cause makes a particular contribution to the properties of the effect. In the case of God's causation, Aquinas says, 'the proper effect of the primary agent is existence, whereas the secondary agents, which as it were make the action of the primary agent particular and determinate, produce as their proper effects further properties which make that being a being of a determinate sort' (*Contra Gentiles*, III, 66). If contingent causes genuinely contribute to the kind of effect which is produced, and do so only at a particular time, then prior to that time those effects are not determinate either, despite the fact that God <cause> those effects in respect of their existence. And if the causal powers of a secondary cause are, as it happens, not actualised (for instance, if something else prevents it from acting) then God <not cause> the existence of that possible effect.

But that, of course, simply makes the problem worse. God, and hence God's creative activity or God's knowledge, cannot be altered by any contingent thing. If, then, God unalterably <cause, know> a contingent effect, then that effect is surely inevitable, no matter what a contingent cause might or might not then do? Aquinas considers the various steps in such an argument, and various possible replies which have been made by his predecessors. The crucial issue is whether the necessity of God's knowledge somehow transfers itself to the things which God knows. Call this a Transfer of Necessity Argument (TNA). The version Aquinas considers goes as follows:[17]

TNA1

1 If it is absolutely necessary that God knew that this contingent future event will take place, then of necessity it will take place.

2 But that God knew that this contingent future event will take place is absolutely necessary for two reasons: i) this truth is eternal; ii) it is expressed in the past tense.

3 Hence it follows that whatever is known by God is necessary, and so cannot be contingent.

Which of the several possible senses of 'necessary' are involved in the various steps of this argument? From the reasons alleged in 2, the first occurrence of 'necessary' in 1 must be taken to mean 'unalterable'; the reference is either to the unalterability of the past, or to the unalterability of God's eternal state. If I am right in my earlier remarks about how Aquinas understands the eternity of God, we shall have to say here that Aquinas allows 'God knew' to be expressed in the past tense as a concession to our natural way of speaking and to the way in which the problem is popularly put, rather than as a strictly accurate account of God's knowledge. The point makes no material difference to the argument, though, since an eternal '<know>' would have just the same consequence.

Aquinas first considers, and rejects, the view that God's eternal (or 'past') knowledge cannot be necessary since the content of what he knows is future, and the future need not turn out that way. He rejects this suggestion on the grounds that 'what has a relationship to the future must have had that relationship, even though what is future does not always follow.' By this somewhat obscure remark, I take it, he is arguing that if God had (or, for that matter <have>) an item of future-related knowledge, then his having had (or <having>) it is unalterable, and hence 'accidentally necessary', whatever the *content* of the knowledge is.[18]

Aquinas next considers the suggestion that 1 is false because God's knowledge is only a remote cause, and the secondary cause is contingent. The best interpretation of his reply is that he thinks the proposed solution is true so far as it goes, but that it fails to deal with the special case in which the remote cause is God's *infallible* knowledge.[19] For surely it is necessarily *true* that if God <know> that *p*, then *p*, whereas it is not necessarily true that if the sun shines, the grass will grow. Aquinas's strategy is to repeat his earlier claim that the necessity of the act of knowing does not show that what is known is similarly necessary, and, crucially, to add that the second occurrence of 'necessary' in 1 is to be read as an assertion that 1 as a whole is *de dicto* necessarily true (since 'X knows that *p*' entails '*p* is true'), and *not* as an indication that the event referred to in *p* happens *de re* necessarily.

Serious problems remain with this solution, however. Recall that God's knowledge is unalterable, in Aquinas's view, and that it is not obtained by seeing what is actually happening. The causal link goes in the opposite direction. God knows what happens by being aware of his eternal activity as the transcendent cause of contingent time-bound effects. Suppose that God <know> my decision in 2000 to go to Scotland. He therefore <know> the proposition, 'To say in 1992 "Gerry Hughes will decide in 2000 to go to Scotland" is to say something which is true'. The following problems at once present themselves.

i)   If it is now true (and indeed has always been true) that I shall go, in what sense is it possible that I shall decide not to go? Aquinas can reply to this that what makes it true that I shall decide to go is the decision I will take. Were I to decide otherwise when the time comes, then it never would have been true that I would decide to go. This ought not to be seen as some kind of retroactive causation on past truths, as though past truths were states of affairs, as it were 'things' that once past can no longer be changed. The connection between what is true and what I decide is logical, not causal. My decision does not alter a past state of affairs, but logically determines what could truly have been said at some previous time.

ii)   But if he makes that reply, it likewise follows that were I to decide not to go, then it would not be the case that God <know> of my going. Does what God <know> then not depend on a decision that I have not yet made, and could make either way? Aquinas could try repeating his previous answer: the dependence is logical, not causal. I do not cause God's knowledge to be other than it <be>. Aquinas, I believe, must reply in this way. But this reply seems only to generate further problems.

iii) At the very least, then, what God <know> could <be> different; and this suggests that God's knowledge is not accidentally necessary. I think Aquinas would reply that indeed God could <know> a different world, since that simply follows from the fact that God could <create> a different world. Aquinas does not hold that this kind of power in God conflicts with God's simplicity as pure act. All right, but once there is a creation, could it *still* be that God might <know> a different world only because *I decide* which world is the actual world? To say 'yes' to that question would at least seem to make God's knowledge *causally* dependent on what I eventually might decide to do. So Aquinas must, to be consistent, say, 'no'.

iv) But then, *up to what* point does it remain open to me to decide differently? I would of course want to say 'right up to the moment of decision'. Up to that point in time, nothing is fixed. But God's causal action, which is the source of God's knowledge of what I shall do, unalterably <create> this universe, not some other possible universe. And in this universe, I go to Scotland. In what sense could I still decide not to go? It seems a very lame answer to say, as Aquinas does, that God's causation leaves me, the contingent cause, undetermined in my choice, but is still sufficient to ground God's infallible knowledge of what I shall do. If God's action as transcendent cause does not determine me, how can it be the ground of determinate, infallible, and not merely conjectural, knowledge in God? And if God's knowledge is only conjectural, how could it possibly be accidentally necessary, and identical with God's essence?

This difficulty stems from the conjunction of the traditional assumptions about God which I outlined at the beginning, plus some others which Aquinas developed in the course of his discussion:

A   God has the attribute of simplicity.
B   God cannot be changed, hence God's knowledge cannot be changed.
C   God <know> everything, and his knowledge of creation is accidentally necessary.
D   Human beings can make free choices.
E   God <exercise> Providence over creation.
F   God is eternal.
G   It is possible at t_1 to make a true statement about some future time t_3.
H   What is past (or eternal) is unalterable.
I   God's action in creating this world leaves some events in this world indeterminate at particular times.

The problem which faced later writers was whether it is possible to alter, or at least modify, some of these assumptions in such a way as to render their conjunction less problematic, while still remaining faithful to what were thought to be undeniable truths about the omniscience and providence of the Christian God.

William of Ockham

An examination of Ockham's treatment of these issues can conveniently begin with some straightforwardly obvious ways in which his view coincides with that of Aquinas as just outlined.[20] Ockham, as it seems to me, accepts most of these assumptions; but he denies F in the sense in which Aquinas understands it, and hence modifies B; and, crucially, he denies the second part of C.

To capture Ockham's view, we must replace the tenseless <know> in C with a tensed 'knows'. This is because Ockham's understanding of being eternal differs sharply from Aquinas's. Perhaps Ockham was convinced by Scotus's criticisms of Aquinas's view. Scotus had argued that it was not coherent to maintain both that moments in time were not simultaneously actual and yet simultaneously present to God. At any rate, Ockham speaks of God's eternity in terms which suggest that he understands it as everlastingness, rather than atemporality. So he can say, 'For example, "the world does not exist" was true from eternity, and nevertheless is false now', implying that eternity in part antedated the creation of the world; and he regularly speaks of what God 'knew' or 'will come to know'.[21] Quite consistently, he maintains that the content of God's knowledge can change. At one time God knows that it is true that Socrates is sitting, and at a later time he knows that Socrates was sitting.[22]

Although Ockham would agree with G, that it is possible to make true statements about the future, he thought this was by no means a simple thesis to maintain. He took it as given that Aristotle, in his famous discussion of fatalism and Tomorrow's Sea Battle, had in the end denied that singular statements about the future were now true, or now false.[23] Aristotle's reasoning, as Ockham understands it, was that what makes a statement true at any given time is that at that time it corresponds to a determinate reality in the world. Now, Aristotle argued, the past and the present are determinate; that is to say fixed, unalterable, actually the way they were, or are. So there is no problem about the truth-conditions of statements about the present or past. But for there now to be true statements about the future, the future would also have to be already fixed, unalterable, not potentially other than it will be. And this would lead to the conclusion that I could not make things turn out differently by any future decision of mine. Aristotle, as Ockham understood him, took this to be an unacceptable conclusion, and concluded that the only escape route was to deny that there are now truths about the future. If the future is genuinely open, then it is indeterminate, and there exists nothing now which could make statements about it true now.[24]

Such a conclusion, in Ockham's view, was incompatible with the Christian belief that God knows the future of all things, and must do so in order to exercise his providential care for them. There must therefore now be truths about the future to be known. Ockham therefore seeks an alternative solution which leaves F intact, and so leaves room for divine foreknowledge and providence. Here is an objection he considers, and his reply to it:

> *Obj*   Whatever is not determinately true in itself is not known by God with determinate cognition.
> But a future contingent is of that sort.
> Therefore [God does not have determinate cognition of a future contingent].
>
> *Reply*   The minor premiss [that a future contingent is not determinately true] is false. Nevertheless, [though a future contingent is determinately true] it is *contingently* true, for it can be false, and it could never have been true.
>
>   (PFC II,1, reply 4)

According to Ockham, what makes a contingent statement about the future true is the occurrence in the future of the determinate event which the statement asserts will occur. It is my determinate-in-the-future sitting at t_n which makes it true to say now that I will be sitting at t_n. But because the truth of that statement will be brought about by my future decision to sit, or not to sit, the future statement is as yet only contingently true, if it is true at all. It still can be false, and so might never have been true. Ockham thinks Aristotle is right that only a determinate reality can make a statement true; but mistaken in not seeing that for a statement about the future to be true, a *future* determinate reality is all that is required. Ockham therefore has no trouble with saying that statements about the future might all along have been false, and be false now.

Consider, then, 'Socrates will sit down at t_3', said at t_1. Ockham insists that

before t_3 it cannot first be true and afterwards false. Rather, if it is true before t_3 it always was true before t_3, for every proposition that is simply true about the future was always true if it is ever true.

(PFC, II, 3, reply 1)

Propositions which are about the future differ from propositions about the present or past. Whereas propositions about the future can be contingent,[25] propositions which are genuinely about the present or past are accidentally necessary; that is to say, their truth or falsity is now fixed and unalterable. Take, for example, a proposition like 'A is now taller than B', which asserts that there is a relation in A now.[26]

> at any rate, it will always be true to say afterwards that there was such a relation in A, since, according to the Philosopher in Book VI of the *Ethics*, 'In this alone God is deprived; to make undone things that have been done.' This is to be understood in the following way. If some assertoric proposition merely about the present that is not equivalent to one about the future is true now, so that it is true of the present, then it will always be true of the past. For if the proposition 'this thing is' (some thing or other having been indicated) is true now, then 'this thing was' will be true forever after, nor can God in his absolute power bring it about that this proposition be false.

Ockham is careful here to point out that what he is saying applies only to present propositions which are '*merely* about the present, and not equivalent to one about the future.' He takes the same line about propositions which are *merely* about the past. What is the point of 'merely' here? The following example might illustrate the kind of proposition which Ockham wishes to exclude. 'Charles is the next King', though it is expressed in the present tense, and so might be taken as stating a present truth, is equivalent to a statement about the future, 'Charles will succeed the present Queen'. But, since this statement is about the future it is contingent, and if it is true now, it is only contingently true. Hence 'Charles is the next King', its equivalent, if true at all, is only contingently true, despite its present-tense form. It is still *possible* that it should turn out never to have been true (for instance, if Charles were to die before being crowned). In contrast, it is not even possible that it should ever turn out that 'Charles is now the Prince of Wales' was never true, if it is true now.

It is clear enough that the basic insight behind this discussion is that 'Time's Arrow' points in only one direction. What is past is irrevocably past, and what is present can no longer be changed. This would be simple enough if only it provided us with a clear criterion for deciding which propositions are 'merely' about the present or past. Obviously, the grammatical form, or the tense of the verb, is not a good test, since present- or past-tense propositions might, despite grammatical appearances, be 'equivalent to a proposition about the future.' So what is the test? The test which Ockham consistently applies is to ask whether there is anything that anyone can do to bring it about that a proposition was never true in the first place.[27] If there is, it is 'equivalent to a proposition about the future'; if not, then it genuinely is about the present or the past, and as Aristotle says, not even God can do anything to undo the present or past. The test, then, is to discover in what ways it is *de re* possible for us to affect the way things turn out.[28]

Further caution is still needed, since it makes a difference whether we are talking about past knowledge, or a past belief. Consider, 'In 1985 John believed that he would be dead before 1995.' That is plainly a statement about John's state of mind in 1985, and as such has the necessity of a proposition which is merely about the past. Yet whether John would or would not die before 1995 was, let us suppose, in 1985 still a contingent matter. Still, though several things might bring it about that his belief was false all along, nothing could bring it about that he did not have that belief, once he had it. Contrast 'John *knew* in 1985 that he would be dead before 1995'. Anything that brought it about that he did not die would thereby bring it about that he never did *know* that he would die. So, on Ockham's criterion, 'John knew in 1985 that he would die before 1995', despite appearances, is not *merely* about the past. It is about the future as well, since it entails 'John will die before 1995', which is about the future, and there might still be something we can do to ensure that John does not die before then. So 'John knew in 1985 that he would die before 1995' is, even if true, only a contingent truth. Right up until 1995, it might well be *de re* possible that John's belief about his death will turn out to have been false. Hence, while John's past beliefs about the future are genuinely past, John's past knowledge about the future is not genuinely past. This, as we shall see, is one source of difficulty for Ockham.

Be that as it may, it still seems very difficult to find a case in which someone does know something about the contingent future. For if the future is genuinely open, then something could still make it turn out that what the person allegedly knew never happened; in which case, he could not have known that it would happen. So even if Aristotle (as Ockham read him) was mistaken in saying that there are as yet no truths about the contingent future, it does not seem to be much of an improvement on his view to say that there are such truths, but nobody will ever be in a position to know which those truths are.

With these thoughts in mind, we may return to Ockham's presentation of God's knowledge and its relationship to God's providence. First, God's knowledge. Ockham maintains that God's knowledge, though immutable,[29] is nonetheless contingent:

> For example, 'God knows that this person will be saved' is true, and yet it is possible that He will never have known that this person will be saved. And so that proposition is immutable, and yet is not necessary but contingent.

But is not God's knowledge identical with God's essence, and hence necessary? No, says Ockham:

> Knowing A is not in God formally, however, but merely through predication. For it is a certain concept or word that is predicated of God, and at other times not. And it is not necessary that it be God, for the word 'Lord' is predicated of God contingently and temporally, and nevertheless is not God.

> (PFC, II, 4, 3)

Knowledge is not an intrinsic property of God himself, but is a relationship between God and things, some of which are changing, and some of which are only contingently as they are. We can truly *say* ('predicate') that God knows A, but in so saying we are not describing God in himself. Similarly, 'God is Lord' is true when there exists a creation; but 'being Lord' is not an intrinsic property of God, and hence not one that God of necessity has. It is for this reason that Ockham could not straightforwardly accept

B   Since God is unchanging, God's knowledge must be unchanging.

which Aquinas asserted. If by 'God's knowledge' one means 'the truths that God knows', and if, as Ockham believes, God is not timeless and can know tensed propositions as such, then God's knowledge does change, since some propositions are at one time true and at another false; and many of the ones which are true are only contingently true. So B must be distinguished, to allow us to accept

> B1   The truths that God can be said to know will vary from time to time, and will depend on which propositions are true at any given time.

B1 in itself is compatible with something Aquinas would admit, namely,

> B2   If the world had been different, it follows that God would have known that different propositions were true.

and with

> B3   If at some future time I decide to do A, it follows that it will never have been true to say that God knew I would not do A

Neither B2 nor B3 of themselves need involve any suggestion that changes in the world, or any free decisions, have a retrospective causal impact on God's mind. As Ockham rightly says, it will consequently be the case that different things can be said about God. But that consequence is a logical consequence, not a causal one. Ockham also accepts, as does Aquinas,

> B4   God's knowledge is immutable, in the sense that the truths that God knows/<know> can never turn out to have been false.

Here, however, Ockham takes 'knows' to be tensed, and admits that at some times the propositions which God knows at that time are at other times false, and known to be false. For Aquinas, God <know> that '*p* is true at one time and false at another', but he does not *at any time* know that *p*. Still, Ockham does not believe that his view involves any intrinsic change in God, since 'knowing that *p*' is not an intrinsic property of God at all.

There are at least two serious problems with this view, however. One, which for the moment I shall postpone, concerns the source of God's knowledge. Call it the Source-Problem. First, though, we need to ask how we are to characterise knowing as it is in God himself.

Call this the Description-Problem. To see the particular way in which this presents itself in the context of Ockham's general position, it is interesting to compare what Ockham says about God's will, and in particular his providential will that a person – say, Peter – should be saved rather than damned.[30]

Consider the suggestion that if God wills that Peter be saved, then God has a property W, consisting in his so willing, and Peter has a property P, consisting in his being predestined for heaven; and consider again the example about Prince Charles. Charles has a property P*, which is the property of being Prince of Wales. But, as the previous discussion made clear, P* is not at all the same property as K, the property of being the next King. Given that Charles went through a particular ceremony, he unalterably now is Prince of Wales, and hence in that sense being Prince of Wales is an accidentally necessary property of Charles. But being the next King is not now a necessary property of Charles, since his succeeding Elizabeth still lies in the future, and even if it is true that he will, it is not unavoidably, or necessarily, true that he will. So K is not the same property as P*.

Well, then, is Peter's property P like Charles's property P*, or is it like Charles's property K? Ockham answers this question by considering an objection:

Obj   Every proposition about the present that is true at some time has [corresponding to it] a necessary proposition about the past. For example, if 'Socrates is seated' is true, 'Socrates was seated' will be necessary forever after. But suppose 'Peter has P' is now true. In that case, 'Peter had P' would always be necessary. Then I ask whether or not it is possible that Peter be damned. If he can be, suppose that he is. 'Then Peter has not-P' is true of the present. Therefore 'Peter had not-P' will always be necessary of the past. Thus, 'Peter had P' and 'Peter had not-P' would be true at one and the same time.

Reply   I maintain that the major premiss is false [that every true proposition about the present has a corresponding *necessary* proposition about the past]. For that proposition that is about the present in such a way that it is nevertheless equivalent to one about the future and its truth depends on the truth of the one about the future does not have a [corresponding] necessary proposition about the past. On the contrary, the one about the past is contingent. All propositions to do with predestination and damnation are of that sort.

(PFC, I, objection 2 and reply)

In short, Peter's being P is like Charles being K, and not like Charles being P*. To say that Peter is predestined for heaven is to talk about something which will happen, but which need not happen. If Peter were to die unrepentant, then Peter will never have had P, just as if Charles dies before being crowned, he will never have been the next King. Now what about God's property W, willing that Peter be predestined? Ockham seems to be in trouble here, at least:

Obj   Since everything that is God, or is in God, is necessary, W is necessary. Therefore necessarily God predestined Peter. Therefore Peter necessarily is predestined, and so not contingently.

Reply   I maintain that 'predestination is necessary' can be understood in two ways. In one way, it says that that which is principally signified by the noun 'predestination' is necessary. In this sense, I grant it, since it [W] is the divine essence, which is necessary and immutable. In another way, it says that someone is predestined by God; in this way, it [W] is not necessary, for just as everyone who is predestined is so contingently, so God contingently predestines everyone.

(PFC, I, objection 4 and reply)

It now turns out that Ockham thinks that 'W' has two referents, 'God's essence', and 'Peter being saved by God's will'. Taken in the first way, W_1 is identical with God and is necessarily and immutably as it is. In contrast, while W_2 is immutable, since, if God wills that Peter be saved Peter will be saved, still, God's saving Peter is not a *necessary* property of God, since it is not a real property in God at all *yet*, any more than being the next King is a real property in Charles yet, even if it is true now that he will be. In short, there are some things which can truly and unchangeably be said about God, which are nevertheless not *necessary* truths about God, since they do not ascribe to God real properties which God has – *yet*.

But how are we to describe W_1 on this account?[31] There seems no good reason for describing it as 'predestination' at all, let alone as 'predestining Peter'. Everything about predestination is contingent on the future choices of the predestined. So it is quite unilluminating (though of course, not false) to say that talk about predestination also involves reference to the divine essence. There is no *special* way in which predestination so refers, no *special* feature in God himself to which such talk corresponds. Would Ockham not have done better to deny the objector's contention that predestination is necessary altogether, rather than try to salvage the traditional position by removing all specific content from the term?

Just the same difficulty, as it seems to me, can be raised about God's knowledge of future contingents, where Ockham makes a similar move:

> I maintain that 'God has necessary knowledge of future contingents' can be understood in two ways. In the first way, 'God's knowledge whereby future contingents are known is necessary'; and this is true, since the divine essence itself is one single necessary and immutable cognition of all things, complexes as well as non-complexes, necessary and contingent. In the second way, 'by God's knowledge future contingents are known necessarily'; and his knowledge is not necessary in that way. It need not be granted that God has necessary knowledge regarding future contingents.
>
> (PFC, II, 4, L)

Of course, in saying 'God necessarily knew that Peter would be saved' we are referring to God, and hence to the essence of God. But, says Ockham, we are not doing so because we are using the word 'knew'; for the term 'knew' involves a contingent relation between a future event and God, and hence does not refer to something necessary in God himself.

So what is it *in God* that is necessary? Not, according to Ockham, what is known. Nor, says Ockham, the act of knowing, since it isn't necessarily an act of *knowing* at all, yet. Nor can Ockham try to get round this difficulty by saying that God necessarily has *beliefs* about anything that he contingently knew. For although the truth of 'X knew that *p*' is logically dependent whether it turns out that *p*, and hence is contingent if *p* is contingent, the truth of 'X believed that *p*' is *not* contingent on the truth of *p*. Whether or not *p* turns out to be true makes no difference to whether someone believed it to be true. If someone were so to act that *p* turned out to be false, that could not bring it about that X did not at one time in the past believe *p* to be true. 'X believed that *p*' is 'merely about the past', as Ockham would put it, and hence is now unavoidable and in that sense necessary. Ockham might, of course, argue that in the special case of God, who cannot have false beliefs, God's past belief that *p is* contingent on the truth of *p*. But in that case, God's belief that *p* could not be necessary either.

It is therefore very difficult to see how Ockham can characterise a cognitive state in God which is essential, and hence necessary, and is a cognition of contingent truths.[32]

What I think this brings out is a real difficulty with

B   God cannot be changed, and hence God's knowledge cannot be changed.

which, as we saw, is something which Aquinas and Ockham both accept. What Ockham does is to accept B, but to distinguish the inference it contains. He agrees with Aquinas that God's knowledge is infallible, and hence immutable. There is nothing that we can do in the future which will *change* anything in God.[33] But he denies that God's knowledge is necessary when it has as its content contingent truths. What is necessary *in God* cannot be described as knowledge so long as its content is contingent. How can we describe what is in God, then, on this account? The Description-Problem remains unsolved. Aquinas, in contrast, understood 'cannot be changed' in B to mean both immutable *and* necessary. The Description-Problem is no problem at all: what God <have> is knowledge, even when its content is contingent. But, Ockham would argue, Aquinas is not entitled to say this, since he fails to explain how knowledge of genuinely contingent truths can be necessary.

It is hard to be sure to what extent Ockham's difficulties with Aquinas are bound up with his view that God is in time. He is no less committed to the past being accidentally necessary, now unchangeable, than Aquinas is to the accidental necessity of what eternally <be>. Both, therefore, have to deal with the difficulty of reconciling the accidental necessity of God's eternal mind with the fact that some truths are still, at a moment in time, accidentally contingent. Both are willing to admit that the truth value of a given proposition can change over time, without this entailing any change in God. Both hold that if a statement about the future is true, it always was true, and will continue to be true until the point in time at which it needs to be replaced by a statement about the present or past. .

The difficulty arises from the way in which Ockham connects knowledge of the contingent with necessity. It is tempting to suppose that all he is saying is that a cognitional state whose content is a contingent truth cannot be *called* knowledge prior to the time at which that contingent truth becomes accidentally necessary. Ockham is willing to describe it as infallible, and as immutable; but is it knowledge? The question is whether this is a question about what *we* from our position in time are able to *say* about what God knows, or whether it is a remark about what God, given *his* position in time, can know. Now, Ockham insists that God does know future contingents, though it is impossible to explain how he knows them; he also insists that, even though his knowledge is only contingently knowledge, it nevertheless is knowledge. So it seems to me likely that he is saying no more than that God's necessary cognition is of all and only those propositions which are, as it will turn out, true; that it is not possible for us to spell out what justifies calling it knowledge when its content is still only contingently true; and yet it does amount to knowledge, though it is not as yet necessarily knowledge. The lack of necessity has to do with the futurity of the contingent event in time, and does not depend on whether God is in time or not. Knowledge of a contingent event can be described as necessary only if the event is already present or past.

I offer the suggestion, then, that the difference between Aquinas and Ockham is less than is commonly supposed, and is little more than a verbal difference about the propriety of describing even immutable knowledge as accidentally necessary. Aquinas's criterion is the immutability of the state of the knower: Ockham's is the actual occurrence of the event known. The contradiction is only apparent, since their use of 'necessary' is different. What Ockham is saying is not, on this point, incompatible with what Aquinas is saying.

The really important difference between Aquinas and Ockham is that Ockham thinks Aquinas has too rapidly concluded that there is no problem about God eternally knowing contingent truths. But there *is* a problem – the Source-Problem, as I have termed it, which Ockham spells out, and admits he is unable to solve. The problem is this. Even if one grants that God immutably knows what is true, and indeed what is true about the future, nevertheless what *is* true about the future is causally dependent on genuinely free decisions, which at present are not determinate in one way or in another. So what God knows seems to be causally determined by free decisions. How could God's knowledge be infallible, indeed how could it be knowledge at all, let alone necessarily, if it were independent of those decisions? Where would it come from? Scotus offers the suggestion that God obtains this knowledge by willing that one of the future alternatives should be the true one. Ockham cannot see that this will work:

> For I ask whether or not the determination of a created will necessarily follows the determination of the divine will. If it does, then the will necessarily acts, just as fire does, and so merit and demerit are done away with. If it does not, then the determination of a created will is required for knowing determinately one or the other part of a contradiction regarding those [future things which depend for their determination on a created will]. . . .
>
> . . . Secondly, when something is determined contingently, so that it is still possible that it is not determined and it is possible that it was never determined, then one cannot have certain and infallible knowledge based on such a determination. . . . For that reason I maintain that it is impossible to express clearly the way in which God knows future contingents.[34]
>
> (PFC, I, assumption 6, P)

But if God does not obtain his knowledge from his own act of determining which events will take place, it would appear that the only alternative source would be to make God's knowledge not merely logically, but also *causally* dependent on what takes place. And that is a move which neither Aquinas nor Ockham is willing to contemplate, since it makes God causally dependent on creatures.

To sum up. Let Fp be a true contingent proposition about the future. Aquinas and Ockham both subscribe to

J   God's mental act, being identical to the essence of God, belongs to God *de re* necessarily.

K   For any Fp, God <know> (Aquinas)/has always known (Ockham) that Fp.

Aquinas claims that J entails

Ka   It is eternally accidentally necessary that God <know>
that *Fp*

whereas Ockham claims that J is compatible with

Ko   It is still accidentally contingent that God has always
known that *Fp*.

Ockham distinguishes between God's act of knowing and what it is
that God knows, in order to show that Ko is compatible with J. So
he might be thought to be in difficulties in trying to show why God's
necessary act in such cases should be described as knowing at all,
since *qua* necessary it seems to have no content whatever. This
difficulty is all the more acute not, indeed, immediately because
Ockham takes God's knowledge to exist in time, but because he takes
it that God knows future *propositions*, and knows them therefore as
future. Moreover, he has simply to admit to having no coherent
account to give of how God comes by his knowledge of *Fp*'s.

Aquinas has less difficulty in moving from J to Ka, in part because
he thinks that God can be said to know *propositions* only in a
metaphorical sense, since what God strictly knows is his own essence
and his causal activity, which together make up the ultimate ground
of the truth of all *p*'s, including *Fp*'s. But Aquinas, in a more pressing
way than Ockham, is faced with the particularly unhappy task of
explaining how it is that God's willing to cause things can cause them
to be contingently, and, in particular, how necessary knowledge of
that activity can be knowledge of things which could be otherwise,
and which his causal activity does not determine one way or the other.

Luis de Molina

Molina inherited these difficulties from his predecessors, and endeavoured to answer them. He does so by means of an extended
commentary on the Aquinas text I, 14, 13 which we have already
considered at length above. In general, he wishes to defend the same
kind of position that Aquinas held against the criticisms or contrary
views which were adopted by intervening thinkers such as Duns
Scotus, Ockham and others. He therefore offers a vital addition as a
friendly amendment to what Aquinas said.

As a piece of preliminary ground clearing, Molina makes it clear
that he believes that God is eternal, in the sense in which I have

attributed to Aquinas (see pp. 69–70).[35] In particular, he wishes to say that all time-bound things 'are from eternity present to God in their own actual existence' provided that this is not interpreted in such a way as to suggest that the 'are' has a temporal sense, and provided especially that it is not supposed that all things past, present, and future are *simultaneous* in eternity. This last phrase he regards as incoherent. Moreover, he holds that 'Adam exists' and 'Adam does not exist' can both <be> true, whereas 'Adam exists' and 'Adam does not exist' of course cannot simultaneously be true.[36]

Secondly, Aquinas, according to Molina, is quite clear that God has two sources of knowledge:

1   God <know> all the possible natures which created things might have, and how those natures could possibly interact with one another.

2   God <know> all the actual things that he <create>, which <be> determinately present to him in their actuality *because* he <create> them. This includes contingent choices, which are actual because God <create> them.

From 1, it follows that God knows everything which is *de re* possible, including the choices which people *could* make; all truths about what is *de re* possible are themselves *de re* necessary truths.[37] From 2, God knows everything which is actual. This includes all those states of affairs which come about by causally necessary interactions between natural things, and those states of affairs which come about contingently because of the free actions of created agents. God knows the choices people actually *do* make. The question Molina asks is whether Aquinas thought that 2 expresses the *only* source of God's knowledge of contingent things. He concludes that Aquinas probably thought it was. But if God knows contingent choices only in causing them, it seems that those choices could not, despite Aquinas's claim to the contrary, be genuinely free. Molina suggests that if it were pointed out to Aquinas that this view imperilled the genuine freedom of human choice, Aquinas might have been willing to change his mind (*Disp.*, 49, 7).

Molina therefore proposes a third source of God's knowledge of contingent events:

He comprehends in Himself – because of the depth of his knowledge – all the things which, as a result of all the secondary causes possible by virtue of his omnipotence, would contingently and freely come to be on the hypothesis that he should will to establish these or those orders of things with these or those circumstances. . . .He comprehended this not only prior to anything's existing in time, but even prior (in our way of conceiving it, with a basis in reality) to any created thing's existing in the duration of eternity.

(*Disp.*, 49, 8)

The key elements in this suggestion are that *i)* God knows everything that *would* come about contingently as a result of the free choices of agents in any universe ('order of things') that he might create; *ii)* as in 1, this knowledge is independent of God's knowing these choices as actual; but *iii)*, unlike what is known from 1, and like what is known from 2, this knowledge extends to what is contingent as well as to what is necessary. Since it thus shares features both of 1 and of 2, he called this knowledge *scientia media*, 'Middle Knowledge'.

Molina offers two philosophical proofs that his suggestion is correct:[38] the first is that God's understanding of his own creative powers entails that God knows everything that is within their scope; and the second is that if God can be said to know our free choices, and if it is the case that he cannot be *caused* to know them by our making them, then even if those choices are actually present to God in eternity, that presence cannot be the explanation of how God is able to know them (*Ibid.*, 11–12). Hence, he sums up,

Just as it falls under God's *omnipotence* to be able to bring into existence creatures who are endowed with free choice and who have control over their acts (as we discern in our experience in our very own selves), so too it falls under his immense and altogether unlimited *knowledge*, by which he comprehends in the deepest and most eminent way whatever falls under his omnipotence, *to penetrate created free choice* in such a way as to discern and intuit with certainty which part it is going to turn itself to by its own innate freedom.

(*Disp.*, 50, 15)

What might Ockham and Aquinas have thought of these two 'proofs'? Firstly, the proof from God's omniscience about his own creative powers. Ockham wrote,

There is no adequate proof that someone who knows some

power perfectly knows all the things to which the power extends itself. For it was proved earlier that that which is the cause can be perfectly known when no effect is known. For it was proved that an adequate non-complex cognition of one thing cannot be had from a non-complex cognition of another thing.

(*Ordinatio*, I, 35, 2)[39]

One can perfectly understand heat in itself ('a non-complex cognition'), Ockham argues, without having a perfect understanding of any distinct effect that heat can produce. This Aquinas, like Molina, would simply deny, perhaps by appealing to the implications of 'perfect'. But Ockham could equally well counter that we are talking about the perfect understanding of some one thing in itself, and not of all its possible relations to distinct things. Neither argument seems conclusive.

As for Molina's second argument, that if God's knowledge is uncaused, it cannot depend on what is or is not actually present to him, Aquinas would doubtless reply that while it is indeed true that God's knowledge of what is actual is not caused by that thing's actual existence, it is still the case that God knows actual things only in causing them to be actual. Molina has not, therefore, shown that the only possibility which is compatible with God's not being affected by creatures is that he know contingent free choices by 'Middle Knowledge'. If to this Molina replies that his suggestion is the only way of making God's knowledge of contingent futures possible while still respecting human freedom, it seems to me that he genuinely does have a point (albeit a purely negative one); for Aquinas indeed doesn't explain how his view is coherent, and Ockham explicitly says he cannot explain how such a view is possible. On purely philosophical grounds, then, Molina's suggestion is relatively unsupported. Perhaps humans are not free, so his suggestion is unnecessary? Or perhaps God is not omniscient about free choices? That these truths are taken as axiomatic on Christian grounds does not amount to a philosophical proof that they must be coherent. But it does explain why Molina thought he had good reasons for his suggestion.

In any event, Molina thinks he has a much stronger argument against alternative views, and in particular against Ockham's view that, although one cannot have power over the past, it is nevertheless true that were some contingent future event E to take place, God would always have known that E would take place; and if E were not to take place, then God would always have known that it would not. Molina thinks this claim inevitably leads to a contradiction, between

a)   The past is fixed, in that nobody can make what was the case cease to have been the case.

and (where *Fp* is a contingent truth about the future)

b)   To say that God contingently knows that *Fp* entails that, if it were to turn out that *Fp* were false, God *could bring it about* that he never had known that *Fp*

As Molina puts it,

> Our opponents, on the other hand, hold that freedom of choice and the contingency of things accord with, and are correctly reconciled with, divine foreknowledge by virtue of the fact that if a thing is going to turn out otherwise, then when it actually occurs, God himself will bring it about that from all eternity he foreknew none other than that very thing that has occurred. But this is as if *i)* God acquired knowledge of future contingents from the very occurrence of the things; and as if *ii)* before the event there was no more certitude in the divine knowledge than there is in an object which is still contingently future; and as if *iii)* God's knowledge did not from eternity have in itself a fixed determination to one part of a contradictory pair of future contingents *before* the thing itself received that same determination in time when it was posited outside its causes.
>
> (*Disp.*, 51, 18)

Although Molina mentions Ockham as someone who holds this view (*Disp.*, 51, 4), it is by no means clear that this is fair. I have earlier remarked that Ockham did indeed hold

B3   If at some future time I decide to do A, it follows that it will never have been true to say that God knew I would not do A.

B3 does not, on the face of it, say what Molina believes Ockham was committed to saying. Ockham would, I believe, have repudiated the suggestion that God could *cause* his own eternal beliefs always to have been other than they always were. Instead of *i)* as Molina has it in the above quotation, Ockham would probably have said that

God's state of mind is properly *described as* knowledge only given that the event foreknown in fact occurs (see p. 83); to *ii)* Ockham might have replied that the mere fact that things *could* turn out differently does not entail that God has not eternally been certain about how they *would* turn out in fact; and to *iii)* he might have tried the same move as in his reply to *i)*, that he has all along held that God's knowledge was 'fixed' in the sense of 'immutable'; all he denies is that it was necessary.

Might Molina be right though? Could Ockham be forced to admit conclusions that he did not himself draw, and would have been unwilling to draw? I have already tried to indicate the difficulty in Ockham's reply to a criticism like *i)*; and although the reply to *ii)* which Ockham might make is correct as far as it goes, it altogether lacks force unless Ockham can give an account of how God achieves this certainty, which is just what Ockham admits he cannot give. It seems to me, then, that although Molina is wrong in attributing to Ockham the view that God can change his own past state of mind, it remains a fair criticism that Ockham gives no alternative account of what that immutable state of mind is, nor exactly *how* we are to reconcile the necessity of God's act of knowing with the contingency of what God can be said to know.

The strength of Molina's position is that, if it works, it provides an immediate answer to all these questions. Molina can make all the following claims:

B1   The truths that God can be said to <know> will vary from time to time, and will depend on which propositions are true at any given time.

B2   If the world had been different, it follows that God would <know> that different propositions were true.

B3   If at some future time I decide to do A, it follows that it will never have been true to say that God <know> I would not do A.

B4   God's knowledge is infallible, in that the truths that God <know> never turn out to have been false.

J   God's act of knowing, being identical to the essence of God, belongs to God *de re* necessarily.

Ka   It is *de re* necessary that God <know> that *Fp*.

It is also worth itemising what Molina takes to be true about Middle Knowledge; he claims

M1   God *de re* necessarily <know> all the *de re* necessary truths which express the natures of everything God could create, and all the *de re* necessary truths about how those things could interact with one another in any possible creation.

M2   God *de re* necessarily <know> all the contingent events which would take place in any creation he chose to create, and which would arise from the manifold interactions of deterministic and free secondary causes.

M3   God accidentally necessarily <know> which creation he <will> to create.

Given M1 and M2, and his decision to create in a particular way, it follows that

M4   God accidentally necessarily <know> all events, contingent and necessary, in this creation.

Note that in M3 and M4, although God's knowledge is only accidentally necessary, given what God <create>, M2 is true no matter what God decides to create. This points to a difference between Aquinas's reading of Ka and Molina's. Aquinas holds that God's knowledge that some particular *Fp* is true is dependent on his free decision about which creation he <create>, and hence only accidentally necessary. In this way, Molina hopes to avoid what he takes to be an unfortunate consequence of Aquinas's reading of Ka as true only given God's creation of this universe, since to read it that way would, as we have seen, make it difficult for Aquinas to explain how God comes by this knowledge other than by determining the free choices of the agents he <create>.

Molina's thesis, then, is immensely powerful – if it can be made to work. But can it?

There are two main questions here. Firstly, how does God know these truths? Secondly (which has seemed to many the more serious problem) *are* there any truths of the kind which Molina requires if the theory is to work as he hopes it will? How does God know what persons will freely decide to do?

Since the faculty of choice thus created and situated in this order of things remains free to turn itself toward one part or the other, God would most assuredly not know determinately which part of a contradiction among contingent states of affairs of this sort was going to obtain unless by the depth, excellence and

perfection of his natural knowledge, through which he comprehends all things, in his essence, in a most excellent manner.

(Disp., 50, 15)

This, however, is more a statement of the position than an explanation or an argument in its favour. It amounts to saying little
more than that although free choices are not knowable by ordinary
knowers, they are knowable by the infinite powers of the divine
mind. It might be fair to say that the main argument in favour of
Molina's overall position is that it would succeed admirably in
reconciling Christian beliefs in a philosophically coherent way
which is not open to the difficulties which apparently beset the
accounts of Aquinas and Ockham. Of course, that a theory has great
explanatory power is in itself a strong reason for taking it to be true.
But one might well recall Hume's warning against the appeal to
'occult powers', not because that warning is in itself an argument for
the contrary view, but because it is particularly in place here, when
so little is said by Molina about how this knowledge is available.

The problem is the more serious in that there seem to be good
reasons for doubting that there actually *are* any truths of the kind
Molina requires. There is a sharp difference between what is required
by Aquinas, and what is required by Molina. Aquinas requires that
omniscience include

Oa   God <know> that P freely does A in C at t_3

by being the actual transcendent cause of P's freely doing A. Molina
requires

Om   God <know> that P would freely do A in C were it ever
       to come about that P is placed in C.

In both cases, C stands for a completely determinate set of circumstances; and it is assumed that P is free to do not-A, given just
those circumstances.

Well, then, what *makes it true* that P would do A rather than not-
A? If one is to respect P's freedom, it cannot be the case that C
necessitates that P do A. Is it enough, then, to say that what makes
it true that P would do A is simply the fact that P does A in C? Of
course it is not required that P *could* do nothing else in C; Molina
makes no such claim, indeed that is precisely what he is afraid that
Aquinas might be forced into saying. No, all Molina needs is that

that is what Peter would in fact do, although he could have done otherwise. Still, on Molina's view, even though God <know> what P does in C, *this* knowledge is irrelevant. It is crucial to Molina's view that God knows what P would do whether or not P even exists, or is ever placed in C. So the truth that A is what P would do cannot depend on any truth about what P actually does do. So what does it depend on?

It is not enough to appeal to the fact that we often know what we ourselves would do in a hypothetical situation, or even that we on occasion know what someone else would do. Firstly, such claims are not easy to substantiate. We are perhaps more often able to say that, whatever P would do, it would certainly not be A; but that, of course, leaves things distressingly open. And even if it is true that we occasionally know what we, or others would do ('Well, she *would* say that, wouldn't she!'), it is very difficult to suppose that we know all such truths. Even in our own case, it is surely obvious enough that often the only way to discover what we would do in C is to discover what we actually do when we find ourselves in C. But Molina's claim is that God knows all the details of all possible cases.

The preceding discussion will, I hope, have amply illustrated the complexities involved in the notion of divine omniscience. The reader might find a quick summary of the problems helpful. Even if one accepts the constraint (which, of course, not everyone would feel bound to accept) that a satisfactory account of omniscience must be at least broadly compatible with traditional Christian beliefs, there are several options, each with its pros and cons:

i)   Does God know propositions in anything other than a metaphorical sense, or does God primarily know actual and possible things?

ii)   Is God's eternity, and hence God's knowledge, to be everlasting or timeless?

iii)   Can we solve the difficulties of God's knowledge of contingent things by allowing that God's knowledge is itself contingent? Or does the doctrine of simplicity require that God's knowledge is itself somehow necessary?

The three writers we have discussed each opt for different combinations of the possible answers to these three key issues. None of them is entirely convincing. It remains to be seen whether it is possible to advance any better solution than the ones they offer.

SOME ANSWERS

The simplicity of God's knowing

The best human analogue of what God's act of knowing is like is to be found in our experience of self-awareness. It is an imperfect analogue, since humans are aware of themselves largely in inter-acting with other things in their environment, whereas I take it that God would be perfectly self-aware even were there no creation, and hence nothing apart from God. Still, through our interactions with other things, we are self-aware – conscious of ourselves as bodily, as the subjects of sensations and feelings, and as the subjects of intentional states. Characteristic of human self-awareness is the fact that, in order to appropriate our self-awareness and our awareness of other things, we have to formulate what we feel and think and believe.[40] For us, mere awareness (itself an abstraction – we are never 'merely aware', at least after infancy) is not knowledge, nor belief, nor perhaps even perception. We have to appropriate our-selves and our environment piecemeal, using language to 'fix' some aspect of our awareness by expressing it in judgments about what we know, or believe, or desire, or remember.

Plato and Aristotle in their different ways speak of knowing as a disposition as well as an activity, and Plato at least on occasions seems to think of us as conducting a kind of 'matching'-process, deciding what to say when we have decided which statements somehow reflect what we already know, somewhat in the way in which we might try out various candidates when trying to remember a name, or a phone number. We try to formulate what we think, or what it is we are obscurely aware of desiring, and we keep trying until we believe we have got it right – until it 'fits'. Although Aristotle does not speak in these terms, he too considers knowledge as something possessed, which we can access by making judgments. We are, in short, only partially aware of ourselves at any given moment, and we can focus that awareness only bit at a time. Plausibly, then, our human self-awareness is limited.

So we might try to imagine what it would be like to be perfectly self-aware, by removing the incompleteness and the piecemeal procedures which we need to employ in order to grasp what we are aware of. Perhaps Aristotle's description of the mind of the Prime

Mover as *gnosis gnoseôs* ('a thinking on thinking') is intended as an attempt to capture this kind of idea.

> It must therefore be of itself that the divine thought thinks, since it is the most excellent of things, and its thinking is a thinking on thinking. . . .
> . . . A further question is left – whether the object of the divine thought is composite; for if it were, thought would change in passing from part to part of the whole. We answer that everything which has not matter is indivisible – as human thought, or rather the thought of composite beings, is in a certain period of time (for it does not possess the good at this moment or that, but its best, being something *different* from it, is attained only in a whole period of time), so throughout eternity is the thought which has *itself* for its object.[41]
>
> (*Metaphysics*, XII, 9, 1175a4–11)

To be sure, what such perfectly appropriated self-awareness might be like is something we can only dimly imagine, at best. Still, I think it is the most suitable model for the divine knowing.[42]

This model allows us to say that God is not aware of himself or of created things by means of numerically distinct judgments. His awareness, though all-inclusive, is simple, unitary, unchanging, non-propositional. I agree that, in order to examine more in detail what the divine self-awareness might be like, we are going to have to speak of the propositions which God might be said to know, and to offer some account of how he might be said to know them. While we can properly point out places in which the necessity of putting things in propositional terms might be misleading, we cannot use this as a manoeuvre which conveniently discounts sheer incoherence. In particular, therefore, any account of the propositions which God might (from our standpoint) be said to know must be consistent with God being unchanging and atemporal, and with whatever is a reasonable account of human responsibility. That being said, though, it is important to remember that God's self-awareness is of things, not of truths about those things. The problems with God's omniscience are primarily problems with ontology, not with logic.

God's untensed knowledge

As I have earlier remarked, I see no good reason to abandon the classical view of the timelessness of God, nor does it seem to me that it is in any way inconsistent with the claim that God has causal and epistemological access to the created world. I am therefore happy to take the consequences of this position so far as God's knowledge is concerned. If God's knowing is atemporal, it follows that God cannot be said to <know> any tensed proposition, since to know a tensed proposition presupposes that the knower is situated in time with respect to the state of affairs which the proposition is about. So God cannot <know> that I am writing now, nor that I was writing an hour ago, nor that I will be writing in five minutes from now, even if all those statements, were I to make them, would be true. Were God to make any of those statements, they would presuppose what is false, namely that God is situated at a time contemporaneous with my present act of writing, subsequent to my earlier writing, and prior to the writing I shall be doing. Those statements, on the impossible assumption that God made them at all, would be false; hence they cannot be suitable ways even for us to express what God <know>.

Hence, although I take Aquinas to be correct in saying that sentences such as 'Gerry Hughes is writing', 'Gerry Hughes was writing' and 'Gerry Hughes will be writing' express different propositions, even if they refer to one and the same state of affairs (say, my writing at 11.30), I think he is wrong to say that God knows all true propositions, if he meant to include such propositions among the 'all'.[43] It would be less misleading to say that God <know> all the true statements which God could make; or better, that God <know> whatever states of affairs underpin the truth of all true statements, both those which God could truly make, and those which I might truly make. He <know> for example that 'The sentence "I am writing now" would express a true statement if said by Gerry Hughes at 11.30'. There is nothing in creation of which God <be> not timelessly aware, and in that sense, there is no event or state of affairs of which God <be> ignorant.[44]

I am inclined to think that it reveals no more than an anthropomorphic bias to suppose that anyone who lacks the knowledge that there is a war going on now, or that the war is at last over, thank goodness, is cripplingly ill-informed about the human condition. We may find the cognitive and emotional roller-coaster of our experience a central component of the richness of human life, for better and for worse, which we would be unwilling to swap for the unchanging sameness of a timeless grasp of all things. So even if God can

<understand> our human emotions of relief and apprehension, eager anticipation and nostalgia, only in the sense, remarked upon earlier, that a man can understand what childbearing is, it seems to me unproblematic to say that our ways of knowing may well be best for us. But we need not suppose that God's total awareness is not best for God. It is surely all but meaningless to make a comparison between an essentially time-bound form of experience and an eternal total awareness of reality, with a view to asking which is better, or as a prelude to suggesting that it is a sad deficiency that God cannot share in what we might find exciting.

Is God's knowledge necessary?

I have already argued that I see no reason to deny that God's eternity is best understood as atemporality; and, furthermore, that there are difficulties in Ockham's suggestion that God's knowledge of what still lies in our future can be described only as accidentally contingent knowledge. Further, God's knowledge is non-propositional, though we need to talk about it in propositional terms. Suppose, then, we try to reformulate the problem about the accidental necessity of God's knowledge, without the misleading implications of saying that God knows propositions, or that God's knowledge is itself in time.[45]

1 Some of the states of affairs known to God are not yet actual.
2 Some of the states of affairs known to God are contingent.
3 To know a contingent state of affairs is to know what need not be actual.
4 God's knowing is necessary.
5 If it might be that S never is an actual state of affairs, and it equally might be that S at some time is an actual state of affairs, then it might be that God <know> S as actual and it might be that God not <know> S as actual.
So,
6 God's knowledge might be other than it <be>.

The problem is that 4 and 6 seem to be inconsistent.

The first thing to note about this argument is that 1 is irrelevant to the derivation of 4. Of course it is true that if the future turns out differently and instead of S it is S1 that comes to be, then it will never have been true to say that God <know> S, and it will always have been true to say that God <know> S1. Equally, however, it will turn out never to have been true to say that S will come about, and it will always have been true to say that S1 will come about. Given the meaning of 'true' and 'know', both sets of statements are *de dicto* necessarily true. But that relationship is a logical relationship, not a causal one. 'Being true' is not an intrinsic property of a contingent statement, neither is 'being an instance of knowledge' an intrinsic property of a cognitive state. Knowing is not a different kind of state from believing. An analogy with a football match might help. Suppose the goalkeeper of a team which has scored the only goal of the match makes a brilliant last-second save. His action has as a logical consequence that the only goal was also the winning goal. But he does not alter any intrinsic property of the earlier event which was the scoring of that goal. Similarly, in bringing about some future state of affairs, we can bring it about that a statement previously made was true; and we can make it false that someone knew all along that we would not do so.

In itself, then, 1 carries no implication that what comes to be actual has a causal effect on the necessary content of God's state of mind. Moreover, 1 is the kind of statement which we find ourselves having to make because of the time-bound nature of our grasp of reality, and our comparative inability to know what still lies in the future. That problem God does not have. The problem is not with the futurity, as we see it, of some S, but with its contingency. For even if S is not known to God as future, it is surely known as contingent. So the core of the problem is the derivation of 6 from 3 and 5.

First, consider the sense of 'might' in 5. How is this to be understood? Take, for instance, 'I might have some soup at lunch-time today' and compare it with 'I might never have come'. Both concern states of affairs which can be brought about; but the first refers to a state of affairs which I am still able to actualise or not, as I choose; the second refers to a state of affairs I could have brought about, but which cannot any longer be brought about by anyone. The difference between them is entirely a function of my position in time, and of the unidirectional nature of temporal causation. This is a real difference, not merely an illusory one, and is rooted in the very nature of time itself. This difference affects when it is open to me to make some state of affairs actual.

That being said, though, just as (in part through my choices, in part through the choices of others, in part by necessity) there is only one actual past, so there will be (again partly through my choices, etc.) only one actual future. A cosmic history different from the actual one is not an impossibility, but it is not an actual history. To speak about it is to refer to nothing more than the powers possessed by beings in the actual world, and to note that these powers are not completely determined in the way in which they act. Given that what God does he immutably does, and looking at the matter from the point of view of God, the 'might' in 5 has the same sense as that in which it is true that I might never have come, or that the history of the cosmos is not the only possible history of the cosmos. 5 does not require that there be another actual history of the cosmos.

Might God's knowledge of the history of the cosmos be other than it <be>? Clearly it might, in the sense that the actual history of the cosmos is not the only possible history of the cosmos. But it is the only actual one. Now, for God there is nothing exactly parallel to the fact which is crucial in my life, that I can affect my future, but can no longer affect my past. Whatever God <can> do, he <can> do equally to the past, present, or future, since God's power is not itself situated in time. The whole of time is causally accessible to God. But, so to speak, it is accessible only once. The parallel in God to my lack of causal access to the past is God's lack of causal access to more than one actual history of a time-bound cosmos.[46] From God's point of view, then, it <be> *not* accidentally possible that there should be another actual history of this cosmos; so 6 is false if it is taken to mean that God's knowledge of the actual cosmos might <be> other than it <be>, in the sense of 'might' in which I might have soup for lunch today. In a slightly extended use of the term, the entire history of the cosmos is, from God's point of view, accidentally necessary.

What I and other undetermined agents collectively bring about is the actual history of the cosmos. Since there is only one such history, it is not in our power to bring it about that the actual history of the cosmos is other than it <be>, though it is in our power to determine what that actual history <be>. How, then, is this power of ours related to God's knowledge? For the sake of simplicity, I shall consider only my own powers; similar considerations will, of course, apply to all other agents whose acts are undetermined.

7   It is not *de re* possible that I should act in such a way that God <know> some other history of the cosmos than God <know>.

But, we must also say that

8   It is *de re* possible for me to act in such a way that God
<know> *this* cosmic history rather than some other one.

and hence

9   Were my choices to be other than they were, are, or will be,
then the actual history of the cosmos would be a different
actual history.

The problem is how 8 and 9 are to be reconciled with 7. For it might
seem obvious that there is a valid Transfer of Necessity Argument:

TNA2

i)   It is eternally accidentally necessary that God <know>
that I will bring about S1 rather than S2.

ii)   It *de dicto* cannot be the case that God <know> that I
bring about S1 were it not the case that I do bring about
S1; nor *de dicto* can it be the case that I bring about S1
were it not the case that God <know> I bring about S1.

So

iii)   It is eternally accidentally necessary that I bring about
S1.

So

iv)   I do not *now* have the power not to bring about S1.

From i) and ii), it seems that iii). follows: and iv) seems to follow
from iii) Now, ii) is true in virtue of the definition of 'know' plus
the assumption that God is omniscient, and I have already conceded
i). However, although iii) does indeed follow from i) and ii), it does
so only provided that 'accidentally necessary' is taken in the same
sense in both i) and iii). In i), what is being denied is that God has
causal access to more than one actual cosmos. He cannot <cause>
the actual history of the cosmos to <be> other than it actually <be>.
Similarly in iii), neither can I cause the actual history of the cosmos
to be other than it <be>. But it does not straightforwardly follow
from iii) that I have no power to bring about S2 rather than S1; it is
precisely in exercising my power to bring about S1 rather than S2
that I contribute to the history of the universe as it <be>. To put the
matter in another way, it does not follow from eternally-accidental-
necessity of God's knowledge that I have no control *in time* over
my future; iv) would follow from iii) only if iii) were to be
understood as saying something about my power at the present
moment in time; but in *that* sense, iii) does not follow from i) and

ii). The reason why it seems plausible to say that iv) follows from iii) is that we tend to think of what is accidentally necessary in eternity as somehow *already* accidentally necessary. But the accidental necessity of eternity is temporally unrelated to what is accidentally necessary or contingent at any given moment in time. There is no contradiction in saying that some temporal event E is both eternally necessary, and as yet accidentally contingent, where the 'as yet' is a temporal expression. I conclude that there is no inconsistency in holding 1–9 together.

God's uncaused knowing

Implicit in the classical position that God is in all respects simple, is the view that the source of God's knowledge cannot be anything other than God himself. God does not know things, nor which propositions about those things are true or false, as a causal consequence of the existence of those things, or of the states of affairs which true propositions describe. Whatever it is that God can be said to know must be known in God's awareness of his own nature, and of his own causal activity in sustaining his creation. This position will to some extent require correction, for reasons which will become apparent. I shall argue that while it is true that the ultimate source of all God's knowledge is God's awareness of his own nature and of his created activity, his knowledge of contingent events within creation must derive from the occurrence of those events themselves. It will follow that God to that extent must be regarded as being acted upon by creation, even though he himself is the ultimate source of the creation with which he interacts. This conclusion could indeed be avoided were it possible to show that none of the ways in which creation interacts with God in accounting for God's knowledge, involved *causal* interactions. But I cannot see any way of establishing this.

One way of putting what has already been argued is to say that God's eternal knowing 'already' (so to speak) takes account of everything that happens in time to contribute to the unique actual history of the cosmos. So it 'already' includes all the ways in which the powers of undetermined agents are exercised in contributing to that history. The central problem, in my view, is not with the consistency of 1–9, despite the enormous literature to which those statements have given rise. The problem arises when they are combined with another classical view, that nothing in God is *caused* by anything outside God. In particular, the classical tradition held that in saying that God's eternal and accidentally necessary knowing 'takes account of' all the ways in which the powers of undetermined creatures are exercised, this 'takes account of' must not be construed in any way which would imply that God's knowledge is the causal result of what creatures do in time. Where, then, does this knowledge come from?

The replies to this question given by Aquinas and Molina both seem to me to be inadequate, attractive as they might at first sight appear.

Aquinas's suggestion is that God knows future contingent events in causing them. His usual illustration, involving the necessary causal action of the sun and the contingent event of the grass growing, is misleading. It wrongly suggests that God's activity and the activity of secondary causes are related in the way in which the activities of two secondary causes are related. Nevertheless, it does at least point to one element which must surely be a part of any solution which he would accept, namely, that the activity of the secondary cause is not casually determined by God's causation. The aim is to find some characterisation of God's transcendent causality which is both causally efficacious, and yet does not wholly determine its effect, and which could be part of an overall explanation of how it is that God knows the complete effect. But can this be done?

Examples of an undetermined, and hence contingent, effect are to be found in physics. It appears that the unpredictability of some events in quantum physics is not simply an apparent indeterminacy because of the limitations of our data. The indeterminacy is real. Hence, even given the existence of the cosmos, there are at least two different types of contingent event: not all physical states of affairs are determined; and there are agents who make free decisions which, we may suppose, are not causally determined either. To avoid the additional problems with the notion of freedom, I think it preferable to concentrate on the problems for the 'transcendent cause/contingent effect' thesis which arise from the undetermined events in nuclear physics, such as the decay of a radioactive atom.[47] The difficulty might be put in the following way. The radioactive element polonium 210 is such that half of it will decay into lead in 140 days. Let A_2 be an atom of lead produced at t by the decay of one particular atom of the lump of polonium; then consider

   i)   God is not causally affected by any created event.

ii)   God is the causal explanation for the existence of all created things.

iii)   God is the causal explanation of the existence of A_2 at t.

iv)   The existence of A_2 at t was undetermined by the state of the world immediately prior to t.

v)   iii) explains how God <know> that A_2 exists at t.

Aquinas hopes that iii), iv) and v) are all true, and that v) is compatible with i). But how can iii) and iv) both be true? If we consider simply iv), and ask what is the explanation for the existence of A_2, the answer is twofold. There is a statistical explanation with which the existence of A_2 is consistent; and that statistical explanation presumably reflects some feature of the nature of polonium – since it has a different half-life from the half-life of other elements, just by virtue of being the element that it is. Secondly, there is no explanation of why it is A_2 that exists at t rather than the similar atom A_n which would have been produced by the decay of some other atom than the one whose decay produced A_2. The event which is the appearance of A_2 need not have as its causal explanation some immediately prior event which determined its occurrence, though it does have a general causal explanation in terms of the nature of the polonium mass in which this event took place at t.

It would, one might suppose, be possible to read iii) in such a way as to make some particular action of God be the explanation for the existence of A_2 rather than some other A_n. But I think this would be an unwise line to pursue, since it would render the existence of A_2, and countless other similar atoms, miraculous. But that runs quite counter to our proper scientific intuitions that this is simply the way things naturally happen. It would be to invoke the activity of God to salvage our preconception that all events must be individually predetermined, when the scientific evidence so strongly suggests that this preconception is false. Rather, the proper scientific reaction to the appearance of A_2 should be that it is simply a brute fact for which nothing other than a general statistical explanation should be sought at all; and the proper theistic reaction ought not to be to replace the notion of God as a transcendent cause with a notion of God as one more causal agent on the same level as the created causal agents known to science. Created causal agents interact in virtue of the natures they have; and the patterns of their interactions can be captured by law-like generalisations, some statistical in character, which explain the features of some effect in terms of the features of the various causal agents involved. What we cannot do, or at any rate have not successfully done, is to capture what it is for things to interact, as distinct from stating the patterns in which they do so.

A transcendent cause does *not* explain the features which individual things from time to time have as a result of the interactions of their various natures. It does not, in short, duplicate the causal explanations known to, or knowable by, science. Rather, the activity of the transcendent cause explains the actuality of the whole system and of all the individual causal agents with their natures belonging to it. There just is no law-like generalisation relating God's transcendental causation to worldly events.

That, of course, is a controversial view, and would not be accepted by anyone who denies that any such transcendental explanation is required at all. But the point I wish to argue for here is that, even if it is accepted, it does not appear to be of much assistance to anyone who wishes to use the notion of transcendent causation to explain God's knowledge of the existence of A_2 at t. Even if it is supposed that God has a complete knowledge of the ways in which natural things could interact one with another, and hence of the statistical facts about the half-life of the polonium from whose decay A_2 was produced, that knowledge of itself provides no basis for knowing that it would be A_2 rather than some other A_n which would exist at t. All that God could know on that basis would be that a certain proportion of the original polonium would decay over a given period of time. In which case, v) is false even if iii) is true. But if we suppose that the basis for God's knowledge of the existence of A_2 at t is the fact that A_2 exists, then God's knowledge seems to depend on created events, contrary to i). That, I believe, is the correct conclusion to draw. I conclude that the following statements are all true:

H1 If it is true that A_2 changed from being an atom of polonium at $t - 1$ to being an atom of lead at t, then it <be> true that that event <occur> at t.

H2 It was always true to say that that event would occur at t; and the grounds for the truth of that statement is the event which took place at t.

H3 There is no causal explanation (either through a secondary or a transcendent cause) of that event taking place at t.

H4 There were, prior to t, no grounds for believing that that event either would, or would not, take place at t.

H5 At all times subsequent to t, and eternally, the ground for believing that that event took place at t simply is the occurrence of the event itself.

H2 might seem contentious. It has been denied that a sentence of the form 'Given the existence of a mass of polonium at $t - n$, then A_2 would decay at t' can be true or false if the decay of A_2 is genuinely undetermined. Of course, if the 'would' is interpreted as suggesting that prior to t there is some *ground for believing* that A_2 would decay at t, then H2 is false, and for that very reason, H5 is true. But to say that, prior to t, there is no ground for *believing* that something will occur is not at all the same as saying that there is no grounding for its *truth*. The only basis I can see for denying H2 would be a very general anti-realism about the future, which I think is an implausible view, for just the kinds of reasons that Ockham gave in commenting on Aristotle. So the reason H4 is true is that H3 is true.

A parallel argument, substituting some free choice for the decay of A_2, shows that there are no grounds for believing statements of the form 'If X is placed in a fully specified situation, she will choose to do A' prior to her actually doing A. But at any time prior to her doing A, it will always have been *true* that, placed in precisely those circumstances, she would do A. But the temptation to read the 'would' here as somehow expressing the character of A in virtue of which she chooses to do A ('Well, she would do that, wouldn't she?') is just that, a temptation.

But isn't it true that, as Molina suggests, knowledge of someone's character gives good grounds for believing that they will do A in those circumstances? There are two considerations which might be urged against this suggestion: *i)* The fact that someone can, if A is genuinely contingent, act out of character prevents these grounds for believing that she will not from being conclusive. It is difficult to assess the weight of this argument without a detailed discussion of the nature of free choices. I am prepared to accept that there might be cases in which knowledge of someone's character could fully justify the belief that they would never do anything other than A in those circumstances, even though they could. And the claim to know that they would do A does not require that any other *possibility* be excluded. So perhaps in these cases Molina might be right. *ii)* Be

111

that as it may, it is still highly implausible to suppose that *all* free choices are of the kind that one can predict even if one knows the person's character well. Molina simply asserts that the complete knowledge of someone's character available to God would provide sufficient grounds for knowing what they would do. But short of assuming that one's character fully explains all one's actions, I can see no grounds for his confidence. And in any case, even if some such account were to work for the free choices we make, there is no reason to suppose that it would work for the undetermined events of quantum physics.

In short, Aquinas seems to be mistaken in his claim that a transcendent cause is of itself insufficient to produce a contingent effect and yet provides sufficient ground for knowing that that effect would take place. Molina asserts, without proof, that there are other grounds than God's causal action for knowing what such contingent effects would be. I conclude that the only grounds for God's eternal and immutable knowledge of what the actual history of the cosmos <be> is his eternal awareness of what it <be>; and that is to say that God depends for his knowledge on the behaviour of creatures. Though obviously it is not the case that God's eternal knowledge of contingent events is incomplete until those events occur, it is the case that the occurrence of those events is logically and epistemologically prior to God's knowledge of them.

This conclusion is clearly in conflict with that element in the classical doctrine of the simplicity of God which requires that God be in no way potential. And even if, as I have suggested, this was not intended to exclude God's active powers, since it was taken to be compatible with the view that God freely creates, it certainly was intended to exclude that God could be in any way dependent on creatures. Is it then the case that to make God's knowledge dependent to some extent on creatures totally undermines the view that God is simple?

I do not believe that it does. It does not undermine the arguments which demonstrate that God exists of necessity, and that he is not a member of any kind. That I take to be the core of the Simplicity-Doctrine. What it does, however, is weaken the sense in which God's knowledge can be said to be in all respects necessarily as it is; and hence it weakens the sense in which God's knowledge can be said to be identical with God's existence. On the other hand, even on the traditional view, God's knowledge could have been other than it

<be>, had God created other than he <create>, since he would have known that another world was the actual world. Yes, it might be replied, but in that case, there is still no question of the difference in God's knowledge being dependent on the activity of creatures. It is quite another matter to say that, *given* a creation, God knows what that creation is like only *because* creatures behave as they do, but need not do.

There are two possible lines of reply, I think. The first is to point out that even in this case, God is still the transcendent cause of whatever it is that happens, including what happens without being predetermined. Even the decay of atoms or the free decisions of humans would not exist at all did God not transcendentally cause their existence. So the extent to which these events are independent of God is limited. Secondly, it is in any case not clear what might be meant by stating that God's knowledge and God's existence are identical, and hence unclear whether the necessity of God's existence automatically transfers to God's knowledge. I think the conclusion must be that it does not.

CHAPTER IV

Omnipotence

As Quine (1961) might have said, the question about God's omnipotence can be put in four very short words: 'What can God do?'
The traditional answer is equally brief: Everything. But there
remains room for disagreement over cases, and so the issue has
stayed alive down the centuries. In practice, there have been many
tacit restrictions on the belief that God can do everything. It was not
– or at least not at first sight – supposed that God can go for a walk
in the garden, or speak Hebrew, or sit upon a throne.[1] It was
commonly accepted that since God is incorporeal, he cannot be
said to be capable of such bodily activities in anything other than
a metaphorical sense. For the same reason, whether God can literally be said to have emotions has depended on different beliefs
about whether emotions (or some emotions) necessarily involved
physical states or not. The issues which have been controversial
are those which seemed to be less peripheral, more closely linked
to the belief that God is infinite, and that his creative powers are
therefore likewise unrestricted. Could God create worlds other than
the one he has created? Can God change the past? Are there any
other kinds of limitation on what God can do? Can God do what is
morally wrong?

It is often suggested that the classical treatments of these views
can roughly be divided into two groups: on the one hand, it is said,
philosophers like Aquinas hold that God is somehow limited by the
laws of logic, and is able to do only what it is logically possible to
do; on the other hand, it is said, philosophers who are more
influenced by nominalism, such as Ockham and perhaps Descartes,
maintained that God could, if he so chose, alter the very laws of logic
themselves. I think it will emerge that, though there are still notable
differences between the three philosophers I have mentioned, the

alleged contrast is much less sharp than is commonly thought. But the details need careful discussion.

THE HISTORY OF THE PROBLEM

Aquinas

THE GENERAL ACCOUNT

Aquinas's overall position is to be found most conveniently in I, 25. The first two articles are by way of a ground-clearing exercise, in which Aquinas is concerned that the concept of 'power', as it is applied to God who is in no way merely potential, is not to be understood as a passivity, nor to refer to something prior to God's action, though it can properly be seen as prior to the effects of God's action. God's power, intellect, and will are all 'one', and are all unlimited, since they belong to no genus. Aquinas takes it that this much follows at once from the simplicity of God which he has already established. The problems come in trying to show that the conclusions which are entailed by this view are mutually coherent, and consonant with traditional Christian belief. It is worth noting that, having already asserted that God's power is infinite (in the sense of totally simple), Aquinas regards it as still to be settled whether God is omnipotent.

Aquinas remarks that although everyone agrees that God is omnipotent, 'omnipotence' is difficult to define. It is no doubt the case that to say that God is omnipotent is to say that God can do whatever is possible. But that is merely to postpone the problem:

'Possible' is said in two ways, as Aristotle points out in *Metaphysics* V. In one way, what is possible is relative to some capacity, as when something lies within a human capacity it is said to be possible for a human being. Now God cannot be called 'omnipotent' [just] because he has all the capacities of created natures, since his divine power extends more widely than that. On the other hand, if God is said to be omnipotent because he can do everything which lies within the powers of his own nature, the account of omnipotence will clearly be circular: God is omnipotent because he can do all that he can do. The only alternative is to say that God is omnipotent because he can do everything that is absolutely possible (which is the other sense of 'possible'). Something is called 'possible' or 'impossible' from the relationship between the terms; 'possible' if the predicate is not incompatible with the subject, e.g. that Socrates is sitting; 'impossible' if it is incompatible, e.g. that a man is an ass.[2]

(I, 25, 3)

I have already suggested that though a passage like this might naturally be taken to be talking about merely logical possibility one should remember that Aquinas, like Aristotle, would hold that at least in most cases logic mirrors ontology. Given that we know the real essences of things, we define our terms for those things in such a way that the *de re* possibilities inherent in things are reflected in the logical compatibility of terms. 'Socrates is sitting' is logically possible because Socrates is able to sit. It is necessarily false that a man is an ass, because it is *de re* impossible that a man-ass should exist. If this is correct, then Aquinas's suggestion is that God can do whatever is *de re* possible. This reading is confirmed by a remark later in the same article, where Aquinas remarks that to say that God cannot do the impossible is not a limitation on God's power; 'it would be more accurate to say that such things cannot come to be than to say that God cannot produce them.'[3]

This account of omnipotence is indeed not narrowly circular, as Aquinas rightly says. But it is nevertheless of somewhat limited value, since it relies on our grasp of what is and what is not *de re* possible. Since whether something is *de re* possible or not is an empirical matter, our grasp of what it is for God to be omnipotent will extend no further than our empirical grasp of the natural universe – about which we might be less clear nowadays than Aquinas thought he could be.[4]

CAN GOD UNDO THE PAST?

Aquinas answers this question by appealing to the general principles he has just set out. If as a matter of fact Socrates was sitting down at t, God cannot bring it about that he was not sitting at t. To do so would entail that it was both true that Socrates was sitting at t, and false that Socrates was sitting at t, which is a contradiction. He considers an objection, that since God can do what is in itself impossible, such as raising someone from the dead, he can surely also do what is only accidentally impossible, such as undoing the past. He replies,

> Although it is [only] accidentally impossible for the past events not to have been if one considers simply the past event itself (e.g. Socrates's running), still, if one considers the past precisely as past, it is not just in itself but absolutely impossible for it not to have been, since it implies a contradiction. So this is even more impossible than for someone who is dead to rise again, which does not imply any contradiction, but is said to be impossible only with respect to some particular power (in this case a natural power). For things of this latter kind do fall within the divine power.
>
> (I, 25, 4, reply 1)

It is not, however, altogether clear that this conclusion is inescapable. It would indeed involve a contradiction if, given that Socrates did run, God then brought it about that he did not. But could God not bring it about that Socrates never did run in the first place? Aquinas seems to assume that if it was true that Socrates did run, then of necessity it will always remain true that he did, no matter what God might do. It might be argued that this simply begs the question against the claim that it might be within God's power to bring it about that it *never was true* in the first place. While it doubtless is a natural *de re* necessity that we no longer have causal access to the past, is it clear that God does not? We shall later see that this assumption has been questioned. Aquinas, however, takes it as obvious that this is impossible, without further explanation. As I have suggested in the previous chapter, God has access to the time-bound universe only once, because of the nature of time.

CAN GOD MAKE OTHER THINGS THAN HE DOES MAKE?

Aquinas's answer to this traditional question depends on two basic distinctions. The first is between what is willed by natural necessity and what can be freely willed or not: and the second is between God's 'ordered power' and God's 'absolute power'. I shall consider each in turn. First, though, we need some explanation of Aquinas's views on what can and cannot be willed.

Aquinas's general theory of the will includes the following assertions:

i) Someone can will only what they believe to be in some respect good.
ii) Someone is naturally necessitated to will whatever they believe to be in all respects good.
iii) Someone can freely will or not will anything which is presented as only in some limited respect good.

Obviously, the controversy about determinism and free-will is still not resolved to everyone's satisfaction, and I cannot give an adequate account of it here. I must content myself simply with elaborating upon the three claims which Aquinas makes. i) is perhaps best understood as a definition of the term 'to will', much in the same way as it might be considered true by definition that only those things will count as actions which the agent *wants* to do – and hence takes to be in some respect worth doing.[5] Willing is therefore a rational activity, dependent upon the agent's beliefs. As for ii), the most obvious example of what Aquinas has in mind is that humans by natural necessity will their own happiness. This is a view he takes over from the early chapters of Aristotle's *Nicomachean Ethics*; and neither in Aristotle nor in Aquinas is it entirely clear what the status of this claim is supposed to be. It might be an empirical remark, to the effect that human beings in all that they do aim at being happy (whatever they take happiness to consist in); or it might be that there is an *a priori* assumption that there must be *one* ultimate end to explain the many ends which we obviously do pursue in life, and that 'happiness' is the best term for it.[6] At any rate, when ii) is applied to the special case of God, Aquinas had no hesitation in identifying the goodness of God himself as the necessary object of the divine will, and as the only such object.

With regard to iii), I think it is Aquinas's view that although one is free to will anything which one can represent to oneself as good, one is not determined to choose any such thing, nor even to choose the thing which one believes to be the best among limited goods. An objection to this libertarian view is that any given choice must therefore be arbitrary. Aquinas might reply that for any given choice the agent will be able to give a reason; and in that sense the choice is not arbitrary. The reason – that what is chosen is worth choosing, since it is good – genuinely explains the choice which was made.

What it does not explain is why this choice was made rather than some other for which a similar reason would have been available. I take it that the lack of an explanation of this latter kind is just what Aquinas believes constitutes free-will.

At any rate, Aquinas can argue on the basis of iii) that God's choices are not necessitated by any possible finite good that he can bring about. God did not therefore create of necessity, nor did he of necessity create precisely this world. It would be equally within his absolute power to create any other *de re* possible world; and since such a world is in some ways good, that would in itself be a sufficient reason for God's being able to choose to create it.

Aquinas then considers the view, which he takes to be mistaken, that God could not do other than he does because his wisdom and justice, which are in God identical with his power,[7] would require that he does what is wisest and most just. He believes this to be mistaken on the grounds that no finite creation could ever exhaust the wisdom of God, and hence could not exhaust his power either. In effect, the claim is that there can be no one 'wisest' or 'best' world.

The other central distinction, between God's absolute power and his ordered power, Aquinas expresses as follows:

Since God's will is not necessitated to create these things rather than those, (except perhaps hypothetically, as has been said above),[8] so neither is his wisdom or his justice bound to the present order of things. There is no reason why something should not be in God's power which he does not will and so is not part of the order he has established in creation. Since 'power' is taken to involve 'executing', 'will' to involve 'commanding' and 'intellect and wisdom' to involve 'directing', whatever is attributed to God's power considered in itself God is said to be able to do in his *absolute* power; this extends to everything which can properly be defined as a being, as has been said. But whatever is attributed to God's power regarded as executing God's just will God is said to be able to do by his *ordered* power. From which it follows that while it is in the absolute power of God to do other than he foreknew and fore-ordained that he would do, it is not possible for God to do anything that he did not foreknow and fore-ordain that he would do. What God does is included in his foreknowledge and fore-ordination; his power in itself is not, since it belongs to him by nature.

The ordered power of God is limited by what God eternally chooses to do, simply because any choice to do A excludes the possibility of doing whatever is incompatible with A. And, since God is eternal and hence unchanging, God cannot alter the choice which he eternally makes. But God could eternally have chosen to act other-wise than he did.[9] Just as our past choices are accidentally necessary, so are God's eternal decisions.

COULD GOD CREATE BETTER?

So put, the form of the question is hardly idiomatic English. It is intended to capture an ambiguity to which Aquinas calls attention, between 'Could God improve on what he has made?' and 'Could God create in a better way?' Aquinas's reply is deceptively simple:

i)   God can certainly make some created thing be a better thing of its kind. For instance, God might assist Peter to be a better person.

ii) God cannot produce an improved version of what it is to be a man; for that would amount to creating something of a different kind altogether.

iii) There are no doubt things which are better than, for example, Man, which God could create.

iv) God creates whatever he creates with infinite wisdom and justice: it is not possible for God to improve his own performance, so to speak.

A full discussion of some of these points will be more appropriate in the context of the problem of evil, in the next chapter. For the moment, it will suffice to point out some of the problems and assumptions which lie behind Aquinas's view.

i) is relatively clear. The major problem which it raises is why, if God could improve things in this way, does he not do so? This will have to be discussed at length later. ii) simply reflects Aquinas's view that there are natural kinds, and that there is therefore a difference between, say, making someone a better person, and making something which is better than, but thereby a different kind of thing from, a person. iii) is much less clear. Even if one accepts Aquinas's view that there are natural kinds, it is surely very hard to

120

see what might be meant by saying that one kind of thing is a better kind of thing than another. Perhaps Aquinas is here, as elsewhere, influenced by Neo-Platonic views, whereby kinds of things are ranked in their degree of perfection; and of course we too are prepared to speak of the 'higher' animals, and 'lower' life-forms. But to speak in this way is to make some assumptions about, for instance, the value of being sensate, or being more complex, or being intelligent. And it is not easy to rebut the suggestion that this value-ranking does little more than reflect our own concerns and interests. But the difficulty with iv) is that it seems to contradict both i) and iii). At the end of the previous section, I outlined Aquinas's opinion that God could have chosen to create some world other than this one. But if it is true that there is a *de re* possible world which would contain better things, or in which existing things would be better examples of their kinds, how is it possible then to say that in creating this world God expresses his wisdom and justice in a way which cannot be improved upon?

Aquinas's reply is hardly convincing: there is no wiser or more just ordering of this world than the order it has, with all its parts in perfect harmony; in short this world could not be better arranged, but there could indeed be a better world, different from this one (I, 25, 6, reply 3). However, he has already admitted that God could improve the things in this world; is his contention then that the perfect harmony of this creation requires that some parts of it be less perfect than they might be? Some elements in the Neo-Platonist tradition did indeed take such a line. But if this is not so, then it would appear that even this world could be better arranged. Moreover, how can it be true that God would be equally wise in creating any of a number of possible worlds, provided that whatever one he created was well-ordered, if it is also true that some of these well-ordered worlds would be better than others? This too will have to be discussed in the next chapter.

William of Ockham

THE GENERAL ACCOUNT

Ockham did not believe that there was a conclusive philosophical proof that God was omnipotent. He believed it as an article of Christian faith.[10] The details of his view are not easy to unravel. His position is intimately connected with his more general views on epistemology and metaphysics. Despite his adherence to the terminology inherited ultimately from Aristotle, Ockham's account of epistemology, metaphysics and logic differs notably from the traditional Aristotelian views of these matters, especially as some of the interpretations of Aristotle were themselves much influenced by Neo-Platonism. Two elements in Ockham's overall view are especially relevant here.

Firstly, Ockham denied the traditional position that universal terms such as 'man' or 'donkey' referred to the real natures or essences of things, whether in the strongest Platonic sense (in which the referents of such terms were separately existing Forms), or in the weaker more Aristotelian sense (in which the referents of such terms were not separately existing entities, but were nevertheless distinct from the individuals which share the same essence or nature). In Ockham's opinion, universal terms of this kind refer simply to the individuals of which they can truly be said; and they can truly be said of those individuals because the individuals are in fact similar to one another. There is nothing more to the 'essence of man' than the brute fact that human beings resemble one another in the relevant ways. Given this, one might at least get the impression that there is no *essential necessity* for humans to be rational or animal; and hence one might be tempted to conclude (mistakenly, as will appear) that in Ockham's view God could create humans who were not animals, or not rational.[11]

We might, secondly, take up the issue as it were from God's end. Aquinas and others had held that God knew all actual and possible things by knowing the Ideas of those things. As we have seen, Aquinas was at pains to claim that the Ideas were not entities existing separately from the divine essence. He thus tried to avoid the Platonism which would result from supposing that God, in the manner of a Platonic Demiurge, contemplated the eternal Ideas in order to create finite things. Still, even Aquinas granted that it was entirely proper to speak of God's simple knowledge involving a plurality of ideas corresponding to the various ways in which his essence can be imitated by created things (I, 15, 1, reply 2).

In Ockham's view, there were several difficulties in this position. In the first place, it seemed to contradict the view that God is totally simple, despite Aquinas's attempted argument that the Ideas were only notionally and not really distinct from God's mind; secondly,

it suggested that the Ideas were real, eternal, beings, which contra-
dicted the common view that everything other than God was created
a finite time ago; and thirdly, it suggested that God could know
individual creatures only in a universal, and therefore inadequate,
way. Finally, Ockham entirely rejected what he would have regarded
as the Platonist position that there are real essences of things, which
are at least in some way independent both of the things themselves
and of a mind which knew them.

Accordingly, in *Ord.*, I, 35, 5 Ockham eventually came to argue that

i) God knows all actual and possible creatures eternally.

ii) God's act of knowing is identical with his essence, hence
is completely simple.

iii) There are no separate Ideas in God.

iv) It could be said that the 'ideas', known by God, simply
are the creatures themselves, known directly and individually.

In Ockham's view, iii) follows from ii); and, given iii), iv) is the
most that Ockham is prepared to concede to the tradition, because of
his view that knowledge of individuals is direct, as opposed to the
Aristotelian view that individuals are known by knowing universal
terms which are truly said of them, and which represent the essence
of those individuals. Marilyn Adams concludes that Ockham's final
interpretation of iv) is that, prior to the existence of creatures, there
exist no ideas of them at all, even though it is true that God eternally
knows those creatures: 'the creature did not have any existence then;
nevertheless it was truly understood then'.[12] Ockham would apply
the same reasoning even to possible creatures. This would seem to
Ockham no stranger than saying that a future state of affairs can be
known now even though it does not exist now.

Well, what is the connection between this discussion and the
issues surrounding God's omnipotence? Suppose, as Aquinas certainly did suppose, that the grounds on which something is possible
or impossible are to be found in the relationships of compatibility
or mutual exclusivity between the ideas which God has. It would
then be natural to say that God's omnipotence is delimited by God's
knowledge of what is possible; in short, that God can do things only
because they are (already, so to speak) possible, rather than that
things are possible because God can do them. It might then seem
that, if Ockham denies that there are any such ideas antecedently

to the actual existence of creatures, he would say that what God knows to be possible is a consequence of what he knows himself to have done. This would be a reading of Ockham which is sharply in contrast with the more traditional views of Aquinas. Ockham would be seen as dispensing in a radical way with anything even remotely similar to the Platonic Demiurge, who looks to the Ideas in order to shape the universe according to their pre-established pattern of what is possible. For God, anything is possible, without any previous logical restriction whatever. But did Ockham in fact go so far?

Ockham's preliminary reply to this question about priorities is clear enough:

> [In all cases of related things which] are related as active power to passive power, or as cause to effect, the correlatives are always naturally simultaneous. Therefore, since they are naturally simultaneous and each entails the other, one is not more the cause of the other than vice versa. . . . It follows that a son is no more a son than a father is a father, nor vice versa. Neither is it more the case that a son is [a son] because a father is [a father] than the other way round.
>
> (*Ord.*, I, 43, 2, A1247)

So, it is just as true to say that something is possible because God can create it as to say that God can create something because it is possible. So far, this reply leaves everything still to play for. It is, however, also noteworthy in this passage that Ockham can move easily from talking about 'natural simultaneity' to talking about 'mutual entailment', which suggests that he thought that logical necessity mirrors the way things naturally are. This sounds considerably less radical than one might have expected. It is therefore not surprising that he says,

> To be possible is something that a creature has of itself, but is not anything real inhering in it. But the creature truly is possible of itself, just as man of himself is not a donkey. . . . Nor is it a very proper way of speaking to say that possible existence belongs to a creature, but rather one properly ought to say that a creature is possible, not because something belongs to it, but because it can exist in reality.
>
> (*Ord.*, I, 20, 1, A1081)

Just as 'animal' does not refer to some real entity over and above individual animals, so 'being possible' is not something over and above actual things, which, since they are actual, are obviously able to exist. What Ockham is objecting to is the tendency he detected in his predecessors to assume that terms like 'nature' or 'possibility' or 'relationship' must refer to items in the world. No doubt he would have objected equally to any tendency to speak of 'possible worlds' as though they had some kind of independent reality; and even more would he have objected to the view that the actual world simply is that one among the possible worlds which the speaker happens to be in. But while wielding his razor in this way,[13] Ockham is quite prepared explicitly to say that a creature can truly said to be possible 'of itself'. And what does this 'of itself' mean? Further clues can be gained from the following passage:

> The omnipotence we are here speaking about does not have to do with *everything* that does not involve a contradiction. That is to say, an omnipotent being cannot produce everything that does not involve a contradiction, because it cannot produce God. Nevertheless, an omnipotent being can produce everything which is *producible* that does not involve a contradiction, and everything other than God that does not involve a contradiction.
>
> (*Ord.*, I, 20, 1, A1155)

God cannot be *produced* without contradiction; so God cannot produce a God; but he can produce anything else which does not involve a contradiction. So it seems clear that Ockham takes non-contradiction to establish some kind of limitation on what God is able to do, or, equivalently in his view, on what can be done. The problem is to see what kind of restriction non-contradiction can be, given Ockham's more general views. He has been interpreted as if the restriction was no restriction at all. On this view saying that 'A human being is not an animal' would amount to nothing more than saying that *as we currently use the words 'human being' and 'animal'*, 'A human being is not an animal' is indeed necessarily false; but since there is no essence of Human Being, there is no reason why God could not create a human being who was not an animal. Were God to have done so, our usage would have been different, and 'A human being is not an animal' would have been true. But this interpretation fails, for several reasons: *i)* On this view,

125

Ockham's frequent insistence that non-contradiction is a genuine restriction becomes simply empty; it would say no more than that if God had created humans otherwise than they now are, then the logic of 'human' would have been different. We cannot say even that he could have created *them* otherwise, since it would no longer be in the same sense humans that would have been created. *ii)* It overstates Ockham's general position. He does believe that human beings are truly similar; indeed, he believes that if an existing thing is human, it is of necessity a rational animal, and hence of necessity similar to all other humans. What he denies is that this similarity has to be explained by something *further* – such as a human nature, or essence, or the Form of Man. Ockham agrees with Aristotle that we can, inductively, discover what is essential to humans; which is to say, in what way each human resembles each other human. Like Aristotle, he believes that statements of essence, provided they are cast in the form 'If any individual is a human, that individual is a rational animal' are necessary truths, and not simply true about the words 'human', 'rational' and 'animal'. But the fact remains that, as Marilyn Adams puts it, 'such an account would be ultimately unsatisfactory' (1988: 1083, and chs 24–5), since Ockham gives no alternative ground for this necessity once he has denied the traditional Aristotelian explanation. Perhaps in the end he can do no more than say that the ground of this necessity lies in the intellect of God which knows all actual and possible truths; but this is to say nothing about what makes a possible truth possible.

CAN GOD UNDO THE PAST?

Ockham argues in the same way as Aquinas, that,

> If the proposition 'This is the case' (referring to whatever it may be) is now true, then 'This was the case' will always be true hereafter, nor can God bring it about that it is false.
>
> (PFC, 1)

He defends this view, following Aristotle, on the grounds that to change the past would bring it about that 'This was the case' and 'This was not the case' would both be true, which would be contradictory. I have already suggested above that though Ockham here appeals to non-contradiction it is perhaps unwise to take this as purely a logical move. Ockham regards the past as (at least) accidentally necessary, I think, because of the one-way direction of Time's Arrow. Plainly, the question is whether the one-way direction of time corresponds to an absolute limit on what can be done, whether by us or by God. Ockham believes that it does. Since, as we have already seen, he holds that what can be done in creation and what God is able to do are strictly correlative notions, neither prior to the other, he would equally assert that to undo the past is impossible, and that God cannot undo it. Nonetheless, it appears to me that, despite Ockham's claim that neither of these truths is ontologically prior to the other, he does believe that there is an epistemological priority. Ockham in fact places the weight of the argument firmly on our experience that the past is beyond any causal control, because of the very nature of time. He believed that this inductive evidence from our experience sufficed to show that there is a natural necessity involved. It is this that the alternative view denies.

GOD'S UNUSUAL POWERS

Ockham wrote,

> 'I believe in God the Father almighty . . . ', which I understand as follows: whatever does not include an obvious contradiction should be attributed to divine power. . . . Further, on that article is based the famous thesis of the theologians, 'Whatever God produces by means of secondary causes, he can produce and conserve immediately without them.'
>
> (*Quod.*, VI, 6, A1234)

To understand how Ockham is prepared to interpret the 'famous thesis', it must be remembered that, in his view, the only entities which exist as absolute and distinct beings are individual substances and individual instances of qualities in substances. These are the only really existing things in his ontology. There are no further entities corresponding to items in other Aristotelian categories – hence, no secondary substances (such as Man), nor motion, nor relations. This is not to say that one cannot give perfectly true descriptions of the relationships between things, or of their movements, and so on; it is simply that in speaking of 'relationships' and 'movements' and the 'natures' of things, one is not talking about any realities other than substances and their quality-instances.

Ockham insists, as I have already said, that experience can give us immediate knowledge of things, and that by induction we can come to know necessary truths about the natures of things and the causal relationships that hold between things. Thus, in his view, we can know that this is a man, and that if something is a man then it is a rational animal, and that administering a particular type of herb has cured this patient; and the last two express a *de re* necessity.

But this last point is where the main problem lies. For Ockham also writes,

> For any absolute thing really distinct from another absolute thing, it should not be denied that the one could be produced without the other by absolute divine power unless there appear to be some evident contradiction in this.
>
> (*Ord.*, I, 1, Prologue, A1249)

As a striking example one might cite,

> God expels and introduces many absolute accidents by means of natural causes in the same patient [i.e. the thing affected] without changing its place. . . . Therefore God can himself and immediately destroy every accident in a piece of wood and conserve its substance without any change of place.
>
> (*Quod.*, IV, 22, A1234)

Perhaps more serious because of its implications is another of Ockham's examples:

> Further, everything absolute, distinct in place and subject from another thing, can by the power of God exist when the other absolute thing is destroyed. But the vision of a star, both sensory and intellectual, is just such a case. Therefore [the vision of a star can exist when the star is destroyed].
>
> (*Quod.*, VI, 6, A1234)

Because a substance is an absolutely distinct entity from its qualities, it belongs to the omnipotence of God to preserve a material object in existence while removing all its accidental properties. Because my experience is a different entity from the object of that experience, one can exist without the other. Other examples, argued on the same grounds, are that God can preserve instances of properties without any substance (*Ord.*, IX, 2) and separate cause and effect (*Quod.*, IV, 15). None of these remarkable states of affairs, according to Ockham, involves an evident contradiction. In some of the examples, natural causes already produce effects (such as the star which causes my visual experience); there can therefore be no contradiction in God by himself producing, by his absolute power, just that effect.

But what is the sense of 'evident contradiction' here? It might seem that it must be purely *logical* contradiction, representing *de dicto* impossibility. For consider what Ockham wishes to say about our knowledge of necessary truths, based on inductive evidence. Recall that these are *necessary* truths, representing the ways in which things *by nature* interact with one another. But in so saying, Ockham is not committing himself to the view that to deny a *de re* necessary truth of this kind involves a *logical* contradiction. And quite rightly: what is *de re* possible is in principle independent of what is logically possible. But there are two problems with this interpretation of what he says:

i)   Why should Ockham then believe that what is logically contradictory should place any limit on the divine power?

ii)   Is it not true that Ockham in general tends to hold that logical contradiction is apt to reflect what is *de re* impossible?

Both problems would be solved were it the case that Ockham throughout is talking about *de re* impossibility (as ii) would suggest) and that it is only for that reason that he believes that what is contradictory is an index to what cannot be done, and hence to what God cannot do. The question is, can this interpretation be reconciled with the text? Perhaps a clue is to be found in his use of the expression 'unless there appear some *evident* contradiction'.

Ockham holds that causal statements such as 'Every instance of heat produces heat' are only *possible* truths. He gives an illustration: .

> If there are two fires and smoke appears to be caused, I no more know that the smoke is caused by one fire rather than by the other, since it can equally well be caused by either one. Even if there is only one fire and smoke appears, it *cannot be evidently known* that it is caused by this fire, since it can be caused by God alone.
>
> (*Report.*, II, 6, A790)

But this passage is to be contrasted with

> For example, suppose that 'Every herb of this species strengthens someone with a fever' is a first principle. This proposition

cannot be proved syllogistically from any better known propositions. Rather, knowledge of it is derived from intuitive cognition, perhaps of many [instances]. For since he saw that after such an herb is eaten health follows in the person with the fever, and since he removed all other causes of the person's health, *he had evident knowledge* that this herb was the cause of health, and then had experience regarding the singular [proposition]. But it is known to him that all individuals of the same species have the same kind of effect in an equally disposed patient. Therefore, *he derives evident knowledge* of the principle that every such herb strengthens someone with a fever.

(*Ord.*, Prologue, 2, A788)

These two passages appear to be inconsistent. But they can be reconciled by the supposition that Ockham assumes both that in general God does not intervene to cause effects which would normally be produced by ordinary secondary causes, and that such intervention cannot be ruled out as a possibility. He takes it that God in general acts in an orderly way, and that it is only on revealed grounds of Christian faith that we have reasons to believe that this is not always the case. Hence he insists that our normal grasp of causal laws will count as knowledge, and that the evidence for such laws amounts to proof. In the second passage, Ockham concedes that 'all other causes of the patient's health' have been excluded', as, in everyday life, will normally be the case. In the earlier passage, he claims that this exclusion is not theoretically complete; it is always *possible*, *de re* and hence logically, that God should act directly.

Ockham's view is that for us to claim knowledge that *p*, it is not required that we should know that not-*p* is *impossible*, but merely that we have sufficient grounds for knowing that *p* is *true*. Hence, he argues that we can discover inductively what is and what is not *de re* possible in this orderly world, and this knowledge is reflected in the terms we use to express the natures of things, as well as in the causal truths which we learn. On the other hand, while such knowledge corresponds to God's ordered power, there is no demonstrative proof that God in his absolute power could not have chosen otherwise. Ockham would claim to know from Christian revelation that God actually did things which are inconsistent with the causal laws which we know; and for that reason there is no demonstrative proof that any of our causal laws are *absolutely* necessary; they state merely the causal powers which things by nature have, rather than the way in which those powers are exercised in every instance.

In short, Ockham holds the following views:

A   God can bring about any state of affairs which it is *de re* possible to bring about.

B   He can bring about any such state of affairs by himself, without any creaturely cause, provided that no true description of that state of affairs entails that a creature is also causally involved (as for instance would be the case if it depended on a human choice).

C   Since any substance and any quality are absolute entities, it is *de re* possible that any one of these should exist without any other.

D   Our evidence for what is and is not *de re* possible is inductive; and while it can suffice for proof and for knowledge, it is in principle incomplete.

E   In particular, Christian revelation contains examples of states of affairs which are actual (and hence must be *de re* possible), which we would otherwise had no reason to believe were possible.

F   Hence, negatively, we should not deny that God can do something unless we know it to be impossible.

There is at least one plain difficulty with this position taken as a whole. Our knowledge of what is *de re* possible can at least in principle be mistaken. Thus, we might, as D suggests, know on the basis of the overwhelming evidence that accidents cannot exist without inhering in a substance, or that our sensory experience of things is caused by those things. On the other hand C denies this; and indeed more strongly, C suggests that *no* causal law could be known to be true, since a cause and its effect are always absolutely distinct entities. Ockham might reply to this that the mere fact that it is *possible* that what we take to be effects might equally have existed without what we take to be their causes does not show that this is *in fact* the case, and hence does not call in question our claim to know that it is not the case. Well, let us accept this weaker definition of what is required for knowledge: the consequence, as it seems to me, is that we now lose our grip on what is and what is not absolutely possible. Suppose I know (in the weak sense) that my sensory experiences are caused by objects in the world, or that such a kind of herb cures fevers, or that accidents inhere in substances, such knowledge no longer gives me any way of knowing what is *de re* possible, as distinct from knowing what is in fact naturally the case. F then becomes useless. If to this Ockham were to reply that we still cannot ascribe to God any power to bring about what involves a contradiction, one can still object that since, by the previous argument, the notion of contradiction has now been severed from that of *de re* impossibility, it is difficult to see what force this restriction can have. For what is or is not logically contradictory depends simply on our existing concepts, which need not reflect anything more than the current state of our beliefs.

Despite the radical implications of his views, Ockham's beliefs in the goodness and ordered wisdom of what God does prevented him from being troubled by the scepticism inherent in his position. Other contemporary and later writers explored this much more radically than did Ockham himself.[14]

Descartes

THE GENERAL PICTURE

There is still considerable debate about precisely which writers in the medieval tradition were influential in Descartes's education and in the Scholasticism which he endeavoured to refute. I shall argue that it is not too misleading to discern some of the views expressed by Ockham and his contemporaries in what Descartes himself was to write. This is hardly surprising, since Descartes's target was at any rate some version of just that Aristotelianism which Ockham was also attacking.

As we have already seen, there were several problems to do with omnipotence which exercised the medieval theologians:

i)   If there are eternal essences, and eternal necessary truths, would it not follow that God was somehow constrained and limited by them in his activities, and hence not all-powerful?

ii) In particular, in what sense, if any, is God constrained by the law of non-contradiction? And how is this related to what is *de re* possible?

iii) If God creates freely, over what does this freedom range? Only over things he *already knows* to be possible?

132

Both Aquinas and Ockham denied that eternal essences, or truths about the relationships between them, exist independently of God; for of Aquinas, such things simply were aspects of the essence of God, which God knows in knowing himself perfectly; for Ockham, abstract entities such as essences simply did not exist as such at all; God knows creatures directly and individually. (It must be admitted, though, that Ockham probably extended this, in so far as he was willing to talk of God knowing possible creatures as well as actual ones.) When Aquinas and Ockham say that only what is not contradictory is creatable by God, it is perhaps best to read both as taking the logical principle of non-contradiction as the linguistic counterpart of what is and is not *de re* possible. But whereas Aquinas believes that logic is an accurate and complete guide, we have seen reason to suppose that in Ockham's view it is less accurate and less complete. Ockham believes that we can indeed know the laws governing what God has in fact created in his wisdom; but this knowledge might turn out to give a false or at least incomplete picture of what is in God's absolute power. Both Aquinas and Ockham would accept that God's power ranges over what is possible: but whereas Aquinas would be willing to accept the suggestion in iii) since we can properly *speak* of God's attributes separately, Ockham would deny the 'already', on the grounds that any such distinction is potentially misleading. God's knowledge of what is actual and what is possible is identical with God, and so is God's will.

Some of these preoccupations can also be found in Descartes:

> As for the eternal truths, I say again that they are true or possible only because God knows them as true or possible. They are not known by God as true in any way which would imply that they are true independently of him. If men really understood the meaning of their words, they could never say without blasphemy that the truth of anything is prior to the knowledge which God has of it. In God willing and knowing are a single thing, in such a way that by the very fact of willing something he knows it, and it is only for that reason that such a thing is true. So we must not say that if God did not exist nevertheless these truths would be true, for the existence of God is the first and most eternal of all possible truths and the one from which alone all the others proceed.
>
> (Letter to Mersenne, 6th May 1630)

In many ways this passage is straightforward, and could have been accepted both by Ockham and by Aquinas. Neither of them wished to suggest that eternal truths are true independently of God, and hence might constitute an external limitation upon God's knowledge or his power. But what Aquinas would not accept is the contention that, even though in God willing and knowing are one, it is only because God wills something that it comes to be true. That Descartes does indeed wish to say just that is clear from the following imaginary dialogue which Descartes constructs with a supposed critic:

> It will be said that, if God established these truths, he could change them as a king does his laws. To this the answer is: Yes he can, if his will can change. 'But I understand them to be eternal and unchangeable.' – I make the same judgement about God. – 'But his will is free.' – Yes, but his power is beyond our grasp. In general we can assert that God can do anything that is within our grasp, but not that he cannot do what is beyond our grasp. It would be rash to think that our imagination reaches as far as his power.[15]
>
> (Letter to Mersenne, 15th April 1630)

It is interesting to compare this, and particularly the example of the King and his laws, with Ockham's comments on the distinction between God's ordered and his absolute power:

> The distinction should be understood in this way: 'To be able to produce something' is sometimes understood according to the laws that are ordered and instituted by God. And God is said to do those things in respect of his ordered power. Otherwise, 'to be able' is understood to refer to the ability to produce anything the producing of which does not involve a contradiction, whether or not God has ordained that he will produce it. . . . God is said to be able to do such things by his absolute power, just as there are some things which the Pope cannot do in accordance with the laws established by him, but can do absolutely.[16]
>
> (*Quod.*, VI, 1, A1198)

There are other parallels, too. I have already suggested that it is not entirely clear what Ockham's opinion is about what would or would not be contradictory, and hence what would nor would not be in God's absolute power. But he does in general believe that we can know necessary truths which describe the way in which God has ordered his creation, even though these truths are not logically necessary. We know that fire, by nature, can cause smoke; but it is always logically possible that, despite appearances, this smoke is being caused, not by this fire, but by God alone. And I cannot know that this visual experience is being caused by some created object, since God is capable of causing such an experience directly, himself.

Consider, then, what has been taken to one of the most extreme of Descartes's claims about God's omnipotence:

> Yet I previously accepted as wholly certain and evident many things which I afterwards realized were doubtful. What were these? The earth, sky, stars, and everything else that I appre- hended with the senses. . . . Even now I am not denying that these ideas occur within me. But there was something else which I used to assert, and which through habitual belief I thought I perceived clearly, although in fact I did not do so. This was that there were things outside me which were the sources of my ideas and which resembled them in all respects. Here was my mistake, or at any rate, if my judgement was true, it was not thanks to the strength of my perception.
>
> But what about when I was considering something very simple and straightforward in arithmetic or geometry, for example that two and three added together make five, and so on? Did I not see at least these things clearly enough to affirm their truth? Indeed the only reason for my latter judgement that they were open to doubt was that it occurred to me that perhaps some God could have given me a nature such that I was deceived even in matters which seemed most evident. And whenever my preconceived belief in the supreme power of God comes to mind, I cannot but admit that it would be easy for him, if he so desired, to bring it about that I could go wrong even in those matters which I think I see utterly clearly in my mind's eye.

> (*Meditations*, III)

What is it that Descartes in this passage thinks that God might do? In the first paragraph, he wonders whether God might produce in him a mistaken belief that there were in the world outside himself objects corresponding to his ideas – such things as the earth, the sky, the stars.[17] Just so, Ockham thought that God could in his absolute power produce in someone a sensation, apparently of some object, without producing the object itself.

In the second paragraph, the claim is that God could bring it about that Descartes is mistaken even about the truths of mathematics. How are we to take this suggestion? To answer this, it will help to consider what Descartes took mathematical truths to be. What he says is not entirely straightforward:

> You ask me by what kind of causality God established the eternal truths. I reply: by the same kind of causality as he created all things, that is to say, as their efficient and total cause. For it is certain that he is the author of the essence of created things no less than of their existence; and this essence is nothing other than the eternal truths. I do not conceive them as emanating from God like rays from the sun; but I know that God is the author of everything and that these truths are something and consequently that he is their author.
>
> (Letter to Mersenne, 27th May 1630)

The mention of efficient causality and the remark that eternal truths are 'something' might at first sight suggest that he thought of eternal truths as some kind of created Platonic objects. But we should be cautious. Descartes is willing to use the expression 'efficient cause' sufficiently broadly to be able say that God is his own 'efficient cause' even while denying that God is in any sense an effect. So too here, he is careful to point out that he means something different from the way in which rays of light are caused by the sun.[18] We should remember that one aspect of the medieval position which he is intent upon rejecting is that God's omnipotence (or his knowledge, which is identical with his omnipotence) is limited by a set of Platonic essences/truths which are independent of him. Ockham's way of avoiding the same position was simply to identify such essences and truths with the actual creatures known by God because created by him, and, by extension, to the things it is in his power to create. What God can and could create is thus a matter of God's knowledgeable power. Perhaps it is this type of view which Descartes is offering here. This would tend to confirm those interpretations of Descartes which seek to exclude necessary truths about God himself from the scope of the truths which might turn out to be otherwise.[19] Though God is the source of (even the 'efficient cause of') *all* truth, it is only with respect to 'created truths', that is the essences of actual and possible creatures and the relations which hold between those essences, that God can freely choose, as Descartes makes clear:[20]

> I turn to the difficulty of conceiving how God would have been acting freely and indifferently if he had made it false that the three angles of a triangle were equal to two right angles, or in general that contradictories could not be true together. It is easy to dispel this difficulty by considering that the power of God cannot have any limits, and that our mind is finite and so created as to be able to conceive as possible the things which God has wished to be in fact possible, but not to be able to conceive as possible things which God could have made possible, but which he has nevertheless willed to make impossible. The first consideration shows us that God cannot have been determined to make it true that contradictories cannot be true together, and therefore that he could have done the opposite. The second shows us that even if this be true, we should not try to comprehend it, since our nature is incapable of doing so. And even if God has willed that some truths should be necessary, this does not mean that he has willed this necessarily, or been necessitated to will it.
>
> (Letter to Mesland, 2nd May 1644)

It was a commonplace view, as we have seen, that God's knowledge of himself is necessary, and that of necessity he wills himself; whereas he is free to create in different ways, even if he eternally and unchangeably creates the world as it in fact is.[21]

What the above passage shows is that, in Descartes's view, God has so created our minds that they are capable of correctly knowing what God has in fact eternally and immutably and freely decided should be actual and possible in creating the universe as he has. In that sense, the truths that our minds can know can properly be said to be eternal truths, and immutable. These truths include both the truths of mathematics, and also the general laws of material beings, which Descartes explicitly says he wishes to assimilate to mathematical truths as closely as possible.[22] These truths are all necessary truths, though their necessity depends upon the free decision of God. Nor is it the case that these truths simply express the way in which our minds are created to think, though they do indeed express this.[23]

137

They express the way in which God has knowingly decided what the world shall be like, though he could have decided otherwise.

Descartes's general position, then, might be summarised as follows:

i)   There are some absolutely necessary truths, which reflect the absolute necessity of the nature of God, together with some few very general metaphysical truths about the nature of causation, and the impossibility of something being brought into being from nothing.

ii) There are also necessary truths which are so because of the knowing decision of God to create this rather than some other world. These are not absolutely necessary, but are hypothetically so; and they are eternal and immutable.

iii) These hypothetically necessary truths are knowable by our minds, which God has made precisely in such a way as to be able to discover them. These truths are such that we see that their negations are contradictory.

iv) The hypothetically necessary truths include the truths of mathematics, and hence also the general axioms of physics, since the essence of matter is geometrical.

v)   Possibility and impossibility, essences, and the truths about the relationships between essences, are not independent real properties of things, still less independent things in themselves; but they can feature in true statements about things.

In short, there are some necessary truths which are necessarily necessary (to do with the nature of God, and the most general truths about causation); and some necessary truths which are only contingently necessary. It seems to me that the ockhamist (with at least a lower-case 'o') flavour of these claims is evident. Similarly, Descartes's epistemological worries about whether we might be mistaken, since God's absolute power enables him to do things about which we would naturally tend to form false beliefs, are not very far removed from Ockham's view that God can produce in us experiences which might lead us to believe that, for instance, this smoke was caused by this fire, when it was in fact directly caused by God. Like Ockham, Descartes also states in so many words that 'the fact that I can clearly understand one thing apart from another is enough to make me certain that the two things are distinct, since they are capable of being separated, at least by God' (*Meditation*

VI).[24] In some ways, too, Descartes's appeal to the goodness of a God who does not deceive is similar to Ockham's assumption that in his ordered power God does not act so as to deceive us and that when he performs miracles he reveals that he has done so.

THE IMPLICATIONS OF THE GENERAL POSITION

The claim that some necessary truths are only hypothetically necessary and that they depend on the free decision of God is spelled out by Descartes with some examples which were as astonishing to his contemporaries as they are to us, suggesting as they do that God's omnipotence knows no bounds whatsoever. Here is a selection, with some comments on each:

A   I would not dare to say that God cannot bring it about that there is a mountain without a valley, or that one and two should not be three; but I say only that he has endowed me with such a mind that it is not possible for me to conceive a mountain without a valley, or an aggregate of one and two which is not three, etc., and that such things involve a contradiction in my conception.
                              (Letter to Arnauld, 29th July 1648)

Notice that Descartes is not making any positive suggestions about what God might be able to do. He is merely saying that there are some things he cannot rule out as being possible for God. Moreover, as Hide Ishiguro has pointed out (1987: 466), Descartes does *not* say that, for all he knows, God might have brought it about that $1 + 2 = 4$; all he says is that God might have brought it about that it was not the case that $1 + 2 = 3$, even though 'It is not the case that $1 + 2 = 3$' is clearly contradictory in my conception. The same comment applies to the next example, too.

B   You ask what necessitated God to create these truths; and I reply that he was free to make it not true that all the radii of the circle are equal – just as free as he was not to create the world.
                              (Letter to Mersenne, 27th May 1630)

C   God cannot have been determined to bring it about that it was true that contradictories cannot be true together, and consequently, he could have done the opposite.
                              (Letter to Mesland, 2nd May 1644)

This example is somewhat more difficult than the previous one. Here, Descartes says that God might have brought it about that contradictories *are* true together: that is to say, that it might have been true that p & $\neg p$. But the general point is much the same. Descartes is not claiming that God can make contradictions true; he is claiming that, for all he knows, it is in God's power to create a world in which what we take to be contradictions would not be contradictions at all. What, then, is the status of what we take to be contradictions? I suppose that Descartes would simply reply that what we take to be contradictions are indeed contradictions, given the nature of the world as it is. Since my conceptions are, by the nature of my God-given mind, an accurate reflection of the way the world actually is, I have no other way of expressing what a radically different world might be like other than by saying that it would be a world in which what is impossible in this world might not be absolutely impossible. Noncontradiction is indeed a good test for what is, as it so happens, possible in our world; it is no test at all for what is absolutely possible, nor for what some mind quite different from ours would then know to be possible in such a quite different world. Of course it cannot be that $2 + 2 = 5$, since all those concepts are concepts that we have formulated with our this-worldly minds, and, given the meanings that those concepts have, such an assertion is necessarily false. Descartes is saying that in a radically different world, '$2 + 2 = 4$' might not express a truth, if for no other reason than that these concepts might have no application at all in such a world. Even here, Descartes believes that there are *some* limits: he says

> Moreover, I showed what the laws of nature were, and, without basing my arguments on any principle other than the infinite perfections of God, I tried to demonstrate all these laws about which we could have any doubt, and to show that they are such that, even if God created many worlds, there could not be any in which these laws failed to be observed. After this I showed how, in consequence of these laws, the greater part of the matter of this chaos had to become disposed and arranged in a certain way which made it resemble our heavens; and how at the same time some of its parts had to form an earth, some planets and comets, and others a sun and fixed stars.
>
> (*Discourse on Method*, 5)

Descartes says he is assuming that the fundamental geometrical laws of matter are essential to *any* material world, since they are a function of the nature of God himself. He does not believe, then, that it is possible for there to be a material world where matter is utterly unlike the geometrically ordered matter of this world. But that still leaves open the possibility of worlds so radically unlike ours that they are not material worlds as we would understand that notion. The last qualification is crucial, though. For on his general principles, it is difficult to see how Descartes could rule out the possibility that our understanding of 'material' was inadequate; and hence that, although we cannot conceive of a material world which does not conform at least to the most general laws of physics, there might nevertheless be such a world.

> D   There are contradictions which are so evident that we cannot put them before our minds without judging them entirely impossible, like the one you suggest: that God might have made creatures independent of himself. But if we would know the immensity of his power, we should not put those thoughts before our minds, nor should we conceive any precedence or priority between his intellect and his will.
>
> (Letter to [Mesland], 2nd May 1644)

This is one of very many passages where Descartes is at pains to stress that our inability even to represent to ourselves what a radically different possible world might be like is a consequence of the limitations of our finite minds. We must take care not to project this limitation on to the immensity of the power of God. But there is another problem about this passage. Is the reader meant to conclude that God could have created creatures independent of himself, even though to us that is manifestly a contradiction, or is the reader meant to conclude that this would be *absolutely* impossible? I think that Curley (1987: 366–7) is probably right to suppose that Descartes would consider this an absolute impossibility on general grounds, but one which might distract us from a proper estimate of the 'immensity of God's power'.

> E   *Question*: Does it follow from this that God could have commanded a creature to hate him, and thereby made this a good thing to do?
> *Answer*: God could not now do this; but we simply do not

141

know what he could have done. In any case, why should he not have been able to give this command to one of his creatures?

(Conversation with Burman: Cottingham 1976: 22)

Ockham also denied that God could do wrong, since to do wrong is to violate one's obligations, and God is obliged to nobody. Hence, no matter what God commanded, he could not command it unjustly, though he could command what we might otherwise have described as 'evil' (*Ord.*, 1, 42 and 47). I take it that Descartes here is making a very similar point. Given the way the world is, and the nature of human beings, there just are some things which are evil, and which it would be wrong for someone to do, and wrong for God to command someone to do. But whether God could have created in such a way that what we now take to be evil would not be evil in that world, that is something that we cannot know, one way or the other.[25]

> F   It is self-contradictory to suppose that the will of God was not indifferent from eternity with respect to everything which has happened or ever will happen; for it is impossible to imagine that anything is thought of in the divine intellect as good or true, or worthy of belief or action or omission, prior to the decision of the divine will to make it so. I am not speaking here of temporal priority: I mean that there is not even any priority of order or nature or of 'rationally determined reason' as they call it, such that God's idea of the good impelled him to choose one thing rather than another. For example, God did not will the creation of the world in time because he saw that it would be better this way than if he had created it from eternity; nor did he will that the three angles of a triangle should be equal to two right angles because he recognised that it could not be otherwise, and so on. On the contrary, it is because he willed to create the world in time that it is better this way than if he had created it from eternity.
>
> (Sixth Set of Replies)

Here again it seem clear that Descartes does believe that truths about God himself are necessarily necessary, since he uses this as the starting-point of his argument. He then proceeds to reject, as Ockham did, the Scotist view that one can at least distinguish 'instants of nature' in God – that is to say, that God 'first' knows and 'then' rationally decides. In God, creating a world and knowing that is a good world are identical – what is known and created is simply the world in question, there just is no prior exemplar which God considers. Elsewhere, though, Descartes does hedge his bets somewhat: he says,

> I do not know that I laid it down that God always does what he knows to be most perfect, and it does not seem to me that a finite mind can judge of that. But I tried to solve the difficulty in question, about the cause of error, on the assumption that God had made the world most perfect, since if one makes the opposite assumption the difficulty disappears altogether.
> (Letter to Mesland, 2nd May 1644)

Perhaps this latter text more typically represents Descartes's view. The view that God in creating a world knows that it is better is expressed in a context where the focus of attention is not on whether God always acts for the best, but on whether phrases like 'the best' can be understood *prior* to God's action. This he denies. Given that God's power is incomprehensible, it follows that so is his notion of 'the best', as Descartes says in the latter passage. I think his view probably was that we are simply incapable of giving any content to the idea of 'the best possible world', simply because we cannot grasp what is included in the notion of a 'possible' world.

SOME ANSWERS

Omnipotence and non-contradiction

Some things have to be held constant if we are to try to deal with these issues at all coherently. Since I have already given grounds for supposing that there are no compelling reasons for abandoning at least the main lines of the classical view of the nature of God, I shall for the sake of this discussion assume that to be God is to be non-bodily, a knower, wise, eternal and simple.

One might think that the obvious next move would be to try to see what followed from saying that God has these attributes. But in order to ask that question, one has to ask what is meant by 'follows from'. One would naturally take 'follows from' to express some logical relationship; so, if *q* 'follows from' *p*, one might mean that it is not the case that p is true and q is false; or more strongly, that it *cannot* be the case that p is true and q is false; and this latter might be further spelt out by saying that 'p & $\neg q$' is contradictory and on that account is necessarily false. But how can we make this move without immediately confronting Descartes's claim that not all contradictions need be necessarily false?

Well, the first stage of a reply to this is to note that Descartes, if I am right, did not precisely say that not all contradictions need be *necessarily* false; he said that not all apparent contradictions need be contradictions. And he said this not as a logical remark, nor as a ruling about our current usage of terms, but as a remark about the way in which God's power transcends our understanding. It seems to me, then, that Descartes is not questioning that 'John is a married bachelor' is a contradiction in terms. Given the definition of 'married' and 'bachelor', it is a contradiction in terms. But if that is not the point, what is? Here is one conjecture. Suppose that we are mistaken in our grasp of what is involved in being one single person – mistaken not about how we currently use the term 'same person', but about the ontology of persons. It might be that it is possible for one and the same person to have two bodies, and that *qua* body$_1$ he is married, and *qua* body$_2$ he is unmarried. Were some such situation to obtain, it might indeed be the case that John is both unmarried and a bachelor; and we would then re-formulate our use of 'bachelor' in such a way that 'being married *qua* body$_1$ and unmarried *qua* body$_2$' is not a contradiction at all, even though it remains a contradiction that John is both married and unmarried with respect to the same body. Our current terminology reflects our current belief that persons *de re* cannot exist bi-corporeally; and it might be that this belief about how persons have to be is mistaken. 'John is a married bachelor' is indeed a contradiction in terms, as we now use those terms. In a world of bi-corporeal persons, that sentence might not express a contradiction, since it would have a slightly different sense, corresponding to the different nature of persons in such a world.

If that is the kind of thing that Descartes had in mind, then his view, rather than being a wholesale attack on logic, amounts rather to a cautionary warning about the extent to which we have grasped what is and what is not *de re* possible. He thinks that, given the goodness of God, we have at least some grasp on what is and is not true, and what is and is not possible in the world as God in fact created it. So he holds that a criterion for what is true or possible in our world is to be found in the clarity and distinctness of what we can see. Aquinas was, in a somewhat different way, even more optimistic in his view of our ability to understand the natures of things, and hence to know their capabilities; and even Ockham, more cautious perhaps, did not doubt that we could come to know the causal laws governing our world.

Our own views about what makes for a reliable scientific method, and about the criteria for scientific truth and for knowledge generally, would no doubt be rather different from those held by all three philosophers. And, despite Quine (1961), we might distinguish rather more sharply between truths which are straightforwardly analytic and those which are empirical. To that extent, we need not, and I suggest should not, take non-contradiction as an infallible test for what is causally possible. Quine (1961: 20–46) is right to suggest that in principle all our views on what is to count as a contradiction are open to revision, some at little cost to our current beliefs, others at much greater cost; but it is not an *arbitrary* matter whether our beliefs, and hence the terminology we use to refer to things in the world, stand in need of such revision; it is a matter of evidence and of truth.

In general, then, non-contradiction is a feature of the way in which we express what we take to be empirical knowledge, rather than a criterion for determining what is empirically possible. To that extent, it is unfortunate that Aquinas, Ockham and Descartes all talk as if it were a criterion, and then discuss to what extent they think it is a reliable criterion, with Aquinas relying upon it most, and Descartes least. Perhaps, though, all three writers, despite all the talk about non-contradiction, were really more intent upon appealing to what is causally possible; and the variations between them are better explained in terms of their varying estimates of how much we in fact know about what is causally possible.

Actions possible for God

So we can properly ask, in the first place, which actions it is possible for an eternal, simple, non-bodily being to perform. In so doing, we are not asking what is implied, or entailed by the *concepts* 'eternal' or 'non-bodily' or 'simple', but about the causal powers of a being which has those attributes. I take it as an *empirical* truth that there are some actions – for instance, walking, or singing, or tasting, which

145

can be performed only by a being with the relevant bodily parts. These things, then, God cannot do.

Moreover, if it is the case that God is simple, and hence cannot be acted upon, then God cannot, as Aquinas, Ockham and Descartes would all have agreed, bring himself into existence, or cause himself to cease to exist; nor can God alter his decisions.

Can God do wrong? This is by no means so straightforward, since there are several different ways in which the question might be understood. I shall discuss three of these.

i) Suppose by 'doing wrong' is meant 'doing some action when one knows that there are conclusive moral reasons why such an action should not be done.' What kind of account are we to give of someone who does wrong in this sense? Of course God cannot be overcome by desire and so do something which is wrong; but this account of what it is even for a human being to do wrong is surely hopelessly inadequate in any case. If a human being does wrong, it must be that they have done something which there are good reasons for doing, even though there are over-riding reasons why it should not be done. It is constitutive of freedom that, while one cannot do something without a good reason, one can simply choose to do something to which one knows there are over-riding moral objections. Further, it is not required that in acting wrongly one must be acting out of self-interest (which, at least on traditional views would not apply to God at all); for it certainly has not been conclusively shown that only reasons concerning one's own interests are reasons for acting. So, one can act unjustly by wrongly choosing to favour the interests of one group rather than another, even if one does not oneself benefit from so doing. One might, for instance, simply decide arbitrarily whom to favour, despite the fact that one knows there are over-riding reasons for some different decision. Well then, could God act in such a way? It seems to me that he could. At least on the traditional views about God's freedom, God is not determined in making any choice between created things; and the reason traditionally given is that any given created good is only a limited good, and hence cannot determine the divine will. This is the premise used to defend the conclusion that God could not create at all, or could have created some world other than this one. By the same token, it seems to me to follow that God has the power to choose some good, knowing that there are over-riding moral reasons for choosing some other instead.

An objection to this conclusion is obvious enough. How could a God who is infinitely wise and infinitely good possibly make such a choice? Geach has argued that 'there is nothing easier than to mention feats which are logically possible, but which God cannot do, if Christianity is true' (1987: 189–92). He offers lying and promise-breaking as examples. 'Christian faith collapses unless we are assured that God cannot lie and cannot break his promises.' He takes the opposite view to hold that 'There must be just a chance that God should do something wicked; no doubt it will be a really infinitesimal chance – after all, God has persevered in the ways of virtue on a vast scale for inconceivably long – but the chance must be there, or God isn't free and isn't therefore laudable for his goodness.'[26] Geach seems to me to be mistaken if he believes that Christian faith would collapse if God *could* break his promises, though it might indeed collapse unless it were the case that God *would not* break them. Similarly, for freedom it is not required that there be 'some infinitesimal chance' that someone *will* do something wicked. It might suffice if someone had the power to do something wicked, even though there is no chance that they ever in fact would. So one might reply that while an infinitely good God would never act wrongly, a free God must have the power to choose wrongly. I do not suppose that this is a conclusive argument, however. There are enough problems with understanding what might be meant by saying that though Jemima could do wrong, she would never choose to do so. One might ask on what evidence one believes that someone has the power to do something which they never in fact do; and one might wonder in what sense to take remarks like 'Jemima just *couldn't* do anything like that!', which we routinely make about someone who never does anything like that. All the more might these questions arise in the case of an infinitely good God. Moreover, it has often been urged that freedom does not require the ability to do otherwise. To examine these issues in detail is beyond the scope of this volume. I must content myself with saying only that I do not believe that the view that I have outlined above is open to any crushing objections, whether theological or philosophical.

ii) It might be argued that if 'wrong' simply means 'forbidden by God', then by definition God cannot act wrongly. I think this argument is simply mistaken. Firstly, even taken on its own terms, it does not seem to follow. Why should it be assumed that God could not act contrary to his own decrees? Plenty of human law-makers can and do, and we are not in the least tempted to conclude that they must have first altered their decrees. Secondly, the argument seems to me mistaken if it is offered as an account of the *meaning* of 'wrong'; at most, it might be said that what is wrong is wrong *because* it is forbidden by God. But to say this at least runs the risk of suggesting that God's commands are arbitrary. Not that the alternative view need be that there is a Platonic Form of the Good, which God can only recognise and revere. I see no reason to deny that what is good, or right, about the ways humans should live and be treated is a feature of the way in which humans and their environments are inter-related; and hence that in creating humans as he has, God thereby brings it about that some states of affairs are morally valuable, and some ways of treating humans are right, others wrong.[27]

iii) But what of the view that if we believed that God had acted in a way we thought to be wrong, we would thereby revise our account of what it is to act wrongly? So put, I suppose the suggestion is quite correct. But things are not so simple. For while it is perfectly possible (and indeed often the case) that we are mistaken about rightness and wrongness, it is equally possible that we are mistaken in our belief that God has done something we think wrong. In practice, *both* beliefs ought to be called in question. At the end of the day, the theist would indeed not wish to conclude that God had in fact acted wrongly; but this result need not be achieved by an unprincipled revision of the moral beliefs involved.

What God can and cannot bring about

If it is the case that for anything other than God to exist is for that thing to be in a relationship of causal dependence on God, then, to answer Descartes's conundrum, it is not possible for God to create something independent of himself; nor is there any being which, if God wills to create it at all, he must will to create it as everlasting. There is no created thing which is such that it cannot altogether cease to be. Hence it is not causally possible for God to create something which once created cannot cease to exist. Or, to put the point more obviously, there is nothing which God can create which he cannot destroy.

I have already argued at some length that it is not possible for God to undo the past, on the grounds that I take it that we know that the nature of time is such that the past is no longer causally accessible.

Or, to put the same claim from the point of view of God, God has causal access only to one actual cosmic history. I will not repeat those arguments here.

Other problems are much more serious, however. Take, for instance, the principle to which Ockham makes such frequent appeal, that God can bring about by his own power anything which he can bring about by means of a creaturely power. Let us grant to Ockham that we are not talking about such things as human free choices which, if they are to be free, must be brought about by the agent. Well then, could God bring it about that I have a visual experience of the Battle of Hastings? Ockham would argue that since my experience and the battle are absolutely distinct entities, there is no impossibility in God producing one of them without the other. Two separate issues are involved here, it seems to me.

a)   Can God, given the physical laws of the world, produce an effect which does not fall under those laws?
b)   How would God do such a thing?

The second question seems to me quite unanswerable. To ask how something is done is to ask for some account of the mechanism by which it is done; and this account would have to be in terms of the laws of the physical universe as we understand them. In the example as proposed, such an account has already been excluded by the way in which a) is formulated. Indeed, more generally, there is surely no way in which we can describe how God brings about anything in the world, or the world itself for that matter. To speak of God as 'cause' is not to commit oneself even in principle to displaying the mechanisms by which God's causality is operative. In the nature of the case, there are no such *mechanisms*.[28]

The first question is also, for different reasons, unanswerable. It could be argued that a God who is capable of bringing about a universe must surely be able to bring about such a comparatively insignificant event as my having a visual experience of the Battle of Hastings long after it took place. But although, if one holds that there are good reasons for believing that God exists, one might also accept that this argument is a plausible one, it does not seem to me to amount to a proof. I think Descartes is right to urge caution if one is inclined to deny that God could do such a thing – for, as he rightly says, how could we establish what is or is not causally possible for God? That such an occurrence would contradict what we believe ourselves to know, or indeed what we correctly claim to know, about the workings of the natural world is, as Descartes says, not a convincing argument to show that such a thing is impossible. Neither, however, am I convinced that the argument which he uses, along with Ockham, is very strong in the opposite direction. They urge that things which are absolutely distinct can be caused to exist independently of one another. I think it is much less obvious to us than it appeared to Ockham and Descartes that things ever *are* absolutely distinct, if by that is meant causally unconnected. Our picture of the universe is much more that of a set of tightly inter-connected causal relationships, so that it is less easy for us to see any event as isolated in the way that this argument might suggest.[29]

On the other hand, I am rather more sceptical about some of Descartes's examples, such as the existence of a mountain without a valley, and in particular the examples he offers of mathematical contradictions. Of course it is true that we can now see that it is not necessarily a mathematical contradiction to say in that the angles of a triangle need not add up to two right angles. To some extent, therefore, we are able to re-formulate our definitions of 'triangle', as Riemannian geometry does; and it might at first sight seem that this is in principle the same kind of move that was made in my example of 'person' above. But it is a highly controversial question to what extent mathematics is an empirical science, or a purely abstract one. To the extent that it is not an empirical science, it would seem that it is a matter of ingenuity whether what would be a contradiction given one way of defining terms and adopting axioms might not turn out to be a truth in some different system. The question whether there are limits to human ingenuity in this kind of inquiry is at least very different from questions about what is causally possible in the world, and whether our knowledge of the laws of the universe is such that what would seem to us now to be impossible (and hence to contradict a law believed to be true) might nevertheless be a genuine causal possibility.

To sum up. If the use of non-contradiction in discussions of God's omnipotence has any real value at all, it is to call attention to two things: *i)* There is an important sense in which we simply cannot coherently express what is *de re* possible outside the realms of our experience and the interpretations of that experience which are expressed in our scientific laws. If there is some action which we believe to be causally possible for God, then we will endeavour to describe that action in ways which do not involve logical contra-diction. To that extent, Aquinas is right to suggest that God can do anything provided there is no true description of it which can be expressed only by a contradiction. He was misleading, or just wrong, to the extent that he suggests that non-contradiction can provide a *criterion* for discovering what it is that God can do. *ii)* Hence, Descartes is also right to the extent that he can be understood to be making just this last point. For all we know, God has it in his power to bring it about that something occur which, given our existing beliefs, can be described only by a contradiction. Even if some of his examples are exaggerated (as I have suggested in the previous paragraph), the overall thrust of his position seems correct. We simply do not have any *a priori* method of determining with any certainty what does and does not lie within the absolute power of God. We do not as yet have more than an imperfect understanding even of what God has actually done and has actually made causally possible, in his ordering of the cosmos as it is.

These rather agnostic conclusions are likely to disappoint readers well versed in the many controversies and conundrums which enliven discussions of omnipotence. In my view, though, these controversies for the most part involve a somewhat misdirected effort, concerned as they are with problems about coherence and non-contradiction. It seems to me that the real issues about omnipotence are to do with what is, in some absolute sense, causally possible. That is an empirical, not a logical, matter, and one where due agnosticism seems to be entirely proper.

CHAPTER V

Goodness

The traditional view of the goodness of God began with the affirmation that, in a non-moral sense of 'good', God is infinitely good because he alone can be said in the fullest sense to exist. The assumption, going back to Aristotle, is that since goodness is a perfection, belonging to what is actual rather than to what is merely potential, any thing or state of affairs can be described as good only if it exists, and indeed only because it exists. To exist is to have some perfection. It was similarly the Aristotelian view that the Prime Mover is the final cause of all other things, and for that reason must be the highest good.[1] In this chapter, I shall not consider this position in any detail. Instead, I shall concentrate on the issues surrounding the claim that God is morally good.

What has come to be known as the 'Problem of Evil' occupies a more central place in contemporary discussions about the credibility of theism than perhaps it did in earlier ages. Not that earlier writers failed to see or to discuss the difficulties; but in the larger context of a religious faith, they believed that the problems must somehow be ultimately soluble, even if the details of God's redemptive plan for the world were obscure. Contemporary discussion is, to say the least, much less optimistic about the possibility of reconciling anything like theism with the existence of evil in the world.[2] It is on the details of this discussion that I shall focus in this chapter. Because the classical writers did not approach the problem in the way in which is normal now, however, the method followed in the earlier chapters is less helpful here. Instead of selecting some classical treatments of the problem for detailed discussion, I shall try to identify the different elements which combine to produce the problem, and discuss these one at a time referring to some of the classical discussion when it is relevant, by way of illustration.

At its simplest, the problem of evil can be put like this: is it possible to reconcile the existence of evil in the world with the existence of a God who is morally admirable, omnipotent, and omniscient? Granted that these three attributes are integral to any conventional conception of God, the problem of evil is regarded as threatening the claim that God can exist at all. If God is omniscient, he knows what this world is like; if he is omnipotent, he could either have created it differently in the first place, or intervened to correct it; and if he does neither of these things, he would seem to be morally at fault, and hence not good. While this will do as a preliminary setting of the scene, the issues are in fact somewhat more complex than this simple outline might suggest. A more detailed breakdown is therefore required.

The central issue is whether or not God can be held to be *morally blameworthy* for creating a world such as ours. So any analysis of the problem of evil must start from some discussion of the conditions under which someone can be said to be morally blameworthy. Before setting these out, however, there are some preliminary issues in moral philosophy which need to be considered. It might be thought sufficient for P to be morally blameworthy for some action A if A is a morally wrong action, and P performed that action knowingly. But this preliminary formulation relies on our being able to *identify* the action that P performed, and this is not at all a straightforward matter.

What is needed, then, is to find some way of spelling out the conditions for being morally to blame which do not beg any important questions about how to identify which action we are talking about. Happily, a completely detailed account of all this is not necessary in order to tackle the issues connected with the problem of evil. But we do at least need some way of distinguishing a question like 'Is God to blame for causing evil?' from 'Is God to blame for creating a world which turned out to contain evil?' In short, we need to know which actions God can properly be said to have performed.

GENERAL CONDITIONS
FOR BLAMEWORTHINESS

To get round these difficulties, I propose a set of severally necessary and jointly sufficient conditions for blaming some agent P. Let S be some state of affairs truly describable as 'S', and A an individual action truly describable as 'A'; then, P will be blameworthy if all the following conditions are satisfied:

1   There is a correct standard of moral relevance which shows that 'A' and 'S' contain just those features which are relevant to the moral assessment of what was done.
2   *Either*   P did A.
    Or   P brought about S.
3   *Either*   P is accountable for A.
    Or   P is accountable for S.
4   P believed that to do A, or to bring about S, was, all things considered, wrong.

The conditions for someone being blameworthy set out above are in some respects complex.[3] Some preliminary explanations are in order.

To begin with, one cannot give any moral assessment simply of 'what was done'; one needs to assess 'what was done' under some description – for instance, that suffering was caused, or a good state of affairs was achieved, or an obligation was satisfied. Moreover, not just any description will do; one needs to have a description which includes precisely those features of 'what was done' which are relevant to a moral assessment. 1 above is formulated with that in mind, while leaving it for further discussion just which features those might be. The 'either/or' in 2 and 3 are intended to be inclusive, not exclusive. 2 is intended to include both the case where P can be said to have, for example, made someone suffer, and the case in which P did something as a result of which someone suffered. The sense of 'did' in 2 is meant to be neutral; in particular, it does not assume that P did the action knowingly, or that P believed that what he did was properly described as 'doing A', or 'bringing about S'. These issues are considered under 3 and 4.

Arguably, it is one thing to assess what was done, and a rather different thing to assess the blameworthiness of the person; to be justified in ascribing blame to someone, one needs to know that they can properly be held to account for what was done under the relevant description. That is what 3 says. Moreover, one needs to know what was done was, all things considered, wrong (as would be the case, for instance, if some better alternative was morally required); and in addition one needs to know that the agent should have known about those features which make what was done wrong, and that the agent was in a position to perform some better action (or to do nothing at all). This is what 4 says. An agent is blameworthy only if all four conditions are satisfied.

None of these matters is uncontroversial, as even a casual acquaintance with moral philosophy makes abundantly clear. In particular, it is highly controversial which features of 'what was done' ought to be included in the description. There are two reasons for this: *i*) Some moral philosophers would reject the view expressed in my previous paragraph that one can separate assessment of what was done and assessment of the agent; or, in different terminology, they would define 'action' in such a way as to include only those things for which an agent can properly be held accountable. *ii*) There is no agreement on precisely which features of any state of affairs are morally relevant: for example, whether the welfare of fetuses, or animals, or plants is morally relevant; or, worse still, exactly what might be meant by 'welfare' whether for humans or for anything else. These controversies cannot be dealt with here. The most that can be done is to present a general view which at least does not make assumptions which would be widely denied, and to pass over the more detailed positions where controversy is most likely. I shall therefore assume some very general notions of welfare; and also assume several moral principles of the form 'Other things being equal, it is wrong to . . .' where the blank can be filled in with such phrases as 'cause suffering', 'fail to help', 'deprive someone of their liberty' and so on. These will be quite enough to enable us to put the problem of evil forcibly. If the problem is insoluble even in these general terms, it will be even more insoluble in terms of some much more specific moral theory; and whatever arguments there are to show that it is not insoluble when so put might be further developed to deal with the requirements of a more specific theory.

The way I have formulated the conditions for blameworthiness presupposes some version of cognitivism in moral philosophy.[4] Thus, condition 1 explicitly speaks of a 'correct' assessment, and 'correct' standards of relevance. I have not presupposed any particular version of cognitivism, however, and I hope that at least most of the following discussion will be readily adaptable to whatever cognitivist position the reader believes to be the most plausible. However, should the reader wish to take a non-cognitivist view of ethical discourse generally, both the conditions for blameworthiness and much of the discussion would have to be fairly radically reformulated in, say, emotivist or prescriptivist terms. I must say that

I have never seen a version of the problem of evil expressed in non-cognitivist terms, and I have some doubts about whether so put it would be as problematic for theism as it is on the cognitivist assumption that moral discourse makes claims to truth.[5] For that reason, if for no other, I think it best to make cognitivist assumptions in all that follows.

I also think it clearer, or at least less question-begging, to separate assessment of actions and the states of affairs resulting from those actions from issues about blameworthiness, responsibility and accountability. I would therefore be happy with a fairly minimal description of 'action', such as 'what is voluntarily done' leaving it for further discussion to discover how that action should be described. It also remains for further discussion to decide to what extent, if any, the agent is properly held to account for all the features of an action so defined (or, alternatively, under which description of what was done is the agent necessarily held accountable for it). Discussion of Condition 1 and 2, then, is a discussion of the state of affairs in the world which either God can be said to have brought about, or which has resulted from God's action in the broad sense; and the remaining conditions are conditions for the assessment of God's blameworthiness for the action or for the resulting state of affairs, so described.

We may now examine these conditions one at a time, to see which of them are met in the case of God creating the world.

CONDITION 1: THE MORALLY RELEVANT DESCRIPTION OF CREATION

First, then, we must ask how the state of the world is to be described from the moral point of view. Is it a world containing evil? Is the world an evil world? It is traditional to deal with these questions under two heads, natural evil and moral evil. The terms are not entirely clear.[6] But we might say roughly that natural evil is any feature of a state of affairs which renders it in some way substandard; and moral evil is any feature of moral agents which renders them morally blameworthy. Well, then, is the world to be described as containing natural and moral evils?

'Natural' evils

Are there states of affairs which are bad in a morally relevant way? At first sight, the answer to this might seem obvious. One needs only to think of the suffering that many sentient beings undergo, humans and other animals alike. But before simply accepting this as obvious, it might help to cast the net somewhat wider.

Consider the following cases: radioactive elements decay over time; animals, including human animals, die; seeds fail to develop into plants; a lion catches and eats a gazelle; a deer experiences pain from a spark produced by an approaching forest fire; animals, including humans, become infected by disease-causing organisms. The first thing to be said about these examples is that they do not all strike us in the same way. Indeed, the reader might have wondered why the first example, the decay of a radioactive element into some other element, was mentioned at all. What could possibly be thought to have gone wrong here? Elements of this type simply decay by nature.[7] But how is that case different from the death of an animal or a human being? Is the fact that an animal dies a 'natural' death (as distinct from a violent death, or a death caused by some other invasive organism) evidence that something has gone wrong? Perhaps we are inclined to think that something is wrong here because we tend to take a teleological view of living organisms and not of inanimate elements. We do not regard uranium as having any in-built purpose, or in-built drives or tendencies, at least not in the way that animals have;[8] organisms, on the other hand, have a purposiveness, and death puts an end to such purposiveness. But even if one allows that such teleological language is in place at all when speaking of organisms (and not all scientists would easily accept this), it might also be argued that to consider teleology at the level of individuals is to take too narrow a view; perhaps modern biology might be willing to accept that the purposiveness of organisms is more intelligible if it is taken to apply to species rather than individuals. What is important is the continuation of the species, rather than that of any individual; indeed it is for the good of the species as a whole that elderly and less efficient individuals should die once they have successfully reproduced. Of course, in our own case, the death of a human being usually seems to be a bad thing,[9] precisely because at least most of us take ourselves to have an interest in continuing to live. But this individualistic point of view is not the only possible one. Why should we not consider ourselves as primarily members of a species, and our individual goods as at least to some extent subordinate to that of the species as a whole?[10]

The general point is that there are various possible standpoints from which the value of something might be assessed. From the standpoint of an individual death might be a bad thing; but from the point of view of the species to which that individual belongs, it might be a good thing. It is at least not clear that one such standpoint is the correct one from which to assess the situation as a whole. Similar considerations apply when the survival of the members of one species is achieved at the expense of members of some other species; and this is true not merely of lions eating gazelles, but also, for instance, of bacteria attacking humans. Of course, we naturally enough assume that our own interests are paramount, because of the unique moral status of human beings. But it does not at once follow that this priority, even if it is justified, suffices to show that in some overall sense it is not a good rather than a bad thing that some beings bring about the deaths or the sufferings of others. We are at least prepared to indulge in some vague talk about an overall ecological balance, thereby giving some credence to the view that there is a standpoint from which an overall, rather than a merely local, sense of what is good can be assessed.

But such talk is indeed vague, and is fraught with difficulties. To begin with, 'good' is too easily identified with what simply happens in the natural course of events, and enables that course of events to continue in a stable fashion. But so far as our present discussion is concerned, that is simply to beg the question; for it might be urged that it is precisely the whole system of nature which is bad because of the sufferings involved in the way it works. The 'ecological balance' could be an evil alliance. Secondly, it ignores the fact that humans are by nature equipped to alter what would otherwise happen automatically; we do feel morally obliged to eliminate disease-causing organisms, for instance, and to make the environment better from the human point of view. While our outlook may be open to accusations of 'speciesism', even the most ardent critic of a too narrow concentration on purely human needs and interests is not going to deny that ideally things could and should be better for us than they are. It follows that our inability instantly to produce at least some of these improvements is a bad thing. John Hick has contested this view, at least put as broadly as I have just done, on the grounds that the effort required to overcome adversity is a requirement for developing the moral and spiritual maturity which is the supreme value for human beings (Hick 1990). This line of argument might be more convincing if such moral and spiritual progress were the universal, or even the predominant, outcome of the struggle against adversity. But this can hardly be a wholly adequate explanation, given the bitterness, depression, and despair which adversity so often produces. Hick himself accepts that his proposed explanation pre-supposes for its plausibility the existence of an ultimately rewarding God, for reasons somewhat similar to Kant's view that the failure of virtue to lead to happiness is morally intolerable unless there is a life after death and a God who will give the virtuous what they deserve.

There are thus problems in the claim that each local evil in the world can be seen as a good from a higher point of view. Attempts have been made, however, to look at things in precisely that way, and to argue that there is a standpoint from which all this can be seen as good. Augustine writes,

> To Thee there is no such thing as evil, and even in thy creation taken as a whole, there is not; because there is nothing from beyond it that can burst in and destroy the order which Thou has appointed for it. But in the parts of creation, some things, because they do not harmonise with others, are considered evil. Yet these same things harmonise with others and are good, and in themselves are good. And all these things which do not harmonise with one another still harmonise with the inferior part of creation which we call the earth, having its own cloudy and windy sky of like nature with itself. Far be it from me, then, to say 'These things should not be.'
>
> (*Confessions*, VII, 13)

The higher standpoint is that of God himself, and the harmony of creation as a whole is not something which can be readily seen by narrow concentration on any of its parts. The very natural laws which produce a stable environment, and which, for that matter, make it possible for animals to exist at all, are the same laws which lead to animals suffering and dying. The importance of the overall harmony is that it puts the local discords into a context in which they are no longer seen as discordant, despite the fact that they are '*considered* evil' by people who take too partial a view. Aquinas writes in similar vein:

> They have failed to take into account the universal cause of all that is, and have looked only at the particular causes of particular effects. That is why, when they found something

159

which was by nature harmful to some other thing, they considered that it must be bad by nature; as though someone were
to say that fire was a bad thing because it burnt someone's house
down. A judgment about the goodness of something ought not
to depend on its relationship to some other particular thing, but
on what it is in itself, and its relationship to the universe as a
whole, in which everything has its perfectly ordered place.

(I, 49, 3)

And, even more in detail,

> God, and nature, and indeed every causal agent, does what is
> best overall, but not what is best in every part, except when the
> part is regarded in its relationship to the whole. But the whole,
> the created universe in its entirety, is better and more perfect
> if it contains some things which can be less than good, and
> which sometimes are so, with God doing nothing to prevent it.
> This is so firstly because divine providence aims not at the
> destruction but the preservation of nature, as Denis says, and
> it is part of the nature of things that those things which can go
> wrong sometimes do. Secondly because, as Augustine says in
> his *Enchiridion*, ch. 11, God is so powerful that he can bring
> good out of things that are evil. So many goods would be lost
> if God did not permit any evil to exist. There would be no fire
> did air not cease to be; the life of the lion would not be
> preserved unless the donkey were killed. There would be no
> praise for the triumph of justice or the patience of suffering,
> were there not moral iniquity.

(I, 48, 2, reply 3)

The difficulty with arguments like this is not, as it seems to me, one
of principle; it is legitimate, indeed essential, to ask from which
standpoint something is considered to be bad, and it is surely true
that something can be good from one standpoint and bad from
another. No, the difficulty is that this kind of argument can easily be
overstated in such a way that, if it is accepted, the problem of evil
simply disappears instead of being taken seriously. To be sure, we
cannot see things from God's standpoint, and it is no doubt helpful
that Augustine and Aquinas remind us to make the effort not to be
too parochial in our outlook. Yet, while it might be true that if we
could see the world with God's eyes we should see the overall

goodness of the 'order Thou hast appointed', and hence see that apparent evils could all be looked at as goods from some other point of view, it is certainly not obvious, to say the least, that every instance of suffering produces benefit, and the theist ought not to be committed to trying to show that it does. At most the theist might try to show that the overall balance is a good one, a point to which we shall return later.[11]

Moral evil

So far as moral evil is concerned, the position is much clearer. It is incontrovertible that the world contains many instances of moral evil, some of them of the most horrendous proportions.

The conclusion is therefore that a correct description of the morally relevant features of the world is that it is a world containing much moral evil, and many other states of affairs which are at least from some points of view undesirable, and hence bad. This description as put does not, I think, make any controversial assumptions about morality, or about moral relevance. On any moral theory, there are instances of moral evil. How many of the other states of affairs which can be described as from some point of view bad are to be seen as *morally* relevant will no doubt be a matter of dispute. For instance, whether the sufferings of every kind of sentient being are of moral significance might perhaps be denied.[12] Be that as it may, it is uncontroversial that the sufferings of human beings are of moral significance. Thus, though there might be differences of opinion on how many states of affairs there are which are both bad and of moral significance, it ought not to be in dispute that there are many such.

But is it true that a morally adequate description of the world is not merely that it contains evil but that it is an evil world? It seems to me that we lack any overall perspective from which such a judgment can safely be made. It is not obvious whether Augustine and Aquinas are correct or mistaken in their assertions that it is not overall an evil world. If they are mistaken, it could be argued that it follows at once that it is wrong without qualification to bring such a world into being.[13] If they are right, it still does not follow that to bring such a world into being is to act in a morally blameless way. There might, for instance, have been better alternatives which should have been chosen instead. All in all, it seems to me that the description 'a world containing much evil' is the one which is undeniably true, and arguably the only morally significant description of whose truth we can be assured. I therefore propose to read Condition 1 in this way.

CONDITION 2: DID GOD BRING ABOUT THE WORLD SO DESCRIBED?

To ask this question is not the same as to ask whether 'to bring about a world in which there are natural and moral evils' was an action which God *intentionally* performed. (That question will be considered later.) Just as there are many things which I might be truly said to have brought about, even though I did not intend to bring them about, so the two questions must be distinguished in the case of God, at least for the sake of clarity, even if it turns out that both must be answered in the same way.

A further distinction is also in order; it is one thing to ask whether God brought about a world in which there are evils, and another to ask whether God brought those evils about. Someone might bring it about that a tree is growing beside a road, without bringing it about that in a gale it fell upon a passing car. Parents might bring it about that a child exists, without bringing it about that the child punched another child in a quarrel. We do not in general accept that each of the causally necessary conditions for some state of affairs can properly be said to bring about that state of affairs. Which among the causally necessary conditions we single out as a cause, or *the* cause, depends on a large number of factors – such as, for example, which of the necessary conditions was unusual, or to whom we believe it appropriate to assign responsibility, or what could be reasonably foreseen.

The theist, who believes that God is the first cause of all created things, is committed to saying that God brought about the existence of a world in which there are evils. But many, indeed perhaps all, theists have sought to deny that we can simply conclude that God caused the evils. A typical example of this line is found in Aquinas:

> That kind of badness which consists in a defective action is not attributable to God. But the kind of badness which consists in some things ceasing to exist does have God as its cause.
> The effect produced by a defective secondary cause is

162

dependent on the non-defective first cause in so far as it exists and is good; but not in so far as it is defective; thus, the movement involved in walking badly is caused by the body's power to move itself, but the limp is not caused by the body's power to move itself, but comes from the misshapen leg. Similarly, in so far as a bad action exists it is caused by God; but in so far as it is bad, it is caused not by God but comes from a defective agent.

(I, 49, and reply 2)

The background to this needs some explanation. Aquinas holds that when something is truly said to be bad, it is because it lacks some feature which it ought to have. Badness is not a positive, but a negative characteristic. In that sense, badness is not a property, and hence not an existing entity. Since only existing entities can be caused, badness cannot be said to be caused, except in what Aristotle calls an accidental, or qualified, sense; something can be caused to exist which happens also to be defective.[14]

The claim is that strictly speaking, *nothing* straightforwardly causes badness, since badness is a lack, not a positive property. Now it is a matter of current dispute whether goodness or badness (whether in a moral or a non-moral sense) are real properties at all. Suppose, though, that they are. It would still seem to be the case that they are relational properties. Something is said to be bad because of some feature F which it has and because of the relation between that feature and the relevant standard of comparison. F is a real property, even if to be F is truly described as failing to meet the standard. To speak of a 'failure to meet a standard' is not thereby to commit oneself to 'failures' as an extra item in one's ontology.[15] So, to cause something to be F is only accidentally to cause that thing to be defective, provided that it is not always or for the most part true that things which are F are defective things. Thus, it is not always or for the most part the case that essays which do not mention Aristotle are defective, and hence to write an essay which does not mention Aristotle is not thereby to write a bad essay. But not to mention Aristotle is indeed a defect in an answer to an examination question on Aristotle. Neither Aquinas nor Aristotle denies that accidental causes of an effect truly are causes; what they deny is that under that description they provide *explanations* of the effect. That a student writes an essay which does not mention Aristotle does not in itself explain why it was a bad essay. That explanation requires some reference to the proper standards for the kind of essay involved. Aquinas's view in general is that failure to meet the relevant standard is not in itself a thing which can be straightforwardly caused.

Secondly, Aquinas holds quite in general that the First Cause straightforwardly explains the *existence* of all things; but their natures and properties are explained by secondary causes. That my eyes are brown rather than blue is explained by characteristics of my parents: but that those brown eyes exist is ultimately explained by the existence of God.

Aquinas tries to apply this general view in the two passages just quoted. In the first, he maintains obviously enough that God's activity cannot itself be defective; but he concedes that God can straightforwardly cause things to cease to exist by causing the existence of their contraries (and regularly does so when, say, the coldness of this water ceases to exist when the water is heated).[16] In the second paragraph, he denies that God straightforwardly causes defective things. That defective things exist is straightforwardly brought about by God as first cause; but that they have that feature which makes them defective is straightforwardly the effect of some secondary cause, and only accidentally the effect of God's causal activity. Hence, he concludes, God does bring about a world in which there is evil; but God can be said to bring about the evil in the world only accidentally. It is not God's causal activity which explains why things in the world are evil.

As will be seen below, it is not clear that Aquinas is correct in saying that God is only the accidental cause of evil. But suppose, for the moment, that Aquinas is right on this point. Even so, an accidental cause is still truly a cause. So God can truly be said to have brought about a world containing those features, and that is sufficient to satisfy Condition 2. God did perform the action of creating which had as its causal outcome that evil exists in the world. And he is at every stage involved in the causal processes of the world which result in both natural and moral evils. Arguments showing that evil is not a positively existing property of things, or that evil is caused only accidentally by God do nothing to show that God (or anyone else, for that matter) is not the cause of evil in the minimal sense required to satisfy Condition 2.

CONDITION 3: IS GOD MORALLY ACCOUNTABLE FOR A WORLD CONTAINING EVIL?

This condition deals with two types of cases. In the first, the action in question can simply be described as 'Doing A'; as for instance, someone might simply be said to shoot someone.[17] The second type of case is that in which someone brings about a situation in which it can be foreseen that something will come about which the agent might, or might not, properly be said to intend; as, for instance, if someone incites a crowd to riot and in the riot someone is killed; or, where someone bombs a military target knowing that it is likely that civilians will also be killed. It is, once again, a matter of dispute in moral philosophy to what extent, if at all, people can be held accountable for the foreseeable bad effects of their actions when those effects are neither desired nor intended; and, indeed, whether foreseen or foreseeable effects must be said to have been in some sense intended.[18] It would be unfortunate so to formulate questions about the problem of evil in such a way that decisions about them presuppose a particularly restricted view in moral philosophy, as for example the view that agents are accountable only for what they intend in the narrow sense. So I shall here assume (what I happen also to believe to be true) that agents can be held morally accountable for the reasonably foreseeable effects of their actions, even if they cannot be said to bring about those effects, or to be in that sense responsible for them, or to desire them.[19]

Now we have just seen that Aquinas is at some pains to establish that God can be said to be the cause of evil only in an accidental sense. Why should he think this an important point to make? Because he believes that someone can (given some other conditions, which need not concern us for the moment) properly be held responsible for what they can be said to bring about, but that it is not equally automatic that someone can be held accountable for what they bring about only accidentally. The digger is accountable for the hole, but not necessarily for finding the buried treasure. That is not something he *did* in the same sense as he did the digging, even though he brought it about that the treasure was discovered. How far does this argument succeed? It contains two claims, which need to be considered.

i) The first claim concerns the relationship between the First Cause and secondary causes. Aquinas makes several assertions about this relationship, which are not easy to reconcile with one another: the First Cause and a secondary cause are not related in the way in which two men rowing a boat together cause the boat to move; the First Cause and a secondary cause do not have distinct effects; the First Cause explains the existence of an effect; and the secondary cause explains the kind of effect that it is. Perhaps an acceptable reading might go like this. It is not the case that God's causation produces a partial effect, supplemented by the causal activity of a creature; it would be better to say that the effect in its entirety depends both on God and on the created agent; but the explanatory force is different in the two cases: God explains the existence and activity of the created cause, and the existence of the created effect; the creature explains the kind of effect which it is. Moreover, God can be said to cause only in an analogous sense to that in which creatures cause. If that is accepted, then God is truly but only accidentally the cause of whatever features an effect has.[20]

ii) The second claim is that an agent's relationship to what he causes without qualification is different from his relation to what he causes accidentally. While it is truly a causal influence in both cases, it is not equally explanatory. Now, what is the connection between this claim and claims about moral responsibility or accountability? The farmer who discovers a treasure is only the accidental cause of their coming to light, since ploughing a field does not of itself constitute an *explanation* of finding a hidden treasure. Though in one sense the farmer is responsible for discovering the treasure, he is not praiseworthy for having discovered it. Neither was the cricketer whose mighty hit happened to kill a passing pigeon blameworthy for killing the pigeon, though he did indeed bring about the pigeon's death. There is no general explanatory relationship between plough-ing and discovering treasure, or between hitting the ball in the air and killing passing birds. I think that Aquinas would see the difference here not primarily in terms of whether the farmer, or the cricketer, *intended* to produce the effect which they brought about, but rather in whether they did something knowing that in general it can be expected to produce such an effect.

In that case, though, to play cricket knowing that one is in close proximity to a greenhouse is to be blameworthy if players then break the glass, even if they had no such intention, because in such a case the player is not an accidental cause of the effect. As Aristotle might have put it, playing cricket close to a greenhouse always or for the most part leads to broken panes of glass. That is why the argument does not seem to me to work when applied to God's responsibility for the bad states of affairs of which he is the accidental cause in creating the world as he did. Aquinas's claims about the accidental nature of God's causal relationship to the features of the world is primarily a thesis about ontology. Even if it is accepted, it does not suffice to show that his causation is accidental in the way required to absolve him from moral responsibility. Recall that the distinction between an accidental and a straightforward cause depends on their explanatory force. In another of Aristotle's examples, a builder is said to be the accidental cause of healing (*Metaphysics*, E 2, 1027a1–3). One might imagine a situation in which a worker on a building site sees a passer-by collapse in the street, rushes down, and successfully administers first aid. Aristotle would say that the builder is only accidentally the cause of healing, since there is nothing about being a builder which explains the healing. The building-site worker is a healer in virtue of his knowledge of first aid, not his knowledge of the construction industry. It is his knowledge of first-aid which explains the healing.

True; but the builder is nevertheless accountable for and indeed praiseworthy for the healing of the passer-by, because there is one true description of him under which description he *is* straightforwardly the cause of the healing. Aquinas would, of course, reply that there is *no* true description of God under which God is straightforwardly the cause of evil. A salient element in Aquinas's account is that the history of the world is brought about not merely by God, but by other agents as well, and that it is *these* agents, not God, who are straightforwardly accountable for evil.

But there are some reasons to suggest that this is a mistake. The agents Aquinas has in mind fall into two classes, those whose actions are determined, and those whose actions are free. We must therefore ask under what conditions an agent can be held accountable for the actions of other agents in each of these two cases. Consider first the snooker player. Which events on the snooker table does the player straightforwardly cause? Aristotle, I believe, would have answered that those events can be said to be straightforwardly caused by the player which are known to be generally correlated with what the player does.[21] We customarily give players credit for shots that they intended and whose effects they could reasonably have foreseen, and ascribe to luck or chance those effects which they could not have foreseen, precisely because they are not correlated always or for the most part which what the player did. I think that the situation is broadly similar when the other agents involved are free agents. If I ask someone to do something in circumstances where such requests are normally acted upon (for instance, I ask someone to pass the salt at table), I and the other person are both accountable for the salt ending up opposite me; and if I provoke someone known to be especially hot tempered into losing his temper and hitting someone, then I am accountable, as well as him, for what he did. Always or for the most part, that is how he reacts. Contrast the situation in which I mention that Jemima has just arrived, and James rushes out of the room. I did bring it about that James left, but only as an accidental cause if I had no reason to suppose that James on no account wished to meet Jemima. Saying that Jemima is coming does not, always or for the most part, have the effect that people rush out of the room. I am not accountable for his leaving.

So, if God is not to be held accountable for the evils in a world which he creates, it needs to be shown that God did not knowingly bring about a kind of world which, always or for the most part, would contain bad states of affairs. To say that God straightforwardly causes the existence those states of affairs, but was only the accidental cause of their badness, or to say that God did not intend to bring about those states of affairs, is either not the right kind of point, or else not true; for God still decided to be the cause of such a world. If he did so knowingly, then he is morally accountable, and hence not in the moral sense an accidental cause.

But *did* God do so knowingly? It has already been argued, in discussing God's omniscience in Chapter 3, that God's knowledge even of time-bound events is a timeless knowledge. It is therefore not accurate to speak of any of the features of the world being *foreseen* by God. But we can speak of those aspects of a world which God knows independently of any decision to create that world, and those which God knows only dependently upon that world being created and agents in it acting as they do. To the extent that events in a world follow a pattern determined by the natures of the entities which that world contains, an omniscient God knows what those features are. The same is true for such events in other possible worlds. It follows that an omniscient God knows of the occurrence of many of those states of affairs which we would describe as natural evils, and that he knows this independently of whether he creates this world or not.

He does not know all the instances of natural evil in this way, however. Some of them occur only because of inherently un-predictable and morally irreprehensible human decisions – such as the decision to meet a friend from whom I catch mumps, or a decision to travel in a ship which sinks in a storm resulting in the person's death. On the other hand, might it be argued that even if individual instances of this last kind cannot be known independently of their actual occurrence, God would still be in a position to know that such instances are likely to occur, given his knowledge of human aims and the ordinary features of the natural world? After all, it is possible to predict that many people will go on holiday to Spain this summer, even if it is not possible to predict that Jemima will choose to go there. And in general, it is possible to predict that many humans will die of disease rather than from other causes, given that they live in a world where it is possible to become infected, even if the circumstances in which a particular human becomes infected result from free decisions. In bringing about a world such as ours, then, an omniscient God must surely know that he is bringing about a world in which there will be many instances of natural evil? The same argument applies also to moral evils. Might an omniscient God know that, as a matter of statistics, so to speak, individuals who are capable of making immoral decisions will at some time or other make them? For while it is logically possible that no human ever makes an immoral decision, it is surely false that nobody will do so in a world which contains a sufficiently large number of humans for the statistical probabilities to be reliable. It follows, then, that although an omniscient God cannot know which particular instances of moral evil there will be other than by discovering which ones there in fact are once the world is created, he can know that there will be such instances, perhaps many such instances. In bringing about a world such as ours an omniscient God knowingly, and hence not accidentally, brings about a world in which there is moral evil.

A counter-argument might be proposed, however. Recall that the crucial point is not whether God knows the free choices humans actually make, but whether his knowledge is independent of their making it, in the way which Molina suggested it was. So the question is, might Molina be mistaken about the most general statistical patterns of human choice, just he is, as I have argued, wrong about God's knowledge of individual choices? To answer this, one has to examine more closely the knowledge we have of large-scale statistics about human choices. We are able to predict the number of holiday-makers in Spain only by an induction on what has previously happened. Our knowledge is not gained independently of the choices people have actually made. If that is all there is to it, then God's knowledge would likewise not be independent of human choice, and Molina would be mistaken here, too. So God would not know 'in advance', so to speak.

But it is just possible that there is more to it than that. It might be argued that the success of our inductive procedures here, and perhaps in general, can be explained only if there is some kind of law – in this case a statistical law – which truly describes our choice-patterns, just as there are statistical laws which truly describe the patterns of radioactive decay, even though individual events in such decay are not governed by laws at all. It might be the case, then, that whatever it is about human beings and their environments which explains the patterned nature of their choices on a large scale, these facts could be known also to God, independently of which choices individuals in fact make. Exactly *why* non-deterministic statistical laws should be true at all, and indeed whether it is sensible even to ask why they should be true, is quite obscure. But it seems at least not out of the question to suppose that there is some basis for their truth. If there is, such a basis would be known to an omniscient God independently of the choices which people make. He would therefore have known that in creating a world such as ours, there would be morally wrong choices made, even if he did not know which ones those would be.

If this is correct, it follows that God must be held morally accountable for bringing about a world in which there are natural and moral evils, and for the foreseeable evils which resulted from his so doing. This is true even though he cannot be said to have perpetrated those evils himself, nor desired (and at least in that sense 'intended') that they should come about, nor to have been their only cause. To say that God should be held accountable, however, is not thereby to say that God is blameworthy. It is to say simply that God must be presumed to have taken all these features of his creation into account in deciding to bring this world about. It remains to be seen whether the good which is also a feature of this world could have been brought about without at the same time bringing about the natural or moral evils which as a matter of fact accompany those goods in the world as we know it; and it also remains to be considered whether

170

to bring about a world in which there is natural and moral evil is a wrong thing to have done.

CONDITION 4: DOES GOD KNOW HE SHOULD HAVE DONE BETTER?

Leibniz, almost alone among the classical philosophers, maintained that God of necessity does the best possible action, and could not have acted otherwise than he did:

> The supreme wisdom, united to a goodness that is no less infinite, cannot but have chosen the best. . . . There would be something to correct in the actions of God were it possible to do better. . . . So it may be said that if this were not the best of all possible worlds, God would not have created any.
>
> > (*Theodicy*, I, 8)

This claim would, of course, solve the problem of evil at a stroke, since if it is true, God fails to satisfy Condition 4. It can hardly be wrong to do the best possible action. Leibniz includes the possibility that God should never have created at all; and his claim is that creating this world must have been better than doing nothing, and hence must be good overall. Moreover, he claims that God acts as he does out of necessity. Leibniz would defend this on the basis of his view of sufficient reason; nothing can come about unless there is a sufficient reason for its coming about. 'No fact can be real or existing, and no proposition true unless there is a sufficient reason why it should be thus and not otherwise, even though in most cases these reasons cannot be known to us' (*Monadology*, 184).

> As there is an infinite number of possible universes in the ideas of God, and as only one can exist, there must be a sufficient reason for God's choice, to determine him to one rather than to another; and this reason can only be found in the *fitness*, or in the degrees of perfection which these worlds contain.
>
> > (*Monadology*, 187)

Why should one not simply leave matters there, and conclude that there is nothing in the world which is incompatible with the goodness of God – indeed, that there simply *cannot* be any such thing? There are two reasons: *i*) although Leibniz considered that he had conclusive arguments to show that there is a God, it might be questioned whether they are as conclusive as he believed them to be; and the same goes for all the other efforts to show that there must be a God. But once it is accepted that the arguments for the existence of God are not utterly conclusive, then the existence of evil in the world cannot be dismissed as easily as Leibniz would think. For it is at least an open question whether the existence of evil should not add additional weight to the difficulties in accepting the force of the arguments in favour of the view that God exists. The point is an important one. What Leibniz's position brings out is that if there are sufficient *independent* grounds for believing that there is an infinitely good God, then the problem of evil can properly be dismissed *a priori*; one can properly argue that God must have his reasons for acting as he does, even if 'these reasons cannot be known to us'. The earlier Christian theologians would have accepted this view of how the issues are related, and would have agreed with Leibniz that the reasons for believing that there exists an infinitely good God are indeed independent of the precise features, good or bad, of the world as we know it. Hence, while they did try to make it to some extent intelligible why God should have created a world in which there is evil, they did not think it necessary to provide a wholly intelligible account, nor did they think that the validity of their proofs for the existence of God depended on their ability to provide such an account. The modern debate is above all characterised by the view that the proofs for the existence of God are not so conclusive that their force can be assessed independently of those features of the world which seem to count against the existence of a good God. The seriousness of the problem of evil for theistic belief does indeed depend on one's view of the independent conclusiveness of the reasons one has for believing that there is a good God. But if the independence, or the conclusiveness, of these reasons can be called in question, then Leibniz's argument cannot be adequate.

ii) Even if there are conclusive grounds for believing that there must exist an omnipotent and omniscient cause of all things, it might be urged that we would need a *separate* argument to show that this omnipotent and omniscient creator is morally admirable; and this is just what cannot be shown independently of considerations about the existence of evil in the world, Leibniz's claim notwithstanding. So the problem recurs. We shall return to this point below, in connection with Hume.

Is Leibniz right in saying that God is determined to choose just one world – the best one – from among the worlds which he could create; or is the older tradition right in supposing that God could equally well have created other worlds? Two assumptions seem to underlie his view:

a)   A morally good agent is obliged to choose the best alternative from those known to be available.

b)   It makes sense to compare worlds, and to say that one is better than another, and to say that there is a best world.

Both assumptions are surely open to question. It might be argued that a) is unjustifiably demanding, and that all that is required of any morally good agent is to do something which is permissible, even if it is not the best that could have been done. There does seem to be a distinction between someone who does good, even if they could have done better, and someone who acts wrongly.[22] As for b), at least it seems to be over-stated, if it is possible to make sense of the thought that there might be worlds so totally unlike ours that there is no common scale on which they could be compared. We might recall Descartes's cautionary remark, that we ought not to suppose that what is possible is limited to what we can imagine or conceive of. Moreover, it may be that even a less radical difference between possible worlds might be sufficient to make it difficult to say which is the better – a point to which we will have to return. But if it is not possible to rank worlds in function of their goodness, then a good God will not be obliged to create one rather than another, provided only that whichever he does create is a good one.

One might compare and contrast Leibniz's opinions on these points with what Aquinas says. As has been pointed out already, Aquinas would disagree with Leibniz's view that God could not have created any world other than the one he did in fact create. But it is not at all clear exactly what Aquinas takes to be the implications of this claim. He considers a difficulty which is very like the argument which Leibniz proposes, that God can do only as he is morally obliged to do, and what it would be just to do; but it cannot be that God has a moral obligation to do other than he does, nor that it would be just for him to act otherwise than he does. Aquinas replies as follows:

God is morally obliged to no-one but himself. So when it is said that God can do only what he is morally obliged to do, this simply means that he can do only what is proper and just for him. But these words 'proper and just' can be taken in two ways: in the first, they are primarily connected with the 'is' understood in the present tense, and only then related to the 'can only'; in this sense it is false, 'God can do only what it is *now* proper and just for him to do.' Secondly, they could be primarily connected with 'can only', broadening its scope, and only then with 'is' which is then taken indefinitely; and in this sense it is true to say 'God can do only what, if he were he to do it, would be proper and just.'

Granted that the present course of events is limited by the things which now exist, God's wisdom and power are not limited to the present course of events. So, even if no other course of events would be good and proper given the things which now exist, God could create different things, and order them differently.

(I, 25, 5, replies 2 and 3)

And, as we have already seen, Aquinas is prepared to say that some possible worlds are better than others, since they contain better things, or because they add better things to the present world (I, 25, 6, reply 3). Aquinas therefore flatly denies assumption a); provided that God does what is proper and just, he violates no moral obligation; but there are many ways in which God could act properly and justly, and some of these involve creating a better world, or creating better things in this world than it presently contains. So God is not obliged to create the best possible world. Aquinas, then, must be willing, just as Leibniz is, to accept b); neither philosopher shows any sign of being troubled by comparing in respect of their goodness worlds which might be quite unlike one another.

As I remarked a moment ago, it is difficult to decide between Aquinas's rejection of a) and Leibniz's insistence on it. But Aquinas's grounds for rejecting it in the case of God might well appear suspect. I have translated Aquinas's reason as 'God can do only what is *now* proper and just for him'; but the Latin might equally well mean 'What he now takes to be proper and just', a more radical suggestion which might fit better with Aquinas's claim that God is obliged by no-one other than himself. This might suggest almost an ockhamist position that God *decides* what is to be proper and just. On balance, though, I think that Aquinas says that God is under an obligation to nobody but himself in order to exclude the common sense of 'obligation' in which one person is under an obligation to another, and can be released only by that other person.[23] He is not arguing that God can simply decide what shall count as 'proper and just'. But whatever Aquinas's view was, it is surely unwise for the theist to take the line that what it is for God to be a moral agent is totally discontinuous from what it is for a human being to be a moral agent. If human beings are to regard God as morally admirable (which they surely must do, if he is to be worthy of worship), they must surely not hold that what it is for God to be morally admirable is quite unlike what we might take to be involved in being such.

Just as what is morally required of us depends upon the kind of beings that we are, and upon the environments with which we interact, so what it is morally right for God to do is a function of his nature and of the natures of the things he creates. Even if we are in no position to say what God owes himself, we are very definitely in a position to know the moral requirements which follow upon the creation of human beings – requirements which, it seems to me, must delimit how God can properly and justly treat us, just as they delimit how we can properly and justly treat one another. It seems to me false to argue that God is under no moral obligation to the human beings that he creates; to create a human being is to create obligations towards that being, just as human beings create moral obligations towards the children they have. So, while it might be true that God is under no obligation to anyone other than himself in deciding whether to create or not, the act of creating brings in its train a set of obligations to the things created.

To sum up so far, then: firstly, it seems to me that there are some grounds for wondering whether it will always make sense to say that one world is better than another, if the worlds in question are very diverse; but it might make sense to compare our world with a very similar world, and to say that one is better than the other. Until that question is settled, it is unclear whether or not God could and should have done better. Moreover, it is not true that any moral agent is obliged to perform only the best action available; and hence it is not clear that God is obliged to produce the best at least among comparable worlds, or whether there are other worlds which he morally could have produced instead. Taken together, these considerations suggest that there is so far no good reason to say that God satisfies Condition 4. On the other hand, two reasons for asserting that God certainly does not satisfy this condition are not good reasons; it is not clear, despite Leibniz, that this is the best possible world; and, despite Aquinas, it cannot be argued that the notion of 'obligation' is inapplicable to God, so that we cannot meaningfully say that God acted wrongly. Those ways of resolving the problem are just too quick.

Plainly, all evils could have been avoided had God decided to create nothing at all. And all the evils of this world could have been avoided had God created a quite different world – for example, a world in which there were no sentient beings,[24] or a quite different world in which the things we describe as evil simply could not occur. But whether such a state of affairs, in which God alone existed, or in which no moral beings other than God existed, would be overall better than the present state of affairs is just the question I think cannot be confidently answered.

Hume would take that last remark to be quite obviously mistaken. He believes that there are general reasons for supposing that this world could have been better, and he has some more detailed suggestions about how this could be achieved. Firstly, the general reasons:

> It must be allowed that, if a very limited intelligence whom we shall suppose utterly unacquainted with the universe, were assured that it were the production of a very good, wise, and powerful Being, however finite, he would, from his con-jectures, form *beforehand* a different notion of it from what we find it to be by experience; nor would he ever imagine merely from these attributes of the cause of which he is informed, that the effect could be so full of vice and misery and disorder, as it appears in this life. . . . But supposing, which is the real case with regard to man, that this creature is not antecedently convinced of a supreme intelligence, benevolent and powerful, but is left to gather such a belief from the appearances of things – this entirely alters the case, nor will he ever find any reason for such a conclusion.[25]
>
> (*Dialogues*, XI)

The key moves in this argument are two: *i)* that it makes a difference whether it is taken as given that (which is what Hume means here by 'were assured that') God exists, or whether it is still taken to be an open question whether God exists or not. This to some extent explains the complete difference in tone between Hume, on the one hand, and Augustine, Aquinas and Leibniz, on the other. If there are conclusive reasons for believing that God exists, then, so far from the presence of evil in the world tending to disconfirm the belief that there is a God, the disconfirmation works in the opposite direction. Once given the existence of God, it must be that what appears evil cannot be as bad as it appears to us. So it does indeed 'entirely alter the case' whether the existence of God is taken as certain, or as still in doubt.[26] But more strongly, *ii)*, Hume further contends that even if one does take it as given that God exists, the world as it is would still fall well short of what one would have expected from a God.

Hume is surely right about *i)*, that it makes all the difference. But I think he is mistaken to suppose (or at least to suggest) that the assured believer's disappointed expectations ought to be a source of worry; rather the believer's assurance should alleviate his disappointment. So what about *ii)*? Suppose that the point were put to Hume that, if he is serious in saying that not to assume the existence of God 'entirely alters the case', he must be willing at least to concede that the convinced believer, though disappointed in the expectations he had formed 'beforehand' about what a universe produced by a God would be like, could still *consistently* hold to his belief in God even when he discovered how things actually were? Hume's view was that such a position might be consistent, but would nevertheless be unreasonable, given the weight of the evidence:

> And from thence I conclude that, however consistent the world may be, allowing certain suppositions and conjectures, with the idea of such a Deity, it can never afford us an inference concerning his existence. The consistency is not absolutely denied, only the inference.[27]
>
> (*Ibid.*)

But might not the believer in turn argue that the evidence has no weight at all if it is clear that there is a God? And if even if that is not clear, the weight to be given to this evidence will depend entirely on the plausibility of the 'conjectures' which someone makes about what a God-created world would be like. So what is the basis for these conjectures? How does one even begin to conjecture *a priori* what is to be expected from a God?[28]

I have suggested that some caution is required in answering this question, lest we over-estimate the importance of our own human interests in assessing the world as a whole, and lest we over-estimate the importance of individuals rather than of species as a whole. Still, it is clear enough that the world contains states of affairs which are, at least from limited points of view, bad states of affairs, even if at least some of these might not be bad from every point of view. Even so, whether the world is overall a good world from a global point of view seems to me an almost unanswerable question; there is no way to decide whether or not something is good unless we have a relevant standard against which it is to be assessed. And, at least in default of a God's eye view, there is no standard available for assessing worlds-as-wholes.[29] The view of Augustine and Aquinas and Leibniz is an *a priori* view which, given the existence of God, would indeed be plausible, even if, perhaps, it is somewhat over-stated. But without that assumption it seems to me to be little more than an assertion. Hume, on the other hand, pays insufficient attention in the above passage to the various possible standpoints against which states of affairs might be judged even independently of any assumptions about the existence of God, and to be too quick to assume that he knows how to judge the world as a whole.

It might nonetheless be argued that the problems about the non-comparability of dissimilar worlds could easily be met if there were a world broadly similar to ours, in which such evils had been avoided. Here, Hume gives four rather stronger reasons for thinking that such is indeed the case:

> The *first* circumstance which introduces evil is that contrivance or economy of the animal creation by which pains, as well as pleasures, are employed to excite all creatures to action, and make them vigilant in the great work of self-preservation. Now pleasure alone, in its various degrees, seems to human understanding sufficient for this purpose. All animals might be constantly in a state of enjoyment; but when urged by any of the necessities of nature, such as thirst, hunger, weariness, instead of pain they might feel a diminution of pleasure. . . .
>
> But a capacity of pain would not alone produce pain were it not for the *second* circumstance, viz., the conducting of the world by general laws; and this seems nowise necessary to a very perfect Being. . . . In short, might not the Deity exterminate all ill, wherever it were to be found, and produce all good, without any preparation or long progress of causes and effects?

178

It scarcely seems possible but some ill must arise in the various shocks of matter and the various concurrence and opposition of general laws; but this ill would be very rare were it not for the *third* circumstance . . . the great frugality with which all powers and faculties are distributed to every particular being. . . . An *indulgent* parent would have bestowed a large stock to guard against accidents. . . .

The *fourth* circumstance whence arises the misery and ill of the universe is the inaccurate workmanship of all the springs and principles of the great machine of nature. . . . None of these parts and principles, however useful, are so accurately adjusted as to keep precisely within those bounds in which their utility consists; but they are, all of them, apt, on every occasion, to run into the one extreme or the other.[30]

(Dialogues, XI)

The first response that might come to mind is that Hume in the first, third and fourth of these suggestions tends to assume that individual features of the world can readily be altered while leaving the remainder untouched. One can no doubt imagine a gazelle which is driven only by a feeling of lesser pleasure, and which is incapable of feeling pain. But if one considers in detail the alterations which would have to be made in order to accomplish this, it is at least more difficult to see that what one would then have would be a gazelle at all. Similarly, to endow all sentient beings with all the powers needed to avoid any situation which might involve suffering would involve a massive alteration in the kinds of things that exist; even human beings, with many more powers than animals have to foresee and control their environment, are nowhere near possessing the faculties which Hume suggests would be needed. And to suppose that one might have the beneficial effects of, say, the earth's atmosphere without the possibility of there being violent winds, or flash floods, is to suppose that there is a wholesale re-write of the laws of physics. Indeed, it has been more recently argued that even a very small alteration in the initial starting-conditions of our universe would have made it impossible to have any form of life as we know it. So far from the adjustment being inaccurate, it seems from some points of view to be accurate in the extreme. In short, in three of these suggestions, it might be alleged, Hume is misled by his powers of imagination to suppose that everything we can imagine is causally possible, or that it could be rendered causally possible with only minimal alterations to the general laws of nature as they at present obtain.

Hume might reply by citing a passage from Descartes which we have already seen:

> It is easy to dispel this difficulty by considering that the power of God cannot have any limits, and that our mind is finite and so created as to be able to conceive as possible the things which God has wished to be in fact possible, but not to be able to conceive as possible things which God could have made possible, but which he has nevertheless willed to make impossible.
>
> (Letter to Mesland, 2nd May 1644)

As I earlier remarked, it is not easy to decide how far an argument of this kind ought to be pushed. It is something of a blockbuster, in that, if it works at all, it would allow anything whatever to be causally possible, even what appears to us to be logically contradictory. And indeed, what appears to us to be contradictory is not really a much better guide to what is causally possible than is Hume's vivid imagination. Perhaps one reason for caution is that what we have so far discovered about this world is that it is governed by a few extremely general laws such that even small changes in them would produce not minor changes (such as animals which were driven only by pleasure), but the unpredictably large-scale changes suggested by chaos theory. So there is perhaps some reason for thinking that even if Descartes is right, Hume might still be mistaken in believing that minor tinkering with the development of the world more or less as we know it to be is a causal possibility.

It is more difficult to know what to make of Hume's second suggestion, that the world might be better were it not governed by general laws at all. Perhaps Hume's claim here is at least in part shaped by his view that the regularities which characterise our world derive not from any necessity in the way in which things interact, but from sheer coincidence. Any other set of coincidences would be in principle no different, and hence no less possible. But if this view is simply incredible, as I believe it to be, then the suggestion as a whole would amount to the proposal that God should intervene as often as necessary to alter the states of affairs which would otherwise have been brought about by natural necessity. But here again, it is not clear just how such regular and massive intervention as would be needed to avoid all cases of natural evil would be causally possible given the world as it is.

The whole question seems to me extremely obscure, therefore. On the whole, I am inclined to think that it is easier to suppose that some completely different world might be causally possible, than it is to suppose that it is causally possible to have a world very like this one with only selective improvements. But it is easy – perhaps too easy – to speculate along such lines, if only because, if Descartes is right, there is no way in which our current language is able to express what such a world would be like; our minds are not 'able to conceive as possible things which God could have made possible, but which he has nevertheless willed to make impossible.'

So the discussion might be summed up in the form of a somewhat uncomfortable dilemma:

Either   i)   We can imagine a better version of this world, but without much confidence that what we imagine would be causally possible.

Or   ii)   We can suppose that a radically different creation might be causally possible; but we would then have no way of knowing whether it would be better or worse than the present one, since it would be beyond our power to describe it.

In short, while there are at least some reasons to suppose that the natural evils of this world might have been avoided by creating a radically different world instead, there is no way of knowing whether such a world would have contained less evils than this one does.

Could the moral evils of this world have been avoided without making our world incomparably different? Obviously they could, if God created us in such a way that we were not free to make immoral choices. Whether, given the moral evil which has resulted from a world in which free moral choices are made, and the moral good which comes from other such choices, God would thereby have created a better world is just the kind of question which I do not think can be answered one way or another.

But could God not have avoided creating a world in which there is moral evil by creating a world in which there are moral beings who always, as a matter of fact, always choose the good, even though they are not determined to do so? If so, all the benefits deriving from free choices would be retained, with none of the evils. The answer to this question depends on several points which we have already considered.

Firstly, is it possible that a free person should never make an immoral choice? It might appear that it must be so. If any particular choice is not causally determined, then it is causally possible that it should be a morally right choice. And if it is causally possible that any particular choice should be a morally right choice, then it must be causally possible that they should all be morally right. But I have already given some reasons for doubting whether this inference is a valid one. For it is the case that the decay of any particular radioactive atom is not causally determined; but we know that it is not causally possible that no atom of a radioactive substance ever decays. They decay at a predictable rate, of necessity. So far as I can see, there is no reason to suppose that free choices might not also have this characteristic;[31] it might not be statistically possible that all of a person's choices should be morally good, even if it is possible that each of them should be. If that is the case, then at least in a world at all like this one, it is not possible that people would make only good choices. And this statistical fact could be known to God independently of the choices people actually make. God would know that a world like ours but lacking in moral evil would be a statistical impossibility.

Secondly, however, suppose that I am mistaken in this view, and that it is quite possible that free choices should all be good. Even in that case, though, if I am right about the limitations on God's omniscience, God would not be able to *know*, independently of the choices people actually make, whether they would be good or bad choices. Molina is, I have argued, mistaken in believing that God knows, independently of what people in fact choose, what they *would* choose in whatever different circumstances they happened to be placed. Even if there is a possible world in which as a matter of fact nobody makes a bad choice, there is no way in which God can know that the world he creates is that world rather than one like ours. It might so happen that God could create a world without moral evil, but there would be no way in which he could *ensure* that he was creating that world.[32] Hence, in that sense, it is not possible for God to *avoid* creating such a world.

Is Condition 4 satisfied, then? Well, it is surely not the case that what God is accountable for is unqualifiedly good. Even if it is in fact good overall, it is not clear to us that it is. Does it follow, then, that God must know that some better action was available to him which he ought to have performed instead? It seems to me that we have at least plausible reasons for doubting that an improved version of *this* world would have been causally possible; and, while, as Descartes pointed out, we cannot entirely rule out the possibility that a quite different world might be possible, and unqualifiedly good, and better than this world, there seems to be no way in which this speculation can be given any content by us. Indeed, if such a world is totally unlike ours, there might not be any coherent sense in which it could be a better world, even in God's eyes. And where moral evils are concerned, I do not see how God could know that a world containing moral beings would be free of such evils; and even if he could know this, it does not appear that God could ensure that this would be the case. On balance, then, I conclude that it is not clear that Condition 4 is satisfied, and that therefore the existence of evils in our world does not provide conclusive grounds for supposing that God is not morally good.

Conclusion

The historical discussions of these five attributes of God are complex and fascinating. I hope to have unravelled at least some of their complexities, and to have offered interpretations of the classical texts which are at least defensible even though, as I am well aware, some of my readings might be challenged, at least in detail if not in their main outlines. Just as important, though, is something else which I hope has emerged from engaging the classical writers in discussion. Despite their considerable differences and their widely disparate assumptions, Aquinas, Ockham, Descartes, Molina, Hume and Kant are in agreement with one another to a somewhat greater extent than is often supposed. Even when they disagree over what has to be said about these attributes, or, indeed, whether anything can properly be said about them at all, they often share similar views on where the main problems lie, and on what are the main difficulties which have to be confronted.

These problems are not new; neither have they by now been conclusively solved. One cannot accuse the medieval philosophers of some naïve failure to spot damning logical or metaphysical flaws in their arguments which any post-Humean or post-Kantian student can easily see; nor, on the other hand, is it easy to show that the claims, and even the unexamined assumptions, of the medieval philosophers can be shown to be correct. In the Introduction, I suggested that the central issues concern the nature of necessity, the nature of knowledge generally, and of our knowledge of necessity in particular; and the connections between necessity, contradiction, and cause. These topics are at the heart of contemporary debate.

However, there is one contemporary issue which has important implications for philosophy of religion and which does not really appear at all in any of the classical philosophers whom I have been discussing. I have in mind the debate between those who hold some kind of foundationalist position in epistemology and those who do not. In their different ways, I think all the classical philosophers who have appeared in the preceding pages were foundationalists; that is to say, they held that all our knowledge claims must be based on truths which are in some sense 'evident' and stand in no need of further justification of any kind. Of course, they differed on what these evident truths were: for Aquinas, they included the Aristotelian 'first principles', which concern truths about the essences of things as well as truths about causation, possibility and necessity; for Descartes, there was only one indubitable truth, that he existed; for Hume, there were the immediate truths of our sense-experience, and so on. Many recent philosophers have sought to bypass such parochial disputes about which truths are foundational by arguing that in the required sense *none* is. Such 'holistic', 'anti-foundationalist' theories in epistemology have been applied also in philosophy of religion in two main ways; one is directly inspired by Wittgenstein and associated especially with D. Z. Phillips and Norman Malcolm; the other, more explicitly linked with theological concerns, is often referred to as 'Reformed Epistemology' and has been developed especially by Alvin Plantinga.[1]

A full discussion of this controversy, even in its relation to philosophy of religion, would require another book. But I ought to say at least a few words here on how I take the discussions in this book to be related to the current debate. Phillips and Malcolm both wish to emphasise that to believe in God is to be *committed* in a particular way, rather than simply to hold certain propositions to be true. Phillips further insists, following Wittgenstein, that the existence of God should not be regarded as some kind of explanatory hypothesis, resting on evidence.[2] I am far from convinced that it makes no sense for someone to believe that God exists while admitting that this belief makes no difference to their life. (There is a somewhat similar problem in ethics: can a person sincerely believe that some action is wrong, while saying that they don't *care* whether it is or isn't?) But even if one insists that belief that there is a God must involve some kind of commitment, it does not seem to me to follow that belief that there is a God cannot be construed as a conclusion that someone has reached on the basis of evidence, or a position which is regarded as true on balance, given the arguments (or evidence). Nor does it follow that one cannot be wholeheartedly committed to act on a belief if one takes that belief to be only on balance true, or more likely to be true than not. In Chapter II I have given some indication of the kind of reasons which might be alleged in favour of believing that God exists, and how such arguments might fit into a wider picture of explanation which is not vulnerable to the criticisms levelled by Hume or, especially, by Kant.

Of course, it will be objected that the kind of position I have argued for ignores much more general Wittgensteinian reasons for holding that religious beliefs, and indeed all other very fundamental beliefs (for instance in the value of science, or the existence of other minds) are all in an important, anti-foundationalist, sense 'groundless'. The very criteria for truth and falsity are given by a set of framework agreements which simply cannot intelligibly be questioned. To question them is to presuppose some further standard of truth external to all forms of life and the beliefs in which those forms of life are expressed. To my mind, two lines of reply are in place here.

The first is to question whether it is accurate to regard religious belief as constituting a complete framework to which all other truths are somehow 'internal'. It may be true that a person who believes that there is a God in anything like the traditional Western sense might agree that that belief offers a new perspective on *everything* else. 'The world is charged with the grandeur of God' who 'has the whole world in his hands', no doubt; belief in God is a cosmic vision which can colour the whole of a person's life. But it does not, as it seems to me, offer much insight into the correct answers to the conundrums of physics, nor any criterion by which we might assess the truth of various scientific theories about the origins of the universe. Nor is it the case that a believer cannot consistently, or on religious grounds should not, ask whether to regard the cosmos in this way is justifiable, or is coherent with other fundamental beliefs which he or she also holds. Many believers, some of them great philosophers, have asked just those questions; if there is some fundamental mistake involved even in the willingness to pose and try to answer these questions, the mistake must be philosophically demonstrated. It is not enough simply to assert *a priori* that true believers cannot question their beliefs, or that they are misguided in the effort to show that their beliefs meet the standards of rationality which would be required in any other area of human thought.

The second is much more tricky. There is a genuine and so far unresolved philosophical dispute between foundationalism and antifoundationalism in epistemology, which is related to further disputes about realism and relativism quite generally. If foundationalists have difficulty in showing which truths are self-evident or in some other way incorrigible, their critics also have difficulties in giving more than historical, psychological, or sociological explanations of why one view of rationality, one world-view, or one conceptual scheme is adopted rather than any other.[3] But it should be said that these considerations apply quite generally, and do not affect issues in philosophy of religion any differently from philosophy of science, for instance. The basic assumptions to which, as we have seen in the preceding chapters, the classical philosophers appealed to, or denied, are assumptions of complete generality, concerning cause, existence, necessity, and the propriety of using language to refer to and describe things which lie beyond the bounds of our direct experience. Quarks are no more and no less problematic than God. And, at least to me, it seems not merely proper but necessary at least to make the attempt to show that some ways of looking at the world are more helpful, or successful, or unavoidable than others. Such, at least, is the view shared by Aquinas, Hume and Kant, though they differ on where this attempt will lead.

As will have become obvious, I believe that a broadly traditional view of God is defensible. I have argued that it is possible to give intelligible content to the notion of a necessary being, provided that the necessity involved is the *de re* necessity of such a being's existing. I have also argued that the notion of *de re* necessity is irreducible to logical necessity, or to the conceptual relationships between the words we use. Rather more strongly, I would suggest that *de re* necessity is closely linked to causal necessity and causal possibility, and that these notions themselves are best taken as primitive. We can to some extent succeed in describing the law-like ways in which some causal necessities reveal themselves in our world; but such success does not, I think, amount to an account of what causal necessity is, nor does it throw much light upon what might in an absolute sense be causally possible.

Still, I have argued that the medieval claim that the attributes of God depend on simplicity, and that simplicity excludes any essential causal dependence is basically right. The problems with it are largely due to the fact that we, and our language, are ill-adapted to describing such a being, which is neither a kind of thing in the Platonic manner, nor an individual of a kind. Our attempts to describe God literally

187

are inevitably couched in language whose normal application is to ordinary everyday things, and hedged about with specific restrictions on how they must *not* be understood. It is unsurprising that the rich language of religion, as distinct from the philosophy of religion, expresses truths about God largely in metaphors, as is also the case in sub-atomic physics, or contemporary cosmogonies.[4]

I have departed from the classical views both on omniscience and omnipotence. So far as omniscience is concerned, I agree with the predominant view of the tradition that it is less misleading to think of God as knowing things rather than truths about things; that his knowledge is such as befits a timeless and unchanging being; but contrary to all the medieval philosophers, it seems to me that his knowledge of undetermined events in the world is dependent on the occurrence of those events, even if it might be argued that he has a general statistical knowledge of the general pattern which such events follow. I do not take this to be a limitation on omniscience, since I think there are good reasons to doubt whether in such cases there is any further knowledge to be had.

On omnipotence, I think there is much to be said for the agnostic position adopted by Descartes, as contrasted with the more confident assertions of Aquinas, and the only somewhat less confident claims of Ockham. Omnipotence does, as all these philosophers would agree, depend on what is absolutely causally possible. But our ability to extrapolate from our present empirical knowledge of what is causally possible in this world is surely very limited. We cannot be sure even of what is causally possible in the universe as it is, let alone what alternative universes might be causally possible.

Contemporary discussion of the goodness of God and the problem of evil has centred on the relationships between infinite goodness, omniscience and omnipotence. I have argued that with respect to all created things God's choices are free, and that it is at least on balance the more probable view that God could do wrong, even if he never in fact would. If those conclusions stand, then it makes sense to speak of God as a moral agent, with moral obligations. I therefore think that a helpful way to consider the goodness of God is to ask whether there is evidence to suggest that he has violated any moral obligation. The answer to this question obviously depends both on the view one takes of what God can know, and on what it is possible for God to bring about. My conclusion, that it cannot be shown that God has acted wrongly, depends both on the restricted view that I take of what

God knows and how, and on the somewhat agnostic line I take on omnipotence. My conclusion is therefore vulnerable to the objection that it fails to show positively that God is good. The most I can assert is that there is no good reason to suppose that he is not.

Modest as these conclusions are, they are sufficiently strong to be highly controversial. My aim in this book has been simply to show that these problems, both in their historical and in their contemporary settings, are well worth serious philosophical examination, and that such an examination offers a fresh approach to many of the issues which are central to any philosophical endeavour.

Notes

I Existence

1 I intend 'attribute' to be taken as neutrally as possible, so as not immediately to take sides in the discussions about whether existence is a predicate, or an attribute, or a property of existing things. On any account, there is *some* difference between assertions such as 'Tigers exist' and assertions such as 'Tigers are striped'. The problem lies in saying just what kind of difference this might be.

2 Aristotle held that 'being' was said in several ways, when we speak of the being of substances, or qualities, or relationships, and so on. The details of his view are controversial, but at least he was making the point that a substance, like Jennifer, exists in a different way from a quality (such as her colour) or a relationship such as 'being taller than'. The term 'Category' derives from the Greek word for 'to predicate of'; Aristotle is classifying the ways in which 'exist' is said of things, and thereby also classifying the various ways in which things exist.

3 See, for instance, his footnote to *Treatise*, I ii, 7, '. . . 'tis far from being true that in every judgment, which we form, we unite two different ideas; since in that proposition, *God is*, or indeed any other, which regards existence, the idea of existence is no distinct idea, which we unite with that of the object'.

4 It is not his only argument. He also argues that, for all we know, a limited being might nevertheless be absolutely necessary. The notion of an *ens realissimum* (a 'most real being') is 'very far from sufficing to show whether I am still thinking anything in the concept of the unconditionally necessary, or perhaps rather nothing at all' (A588, A593).

5 Kant's use of 'logical' here is confusing. I think it is best understood as 'grammatical' rather than 'logical' in the technical sense of that term.

6 It is not clear what he would have said about identity statements where the predicate is a definite description, like 'John is the person I was speaking to ten minutes ago.' He says that identity statements do not have real predicates; but I suspect that he was considering only the simplest kind of identity statements.

7 An essential attribute is one which an individual must have; Socrates

190

cannot cease to be an animal without thereby ceasing to be Socrates; accidental attributes are ones, like being tired, which Socrates can have or not, as it happens.

8 Accidents have essences only in a secondary sense, since accidents themselves exist only dependently upon the existence of the substances to which they belong (*Metaphysics*, Z, 5, 1031a10ff).

9 It might therefore be argued that, in cases like 'mermaid' or 'goal' the question 'What is X?' and 'Is there an X?' are not distinct at all; there are such things just if the terms have been defined. There is no question, in such cases, of any need to examine instances (or alleged instances), of mermaids or goals in order to discover what they essentially are. They are whatever we deem them to be. On the other hand, it might be argued that the sense in which there 'are' such things is not the sense in which we should speak of things *existing*. On this, see my discussion later in this chapter. At any rate, the traditional distinction between the two questions seems to me sustainable in those cases in which it is proper to speak of *discovering* the real essence of something.

10 The notion of *de re* necessity is far from clear, as it seems to me. But at any rate, it is a necessity which is built into the natures of things which exist in the world, and is not reducible to logical necessity. On this controversial topic, see Kripke (1972). His discussion has been very influential in rehabilitating the view that there are real essences, and the corresponding notion of *de re* necessity.

11 T. Irwin (1982) argues that Aristotle's notion of signification cannot simply be identified with our notion of 'meaning'. He concludes, 'Inquiry into words and their signification is part of inquiry into the world and the real essences in it' (p. 266). This seems to me quite right, and a useful corrective to the common over-verbal reading of Aristotle. The same applies, I would argue, also to Aquinas.

12 Whether Aquinas would have agreed that the principles of causation and non-contradiction were *synthetic* is perhaps open to doubt: Aquinas tends to suppose that we would redefine the terms involved in order that the principles would turn out to be analytic. This I take to be a small point. Neither would Aquinas hold that these principles were known *a priori* in the Kantian sense. He believed that they were grasped by inductive insight into the way the world is.

13 It is not entirely clear from the somewhat repetitive text just how many distinct difficulties Kant in fact invokes. I take it that in A608 he gives the most formal version of the argument and of the criticisms he makes of it, thus summarising the more general remarks which have gone before. I think his criticisms 1, 3, and 4 are fundamentally the same, and that 2 is different.

14 This is true even in the case where what is said to exist is itself a property; for it is essential to an existing property that it is the property of something; and any existing property will therefore also have the property (whether essentially, or accidentally) of being the property of this particular individual thing.

15 I realise that this account denies that such things as merely possible

worlds, numbers, sets or the Equator exist, unless, like Plato, one is willing to say that such things, too, can be involved in causal relationships. This, to my mind, is a welcome consequence. Not all our concepts, not even all our useful concepts, need be of existing things. (Notice, though, that even Plato was willing to define existence in terms of the possession of causal powers. See *Sophist* 247d8–e4, 248c4–5.) This whole question is much disputed, however; many philosophers are quite happy to speak of the existence of possible worlds, or to be Platonists about numbers. I take the view that the important distinction is between those things which have causal powers and those which do not, and I formulate my definition of 'exist' accordingly. Others would hold that the important line has to be drawn elsewhere.

16 It might be objected that some things, for example ghosts, can cause fear, and must therefore in some sense exist; and perhaps Anselm could use such an argument to support the view that there is such a state as 'existence in the mind'. I would reply that what is causally operative in such cases is the existing belief which has such a thing as its intentional content.

17 Exemplified, for instance, by the view that the actual world is simply the one among the many possible worlds which we are in now.

18 What is supposed to be the sense of, for instance, '—— is □(unmarried)'? Is the property involved in 'Tom is unmarried' a different property from the property possessed by, say, a stone? If it is, then the difference is not simply a difference in the scope of 'necessarily'.

19 I am not here considering further questions about individual immortality.

20 It might be thought that the traditional reply would be simpler than this, in that matter/energy is nothing more than the potentiality for there being substances constituted of matter; and that as such matter/energy cannot exist at all. Appeal might be made to Aquinas's views on prime matter (which he interprets as pure potentiality – which may or may not be a correct reading of Aristotle), for example, in I, 7, 2, reply 3, and I, 4, 1. This would, I think, be a mistake; at least as I understand it, the energy/matter of the universe is *structured*, in that it by nature obeys certain laws; and if this is so, then it cannot be the wholly unstructured prime matter postulated by Aquinas.

21 This last point is crucial. The traditional view is not merely that created things can be annihilated because of what they are: it is that they *de re* could not exist unless caused to exist. Cosmological arguments are often presented as presupposing the Principle of Sufficient Reason, or the Principle of Intelligibility, as though the central step was the claim that unless God exists, the world would not be fully explained, and so would not be fully intelligible. Such a claim may or not be true; and it may further be true that we cannot be satisfied unless we have a complete explanation, as Kant suggests. But at least in Aquinas the point of the cosmological arguments does not depend on this kind of claim, but on the view that the universe is such that it *de re could not* exist unless God exists.

II Simplicity

1 Some notable recent exceptions to this generalization are Robert Adams, Robert Burns, and Eleonore Stump and Norman Kretzmann, for whom see the Bibliography. In particular, we now have the detailed and scholarly book by Christopher Hughes (1989), from which I have learnt an enormous amount, even though, as will be evident, I disagree with some of Hughes's conclusions.

2 I, 3, 2. *Demonstratio* is Aquinas's equivalent to the Aristotelian *apodeixis*, and refers to the kind of argument which displays knowledge as scientific – by which is meant, knowledge of what is necessarily the case.

3 And even if it were, the explanation would no doubt be of the kind which Aquinas, following Aristotle, thinks is properly involved in the explanation of actions, since it is the free action of God which explains the way the created world is. Practical reasoning, even divine practical reasoning, should not be expected to have the kind of necessity which characterises theoretical reasoning. Even if, *per impossibile*, we knew the divine essence, the explanation of why there is, for instance, evil in the universe would be an explanation in terms of practical reasoning rather than theoretical science.

4 It is with some hesitation that I offer an interpretation of the cosmological arguments differing considerably from that proposed by J. Owens (in Catan 1980). I believe that all five 'Ways' are but variations on single theme, which is expressed in its basic form in the Third Way. I also hold that Aquinas did not consider that the argument so put would immediately justify identifying the ultimate explanation of the things we experience with the Christian God; the justification for this final step comes only in the following Questions.

5 I, 3. See also *De Potentia*, 7.

6 I, 13, 7. My summary in the text is, I believe, faithful to Aquinas's general intentions. There are points of detail which remain unclear. For instance, the correspondence between Aquinas's view and Geach's account of Cambridge change is not exact, since Socrates can come to be smaller than Callias if Callias grows and Socrates remains the same size. But it is Aquinas's view that my being taller than my brother is an intrinsic accidental property of both of us, since it depends on the sizes which we both happen to have. I do not believe that the overall argument depends on sorting out this particular detail, however.

7 I, 13, 7. 'All relations between an actual thing and a non-actual thing are, similarly, [conceptual relationships and not real,] since the mind conceives of these by thinking of what is not actual as a kind of term of the relationship.' *Ens* and *non ens* in this passage must surely mean 'actual' and 'non-actual'.

8 I, 19, 3, reply 4. 'Though God's willing a thing is not absolutely necessary, nevertheless. . .it is necessary on a supposition, on account of the immutability of the divine will'. That is to say, God's choice, supposing it to be made, cannot be revoked. This quasi-temporal sense of 'necessity' will be discussed in the chapter on omniscience.

9 *Commentary on De Anima* 406a30. His point depends on what is at least a plausible reading of Aristotle's distinction between two kinds of alterations, one of which involves a process of being changed, and the other of which does not. See Aristotle's *De Anima*, II, 5, 417a21ff.

10 So far as I can see, I, 3, 6, and I, 19, 3 are simply inconsistent. In the text, I have resolved the inconsistency in favour of the latter passage, which seems to me better to represent Aquinas's position as a whole. Similar problems can be raised about God's knowledge of contingent things; these will be dealt with in the chapter on Omniscience.

11 Given the resources of genetic technology, Aquinas might have concluded that there are species without any actual members, in so far as it is immediately possible to produce individuals of that kind. 'Immediately' is required, since Aquinas, like Aristotle, does not consider as potentialities in the relevant sense those which require several intervening stages before they can be actualised. A log at the bottom of the sea is not in the relevant sense capable of being burnt. Aquinas, like Aristotle, never envisaged the possibility of the development of new species, and hence never considered what state of the world would be immediately required for it to be possible to produce the first individual of a new species. Species-terms were theoretical terms required to explain the causally necessary similarities between actual individuals (since the offspring of two items in the same species is of necessity itself a member of that species) without relapsing into Platonism.

12 This of course leaves quite open the further and disputed question which natural kinds there might be, and which kinds are properly construed as natural kinds.

13 See the introduction to I, 3. David Burrell (1979) has taken the view that Aquinas's position amounts to a 'dreadfully austere doctrine of God' if it is a doctrine of God at all.

14 The words used of God are inadequate in their powers of expression precisely because God is not in any genus, and hence not even generically similar to creatures; and also in their way of referring, since we must speak of God either in individual terms, or in universal terms, and neither kind of term refers in the required way. (I take *intelligatur vel significatur* in the last line of the paragraph here cited to make *both* these points: see I, 13, 1, reply 2.) For a more extended treatment of Aquinas's views on theological language, see G. J. Hughes (1987).

15 Aquinas's view is in fact more complicated than this oversimplified comment suggests. Aquinas was willing to countenance the suggestion that there might also be non-material individuals; but if there are, he thought there could be only one of any given kind; for the only fundamental way of distinguishing between different individuals of the same kind is that each of them consists of different material, but this criterion is not available for immaterial things.

16 One might note, in passing, that there is no one universal term to cover God's mercy and the mercy of a human being, since, on Aquinas's view, the terms do not have the same sense. God does not, therefore, belong to the class of merciful beings.

17 It must be admitted, though, that even if this interpretation of the text is correct, Aquinas does not seem in the least inhibited from trying to develop various notions of identity, especially when dealing with the conceptual problems involved with the Trinity and the Incarnation. It might be argued that the very existence of these many attempts undermines the interpretation I have just given. To which my reply would be that the passage in I, 13, 4, like much else in the early part of the *Summa*, is intended to provide the theoretical framework within which everything that comes later is to be understood. In this case, that all his attempts to explain identity and non-identity in theology must be read against his cautionary remarks in I, 13, 1.

18 For the strict requirements on 'explanation', see pp. 35–6.

19 I put it this way, rather than saying that B has some accidental property, since 'proper accidents' such as the whiteness of snow, or the ability of humans to laugh are, as Aquinas puts it, 'caused by the essence of the thing', with the consequence that this property cannot be changed. I suspect that Aquinas's view of the relationship between a proper accident and the essence of something is much like what would now be termed 'supervenience'. I have also so phrased this requirement so as to avoid the problem, mentioned earlier, of attributes of God consisting in the exercise of his own active power – for instance, in choosing.

20 This also presents some problems. In general, Aquinas is clear that material things are constituted from matter which could equally go to make up something else. However, Aquinas believed that the heavenly bodies were both material bodies, and unchangeable. So it follows that in his view, being composed of matter does not of itself entail that matter could form some other thing instead. It looks as if he somewhat inconsistently holds that matter as such involves a real potentiality for change, while denying this in the special case of the heavenly bodies. His remark that even the heavenly bodies can be moved in space might have seemed to him to involve the possibility of an intrinsic change; but this is surely a mistake?

21 Not even the category of substance, if substance is taken to be a *tode ti*, an individual; and certainly not substance if substance is understood as an Aristotelian secondary substance, for the reasons already given.

22 Total annihilation, rather than the mere re-arrangement of its constituent stuff into some other thing, must be what Aquinas has in mind in the Third Way:

> Some of the things we come across can be but need not be, for we find them springing up and dying away, thus sometimes in being and sometimes not. Now everything cannot be like this, for a thing that need not be once was not; and if everything need not be, there was a time when there was nothing.
>
> (I, 2, 3)

However, if he does intend 'need not be' to be synonymous with 'can be annihilated' as distinct from 'consists of material which could come to constitute something else', then his claim that we 'come across' such things is difficult to substantiate. It certainly is not simply a matter of observation, as Aquinas thinks it is.

23 It seems that 'absolute necessity' and being totally 'unconditioned' must involve some notion of *de re* necessity if Kant's argument is to work at all here. So I interpret him in this way, despite the absence of explicit indication in the text.

24 The details of the argument are too complex to reproduce here. The step about *prior* understanding of 'Fido' and '—— exists' is supported by the claim that it is quite proper to regard these as Fregean 'constituents' of 'Fido exists'. Miller then points out that unless Fido *already* exists (or has existed) we cannot conceive of Fido; the most we can do is form a description which could be satisfied by Fido and indefinitely many other dogs. How then is it possible to understand 'Fido exists' on the Fregean scheme? Miller's contention is that we must make a distinction between Fido's capacity to exist and the fact that Fido exists; Fido has that capacity neither in virtue of being an individual, nor in virtue of being an existing individual. Therefore Fido's existence must have been caused.

25 Moreover, if Aristotle (and Aquinas, who followed him on the point) is right in saying that 'exists' is not a generic term, since what it is for substances, qualities, relationships and so on to exist is different in each case, then it will follow that what it is for each of these to be a cause will likewise differ. That I take to be quite an interesting idea.

26 I say that he rightly sees this; I am not thereby endorsing the details of the reasons he would give, that we cannot justify our use of the concept of cause, nor, I take it, of *de re* necessity, outside the realm of sense. I would make a similar point on the grounds that the Conservation of Energy is too fundamental an axiom in our scientific picture of the world for us to consider replacing it with some other.

27 I use the term 'transcendence' as a convenient shorthand for 'non-membership of any kind'.

28 See his treatment of simplicity in I, 3. Membership of kinds is considered in article 5; that God is not an individual is implicit in the denial that God is properly to be called a substance, since a substance is paradigmatically an individual.

29 Notice that the notion of *de re* possibility which I am appealing to here is stronger than that often invoked – for instance by Plantinga. Plantinga's notion is that it is *de re* possible for X to be F just if being F is compatible with X's essential properties; and X's essential properties are those properties possessed by X in every world in which X exists. On this view, as Linda Zagzebski has pointed out to me, existence must be an essential property of X, since X has existence in every world in which X exists. In contrast, I would not wish to appeal to a prior notion of 'possible worlds', as I have argued in Chapter I, though if the point had to be made in those terms, I would say that if X's non-existence is *de re* impossible, X must exist in all possible worlds, and not merely in all those possible worlds in which X exists. I would prefer to say, though, that if X's existence is *de re* necessary, nothing can bring it about that X does not exist.

30 For a full and admirable treatment of the use of models and metaphors, see Janet Martin Soskice (1985); and also the papers by Richard Boyd, T. S. Kuhn, and Z. W. Pylyshyn in Ortony (1985). In particular, McMullin (1984) gives an excellent account both of the way in which the postulation of an entity whose properties are hardly understood is compatible with realism, and also of the role of models and metaphors in scientific language. I think that similar points can be made both about theological realism and the use of metaphor in the languages of theology and religious practice.

III Omniscience

1 This is not to deny that Aquinas certainly adds features to the Aristotelian account – notably, for instance, his views about abstraction – which may, or may not, be consistent with Aristotle's intentions, or the correct interpretation of Aristotle's text. See, for example, D. W. Hamlyn's (1968) commentary on Aristotle's *De Anima*, III, 4–5 for the view that Aquinas misreads Aristotle. One might also suggest that Aristotle's own account is so fragmentary, and at one crucial place irrecoverable from the corrupted text, that it is difficult to know in detail what his account in fact was.

2 He does not make the sharp distinction between these two activities which we might wish to.

3 The details of this are a matter of considerable controversy, which need not concern us here.

4 I, 14, 6. The reason Aquinas gives is that otherwise God's knowledge would be incomplete; and since his knowledge is himself, he would be essentially incomplete, which Aquinas thinks he has shown to be false. He rejects the comparison with light which gives rise to the various different colours, since merely to know (white) light is not thereby to know all the colours in which it is variously reflected. But God is aware of *all* the ways in which his being can be reflected in creatures.

5 I, 14, 11. Aquinas's argument here is surely somewhat shaky. He advances several reasons: i) that to know individual things is a perfection in us, and is therefore something we must also attribute to God. ii) God's causation extends also to the material which distinguishes one individual of a species from another in the same species. Against i), it might be urged that we know individuals as such only through our senses, and that to have senses is not, in Aquinas's view, a perfection, but a consequence of being material beings. Against ii), it could be argued that the very concept of knowing entails having concepts, and these must be universal. Aquinas might reply firstly that each individual has an individual essence which can be known; and secondly that God's knowledge does not involve concepts in this way, and hence God does not need a different concept in order to know each individual. On which see pp. 100–1.

6 Even human beings are considered by Aquinas to be immaterial as well

as material substances, albeit in a very limited way. Aquinas greatly extends the scope of Aristotle's very brief remarks that knowing is not the activity of a material organ, as sensing is, into a much more definite view that the human soul is capable of subsisting independently of the body, even though it is dependent on the body for its functions, including the sensory input from which knowledge is gained.

7 We may ignore, as Aquinas does, the additional complexities required to deal with sentences expressing questions or wishes, which might equally count as *enuntiabilia*. In the passage quoted, Aquinas also uses the word *oratio* (which I have translated as 'saying') in such a way that he must be taking it to be equivalent to *enuntiabile*. In which case, perhaps the best translation of *enuntiabile* might be 'statement'. It is not clear whether Aquinas understood this to refer to types or tokens. If I write the same sentence twice, does that count as one *enuntiabile* or two?

8 'Just as there is no change in the divine knowledge through his knowing that one and the same thing at one time exists and at another does not, so there is no change in the divine knowledge through his knowing that a proposition is at one time true and at another false. There would be a change if God knew propositions in the way that our minds do by putting together and separating' (I, 14, 15, reply 3).

9 A distinction is often made between two sets of temporal terms: the A-set contains such words as 'ago', 'yesterday', 'now', and tensed verbs. The B-series contains none of these, but does contain untensed verbs, and references to times. The three sentences I have offered here are not tensed, though they do contain three expressions referring to times.

10 See the excellent discussion in Christopher Hughes (1989: 114–20).

11 See Christopher Hughes's formulation of this point, (1989: 115). Anthony Kenny (1979: 38–40) reiterates his earlier view that this account of eternity is radically incoherent. But his argument presupposes that to say that the whole of time is present to eternity is to say that eternity is *simultaneous* with every moment of time. I see no reason to make this assumption.

12 Though the matter is not beyond dispute, it seems clear to me that Aquinas makes it clear enough that the source of God's knowledge of things is his complete awareness of his own causal powers and activities. The analogy with vision is unfortunate, to the extent that it suggests that the source of God's knowledge is created things themselves, just as the things we see cause our seeing of them. Such a view would be quite inconsistent with Aquinas's clear view that God cannot be acted upon by anything whatever. Aquinas makes it clear that the analogy with vision is intended only to point to the difference between things which exist separately from God in that he has willed to create them, and things which God knows in knowing simply his own causal powers. It is central to Aquinas's entire position that God does not obtain his knowledge of created things from those things themselves. I shall later offer reasons for thinking this view is a mistaken one.

13 See note 7.

14 Were he to be asked whether it was a consequence of his view that future

events were just as real as present or past events, it seems to me that Aquinas would have said 'no' to the question as put. At any given moment in time, the future is to a large degree indeterminate, not yet fixed or settled, in sharp contrast to the present and past. There is nothing illusory about the direction of 'Time's Arrow'. Moreover, God <know> that this is the case. True, God also <know> that some of the things which are merely possible at a given moment in time will be actual at some later time. But that is not, in Aquinas's view, to say that those things are fixed *already*; it is merely to <know> that as a matter of contingent fact they become fixed at some particular time and not before. For a contrary view, see for instance Marilyn McCord Adams (1987: II, 1120–1). See also the following note.

15 Linda Zagzebski discusses at some length whether Aquinas thinks that all temporal events have the 'same ontological status' (1991: 47–56). I think she is quite right in her contention that nothing in Aquinas suggests that temporal becoming is an illusion, nor that God sees everything as simultaneously actual. I do think, though, that it is Aquinas's view that all the events which we would describe as past, present, and future do in one sense have the same ontological status, in that they all form part of the history of the actual world; they are therefore all alike distinguished from events which might have, but never actually do, form part of that history. But that, of course, is a far cry from saying that they are all simultaneously actual, if that is what is meant by 'having the same ontological status'. It is not clear to me from what she says on p. 49 whether Zagzebski would agree with this interpretation of Aquinas or not.

16 There is a problem about the sense of 'necessary' here. The comparison in the text is to the movement of the sun, which of necessity moves as it does. It seems to me that this is at best an imperfect model for God's creative activity, since Aquinas holds that God could <create> other things than he in fact <create>, even though his action in creating is unchangeable. I take it, then, that 'necessary' here means 'unchangeable' or 'irreversible', and hence that God's knowledge is 'accidentally necessary' (for discussion of this phrase, see pp. 76–82). What it plainly does not mean is that the action of the First Cause *of itself necessitates* all its effects, since this is incompatible with Aquinas's view that the effects are contingent because the secondary cause may act contingently.

17 I have given here an outline of the argument proposed as a difficulty by Aquinas at I, 14, 13, objection 2, and answered in the corresponding reply.

18 As will appear, this is a direct rejection of the view for which Ockham later was to argue. In contemporary jargon, Aquinas believes that it is a 'hard fact' that God knew that a future event would take place.

19 The translation of the text, and hence reconstruction of the very condensed and elliptical argument, is somewhat problematic. The text reads:

> Nec tamen sequitur, ut quidam dicunt, quod consequens sit necessarium absolute, quia antecedens est causa remota consequentis, quod propter causam proximam contingens est. Sed hoc

nihil est: esset enim conditionalis falsa cujus antecedens esset causa remota necessaria et consequens effectus contingens; ut puta, si dicerem 'Si sol movetur, herba germinabit'.

With some hesitation, I propose the following translation, with some comments on it:

> But, according to some, it does not follow that the consequent is absolutely necessary, because the antecedent is the remote cause of the consequent, and the consequent is contingent because of its proximate cause. But this [explanation] is no use; a conditional would be *false* if it had a remote cause as its antecedent and a contingent effect as its consequent, as, for instance, if I were to say 'If the sun moves, the grass will grow'.

The first problem is to decide what it is that the 'some' believe. Do they believe that the consequent is necessary, which Aquinas denies? Or do they believe that it does not follow that the consequent is necessary, but for a reason which is not (in Aquinas's view) a good reason? The first is perhaps a more natural reading of the Latin, whereas the second has to take *Nec tamen sequitur* ('It does not follow') as part of the quotation, which feels awkward; on the other hand, *Sed hoc nihil est* ('But this is no use') does seem to refer to the whole preceding sentence, as it does in the two previous places in the reply where the same phrase occurs. However, the situation is complicated in this case by the fact that Aquinas *agrees* that in some cases the necessity of the consequent does not follow from the necessity of the antecedent; the reason given here by 'some people' is just the one he himself has already given in reply to the first objection. Necessary causes *can* have contingent effects. So the point of *Sed hoc nihil est* must be restricted to the *scope* rather than the truth of the reason given in the first sentence; true as far as it goes, it is not sufficient here. Aquinas holds that 'If the sun moves, the grass will grow' is simply false, since the grass might well not grow, for some contingent cause; and the reason why that explanation is 'no use' in the present case, I suggest, is because, unlike the sun example, 'If God <know> that p, then p' is *true*, and indeed necessarily true. So Aquinas then goes on to discuss the best interpretation of *this* conditional.

20 In this whole section on Ockham, I am much indebted to the pioneering work of Marilyn McCord Adams and Norman Kretzmann (1969) in which they provided a serviceable English translation, with notes and commentary, of Ockham's little treatise on God's foreknowledge, and to Marilyn McCord Adams's later full-length study (1987).

21 *Predestination, God's Foreknowledge, and Future Contingents* (hereafter PFC), I, reply 4, and II, reply 2, are two of many such instances.

22 He maintains that this is compatible with there being no change in God, since the change is in things, but not in the mind of God, in just the same way as God does not change in himself by creating, though things come to be outside God. This position is in some respects similar to Aquinas's suggestion that acts of will do not involve any passivity, even though

they do involve an alteration, and that although things come to be related to God, this relationship is nothing intrinsic to God. Ockham's view of God's knowledge would perhaps have been easier to defend were it the case that what God knows are states of affairs rather than propositions about those states of affairs. But Ockham is quite happy to say that God knows propositions, perhaps because of his general view that God is everlasting rather than timeless. Contrast Aquinas, who severely restricts the sense in which God can be said to know propositions, precisely because he insists that God is timeless.

23 Aristotle, *De Interpretatione*, I, 9. Aristotle's example of such a singular statement about the future is 'There will be a sea-battle tomorrow'. Whether Aristotle does hold the view which was commonly attributed to him is still a matter of dispute.

24 See Ockham's Commentary on Aristotle's text, and his own shorter summary of his interpretation of Aristotle, conveniently printed as Appendices II and III in Adams and Kretzmann (1969).

25 Of course they *need* not be contingent, and are not in those cases where a future state of affairs is already causally determined by a present or past cause, as for example that the sun will rise tomorrow.

26 I have taken a different example from Ockham's, and modified the text accordingly, so as not to introduce too many issues at once. Ockham's example concerns 'being predestined by God' rather than 'being taller than'.

27 Ockham frequently asks whether it is still true that Peter can choose not to sin; and if he can, Ockham takes it to follow that 'It was always true that Peter would sin' cannot be merely about the past. To be sure, Ockham expresses this criterion in terms of bringing it about that a statement never was true. But it is surely important to remember his very realist view about what makes statements true. To make a statement about the past never to have been true, some past state of affairs would have to be altered. It seems to me that Ockham took it as obvious that the flow of time is such that we cannot now causally affect those past states of affairs which we could at one time have brought about differently. The 'cannot' here is a matter of *de re* impossibility. The past, *qua* past, is necessarily beyond our causal control. That, of course, is not at all the same as saying that all events in the past took place by causal necessity, which Ockham would have thought they plainly did not. Nor, of course, would Ockham have denied that there are some past states of affairs which it was never in our power to have affected, since they were necessary all along – for example, the rising of the sun on one day last year. His concern is only with what we could once have causally affected, and can no longer causally affect simply because of the passage of time.

It seems to me that much of the discussion of this whole issue is bedevilled by two thoughts; one is that the accidental necessity of the past is primarily to do with *propositions* rather than states of affairs; and the second is that counter-factual dependence will provide an adequate account of causation. I do not believe that consideration of the relations between future and past counter-factual propositions is the right kind of approach to the causal inaccessibility of the past as Ockham would have regarded it.

28 Adams and Kretzmann (1969: 7–8) take it that Ockham's view is that the impossibility here is *logical*. While I would not deny this, I would suggest that some caution is required in interpreting the way in which medieval philosophers understood logical possibility. Aquinas, for instance, maintains that God cannot change the past, because to do so would involve a contradiction, in that it would be true both that Socrates was sitting, and (if the past is changed) false that Socrates was sitting. But, like Aristotle in his discussion of non-contradiction, Aquinas believes that logic here depends on the *de re* impossibility of things being in incompossible ways.

29 See note 22 for the sense in which Ockham intends 'immutable'.

30 Whether this should have been quite as difficult a problem for the medieval theologians as it was is another question. But they took it both on Biblical grounds and as a fixed datum of Christian tradition that God did predestine some, but not all, people to salvation. Yet they also believed themselves to be committed, on equally Biblical grounds, to holding that God wills the salvation of all. They therefore tried to distinguish between God's 'antecedent' will that all be saved; and his 'consequent' will to save those who repented of their sins.

31 It is tempting to say that Ockham must here have in mind God's necessary will that all should be saved, and his necessary will to make this possible for all. Cf. Adams and Kretzmann (1969: 17–20) and the texts from elsewhere in Ockham's writings which they cite. I am inclined to agree, though, that Ockham's replies here do not make use of the distinction between God's antecedent and his consequent will.

32 In PFC, II, 2 and 3, Ockham does try to distinguish, not always consistently, between two terms, *scire* and *cognoscere*, or between a broader and a narrower sense of *scire*. In the narrow sense, *scire* is 'to know'; whereas in a broader sense, equivalent to *cognoscere*, it merely means 'to have some intellectual grasp of'; so Adams and Kretzmann simply transliterate, 'cognize'. I do not think that Ockham manages to explain or justify any cognitive terminology at all in the places in which he uses 'cognize'.

33 I see nothing in Ockham's text to suggest that he ever considered any kind of 'backwards causation' in time to be possible. Mavrodes (1984) seems to me to do nothing more than show that the 'Nobody can change the past' is not a *logically* necessary truth. Plantinga's definition of 'accidentally necessary at *t*' (1986: 254) also suggests that there could be such a power; for if there were not, nothing about the past, including God's beliefs could be accidentally contingent.

34 Ockham does make the suggestion that God somehow in himself manages to see intuitively all things, past, present and future. But this still does not explain the source of his knowledge of what is contingent.

35 *Disp.*, 48, 9–13. In this section, I am very much indebted to the translation and commentary offered by Alfred J. Freddoso (1988) which

makes available a work of great philosophical interest which would otherwise be much less accessible. Though I am less convinced than Freddoso that Molina is right, this in no way lessens my admiration for his commentary.

36 Molina does not put matters in this way, using the <Verb> convention to express a non-tensed verb to make assertions which are true in eternity. But I think that what he says in 48, 18–21 is conveniently expressed as I have it in the text.

37 Note, though, that although I believe that this is Aquinas's position, I am not thereby saying that he believes $\Diamond p \to \Box \Diamond p$, nor that he believes $\Box p \to \Box \Box p$. These controversial statements are normally understood in terms of logical necessity/possibility, not *de re* necessity/possibility, and at least it is not entirely clear what the relations might be between a *de re* and a logical interpretation of the modal operators in this case. It may be that Aquinas did believe that what is *de re* possible or necessary is *de re* necessarily so, since in his view the ground of all such possibility and necessity just is the essence of God. On this, see the chapter on omnipotence.

38 He offers other proofs as well, but these are designed to show that his suggestion harmonises with, or even is required by, various statements in the Bible.

39 Cited in Marilyn McCord Adams (1987: II, 1028)

40 I do not mean to imply that other animals lack this characteristic. On the contrary, to the extent that they have reflective reactions to their environment, and especially to the extent that it is proper to speak of other animals as having language, I assume that my remarks will apply also to them.

41 For other modern attempts to express similar ideas, see William P. Alston (1986) and Linda Zagzebski (1991: 85–91).

42 Of course, as with any model, it needs to be used with caution, and not simply as a convenient way of obfuscating other, pressing, problems which need to be addressed.

43 It is not, however, entirely clear that he does intend to include these. Although at I, 14, 14 he says that God knows 'all possible *enuntiabilia*' he goes on to say that he does not know them as such (*per modum enuntiabilium*); and in I, 14, 15, while insisting that 'Christ was born', Christ is being born' and 'Christ will be born' make different statements despite the fact that they are all about the same event, he denies that God's knowledge of all three involves any change in God; what is involved is that God knows that any one of these is false at one time, and true at another. His view might simply be that since 'God knows all possible *enuntiabilia*' does not express God's manner of knowing, so neither could God use any of these *enuntiabilia* to make a true statement.

44 A similar conclusion is argued for by Zagzebski (1991: 52–6), in agreement with Alston (1986), and in disagreement with Sorabji (1980: 125–6), and Prior (1968). Kenny (1979: 39–40) notes that Pike (1970) offers a reply to Prior; but Kenny himself now believes that the issue can be bypassed, since he takes the notion of a timeless God to be

incoherent in the first place. In my view, Zagzebski's assessment of the debate is more accurate.

45 To avoid the clumsiness of frequent repetition of the phrases 'accidentally necessary', 'accidentally contingent', 'eternally accidentally necessary' and 'eternally accidentally contingent', I shall simply use 'necessary' and 'contingent' where it would not in the context be misleading to do so. I shall also speak of events and states of affairs as seems most natural in a given context, with the intention of referring to features of the world, rather than to the propositions or phrases by which those features might be picked out. I hope to do so without making any controversial presuppositions about how events and states of affairs are to be individuated, or how, indeed, events and states of affairs might be related to one another.

46 I am not here concerned with whether it is possible that there exist several temporally unrelated creations, each with its own unique cosmic history. I am arguing simply for the principle 'One cosmos, one actual history' as a necessary truth about the nature of time.

47 It makes no difference whether such an event truly is undetermined; it is enough for my present purposes to suppose that it very well might be, as at least many physicists assert that it is. If it is undetermined, then an adequate philosophy of religion must be able to take this on board.

IV Omnipotence

1 I am not here concerned with the particular problems connected with the belief that Jesus is God and could have done these things.

2 The reference is to *Metaphysics*, V, 12. Aristotle gives several different senses of *dunamis* ('capacity') and *dunaton* ('capable'); Aquinas regards them as falling into two main groups, the first being those dealt with from 1019a15–b15, the second from 1019b15–32. Aristotle's treatment is in some respects confused (see the commentary in Ackrill (1963) on the passage), but not in ways which would affect the main argument here.

3 See also the reply to the third objection, where what is possible or impossible is said to be so 'by nature', and hence as related to what can and cannot be *caused*.

4 Or, indeed, than Wittgenstein thought he could be. He once remarked that 'We believe it isn't possible to go to the moon; but there might be people who believe that it is possible, and that it sometimes happens. We say: these people don't know a lot that we know. And, let them be never so sure of their belief – they are wrong, and we know it. If we compare their system of knowledge with theirs, then theirs is evidently the poorer by far' (*On Certainty*, 286).

5 Contrast this claim with the claim that only those things are to count as actions which the agent *feels inclined* to do, which does not seem to be a tautology at all and which some philosophers – Kant, for instance – would deny was even true.

6 Perhaps Aristotle begins by assuming it as a dialectical starting-point, and then proceeds to try to prove it. Perhaps, too, it was easier for Aquinas to accept the conclusion as obvious, given his Christian belief that there is one final destiny of humans, which is the vision of God.

7 For the difficulties involved in this view, see the discussion of God's simplicity in Chapter II.

8 The reference is to I, 19, 3: on the hypothesis that God wills some end, he of necessity wills any means which are required to achieve that end.

9 In discussing all this, I have retained the tensed language which Aquinas uses, rather than complicate matters by rephrasing it all in untensed verbs. It should be remembered that Aquinas regards tensed language as natural for us to use, but as inadequate to describe God as he is.

10 One of the Christian creeds begins 'I believe in God, the Father almighty'. In common with the medieval tradition generally, Ockham took 'almighty' to mean 'omnipotent'. For a different, contemporary, understanding, see Geach (1977a).

11 This point should not be confused with a quite different issue. Ockham says that 'All humans are rational animals' is not a necessary truth, on the grounds that there need not exist any humans at all; this point is, in his view, quite distinct from the question I have raised in the text, which for Ockham is about the status of 'If anything is a human, then it is an animal'. As will be seen later, he *does* regard this as a necessary truth. The point turns on the fact that the medieval logicians usually took 'All X's are Y' to involve an existential commitment.

12 *Ord.*, I, 36, 1 = A1059. In addition to the citation from Ockham's works, I give in this chapter page references to Marilyn McCord Adams, *William Ockham*, where the text in question is cited in her translation.

13 Not that Ockham invented the razor, early versions of which are to be found in Aristotle, and in many of the earlier medieval philosophers.

14 For a good account, see Marilyn McCord Adams (1987: ch. 14).

15 E. M. Curley (1987: 341–69) suggests that Descartes's immediate target here might be the Jesuit theologian Francisco Suarez. Suarez explicitly rejects the ockhamist view that 'All men are mortal' is to be understood as true only if at least one man exists, and claims that it is true even if none does, and also claims that this would be true 'even if, *per. impossibile*, God did not exist'. Curley may well be right; I am suggesting in addition that Ockham, or another writer in the ockhamist tradition, might have provided Descartes with the kinds of arguments that he uses here.

16 It is not clear whether Ockham thinks that God can alter his ordered decisions once made, as Descartes clearly says he cannot.

17 He does not here explicitly say that God might bring this about: but in the second paragraph he does say, of mathematical truths, that '*even*' about these God might bring it about that Descartes's beliefs were false.

18 See First Set of Replies, AT VII,110–11, and especially Fourth Set of Replies, AT VII, 243–4, where 'efficient cause of an essence' is assimilated to 'formal cause'.

19 And perhaps also such truths as that like causes produce like effects, or that causes must contain at least as much power as their effects, which Ockham also appears to take to be beyond all possible questioning.

20 The use of 'indifferently' in the first sentence refers to that account of freedom which involves the power to choose otherwise, for which the traditional term was *libertas indifferentiae*, 'liberty of indifference'.

21 I therefore disagree with H. Frankfurt (1987: 6–57), and agree with E. M. Curley (1987: 569–97). Descartes's echoing of traditional terminology in my view clearly indicates that the eternal truths which are created and freely chosen are precisely those which concern creatures. Truths about God, and the nature of causality (which is also a feature of God himself), were never traditionally included within the scope of God's freedom. Descartes similarly repeats the traditional view that what God freely chooses to do, he does eternally and unchangeably. See Fifth Set of Replies, AT VII, 380.

22 Letter to Clerselier, Appendix to Fifth Set of Replies, AT IXA, 213. Hide Ishiguro, in her interesting paper (1988: 371–83) would argue for a sharper distinction between the truths of physics and those of mathematics than my account would suggest. I would incline rather to side with Daniel Garber's view (1986: 81–116) when he says that the contrast between physics, astronomy, medicine and all the other sciences on the one hand, and the certainty of geometry and arithmetic on the other, mentioned in the *First Meditation*, AT VII, 20, does not presuppose that these latter 'concern truths that are wholly independent of the real world. Rather they can be certain despite the fact that they don't give sufficient consideration to the question whether or not circles or triangles exist in nature' (p. 95). God has decided that the laws of geometry define the very essence of matter, and gives us minds which can grasp this more certainly than we can grasp the contingent facts about material existents.

23 Again, this would be disputed by Hide Ishiguro (1987: 375). She cites Descartes, *Principles of Philosophy*, I, 49, and also Second Set of Replies, AT VII, 152: 'All self-contradictoriness or impossibility resides solely in our thought, when we make the mistake of joining together mutually inconsistent ideas; it cannot occur in anything that is outside the intellect. For the very fact that something exists outside the intellect manifestly shows that it is not self-contradictory but possible.' I suggest instead that this passage is not concerned with whether these truths are *constituted* by the nature of our minds, but with the traditional problem about whether possibilities and impossibilities exist independently of actual things. Descartes's point is very like what Ockham held in denying that possibility and impossibility were real attributes of things, somehow separate from the things themselves. Here he says that possibilities just are existing things, and that impossibilities do not exist at all, other than in our minds. Neither remark suggests that possibilities and impossibilities are constituted by our minds. Descartes's parallel view, that necessity is imposed on our minds rather than simply deriving from our minds, is expressed in *Meditation*, V, AT VII, 67, and Sixth Set of Replies, AT VII, 436.

24 It should be noted, though, that unlike Ockham, Descartes denies that *any* accidents are absolutely distinct from substances, while Ockham thought that qualities were. See Sixth Set of Replies, AT VII, 434–5.

25 Quite what the last sentence in this passage is intended to say is less clear. Descartes might simply be being provocative, and asking what is so wrong with hatred. More plausibly, it might be that he thought God could test someone by giving such a command, much as he tested Abraham by commanding him to sacrifice his son. But that is simply speculation on my part.

26 He is criticising what he takes to be the views of the Anglican theologian Richard Price.

27 For an excellent discussion of divine command theories of ethics and a defence of such theories against their critics, see Quinn (1978).

28 It might be remarked that even everyday accounts of causal mechanisms fall short of a complete account of what causal activity consists in. That seems to me to be the truth in Hume's position.

29 I am not here concerned with the epistemological problem about how we would actually recognise such an occurrence as one caused by God, nor with what is perhaps basically a theological problem about why God should ever find it necessary to do such things. I would remark only that if the arguments I offer in the text are sound, then one cannot *a priori* argue that such occurrences are impossible. Individual cases would have to be examined on their merits.

V Goodness

1 Details of this view are to found in Aquinas, I, qq. 4–6.

2 For a contemporary attempt to situate the philosophical problem of evil in the context of Christian belief, see Marilyn McCord Adams (1986: 248–67).

3 I have also ignored considerations to do with cases where the agent is negligent, in the interests of reducing the complexity somewhat. It may be assumed that no adequate resolution of the Problem of Evil could turn on whether or not God acted negligently.

4 By 'cognitivism' I understand the meta-ethical view that holds that moral utterances can be true or false, as distinct from expressions of the speaker's attitudes or decisions. There are, of course, various different views about what truth in ethics might consist in, and on what the criteria for truth in ethics might be. In what follows, I make no particular assumptions on these last points.

5 Such a formulation would have to be along the following lines: 'In saying that a good God should not have created the world as it is, someone is expressing his or her own attitude to creation, and hence to God; or, is expressing a moral decision of policy about how one ought to live.' But it would have to be admitted that God's attitudes might well be different, or his decisions different, and that there is no logical constraint which God would violate if his attitudes or decisions were different, nor any reason to suppose that 'good' or 'right' would be applied to the same

things by God and anyone else. While the non-cognitivist might well point out that he or she cannot approve of a God who does such things, it seems to me more difficult to argue that it follows that the existence of such a God is thereby made less likely, which is what the problem of evil is normally taken to do.

6 Alvin Plantinga's definitions (1974a: 166) differ from mine, in that he defines as moral evil any state of affairs resulting from an immoral choice made by a human being. But he does not insist on the details. I think that my way of distinguishing the two is clearer.

7 Even here, Aquinas would have said that it is in itself a bad thing that something ceases to exist, since existence is a perfection (I, 48,2).

8 Any substance will have a nature, and hence a way of being organised, and hence some tendencies to behave in particular kinds of ways. Perhaps we think the organisation of organic substances is somehow 'tighter'?

9 Perhaps not in every case: we are inclined to see some deaths as a fitting end to a life.

10 Of course, one could refuse to take such a narrowly biological view of human nature. But short of postulating some version of life after death, it is hard to see why the more biological view of the human race is mistaken, even if it is true that we attach unique moral value to individuals so long as they remain alive. And if one does postulate a life after death, then the view that death is an evil, or evidence that something has gone wrong, is less easy to sustain.

11 It is important to keep the two issues separate. It might be the case that the universe is good overall and on balance, even if it is not the case that each individual case of evil can be seen as a good, or even as contributing to the overall goodness of the world.

12 As it is by Kant, for instance: see his *Doctrine of Virtue*, 441–2.

13 The conclusion does not, perhaps, follow *immediately*. It might still be countered that the consequences of bringing into being an evil world are outweighed by some good to be achieved. But it is not clear that there are such consequences; and even if they were, it would still on many ethical theories be wrong to achieve such an end by these means.

14 Aquinas argues that badness can have only an accidental cause (I, 49, 1). He uses 'accidental cause' in the Aristotelian sense. In the kind of case which is relevant here, an accidental cause explains the effect under one description of the effect, but not under another. Thus, to take Aristotle's example, digging explains the existence of a hole, but does not explain the uncovering of a buried treasure (*Metaphysics*, V, 30). Aristotle describes the digging as a cause *kata sumbebekos*, which is contrasted with being a cause *haplôs*; the first phrase can be translated as 'accidentally' or 'only with qualification'; the second is sometimes rendered 'baldly'; but I prefer either 'without qualification' or 'straight-forwardly'.

15 Though Aquinas followed Aristotle in thinking that even relations had some ontological status, since they fall under one of Aristotle's categories of being.

16 It is noteworthy that even in such an example he does not scruple to describe loss of existence as 'a kind of badness'. He does so because he holds that something is less than perfect if it can cease to exist: evidence of the extent to which he was influenced by versions of Platonism.

17 No doubt the person might also be said to have moved their trigger-finger; but in most circumstances we are quite happy to say that they shot the gun, rather than saying that the firing of the gun is a consequence of what they did. I do not intend here to beg any important questions about the precise way in which the act/consequence distinction is to be drawn, and hence make no assumptions about which form of Condition 3 might be applicable in any given case. For a discussion of some of the problems about action-descriptions in this kind of situation, see D'Arcy (1963: chs 1 and 2).

18 The notion of 'intend' is far from clear; it is sometimes used to mean 'desired as an end'; in which case the doctor does not intend to cause foreseen post-operative pain in his patient; but 'intend' is also used to mean 'include in one's honest description of what one is doing'; in which case, the doctor might be said to intend 'to cure the patient despite the fact that this will involve post-operative pain'; since the pain is something the doctor would have felt bound at least to take into account, it will be intended in the second sense, but, since it is not desired, it will not be intended in the first sense.

19 For a good discussion of some of these issues, see Duff (1982).

20 The precise interpretation of the many and various passages is a matter of considerable controversy I offer here only one possible way of taking them. And it must be recalled that for Aquinas a transcendental cause, such as God is, is not a cause in the same sense as a univocal cause. He believes that God causes a child, and the parents cause that child, in a different sense of 'cause'; and this is why he does not think of the situation as parallel to the two people rowing a single boat.

21 For a good account of accidental causation in Aristotle, see Cynthia A. Freeland (1991). She argues that Aristotle is a realist about causes and about explanations; but that the distinction between accidental and straightforward causes is made by us on the basis of our own interests and concerns.

22 The issue is not open and shut, however. For a succinct discussion, in the context of utilitarianism (which has often been interpreted as saying that it is obligatory to perform the action with the best consequences), see Sprigge (1988: 12–15). It is important to notice, however, that it is one thing to claim that a good agent need not do the best of various good actions available; it is quite another to claim that someone could equally well do an action which has some bad consequences, even if it is good overall, and one which has no such consequences. At least on some views, one has a duty to minimise evil which is prior to the duty to maximise good.

23 Some contemporary moralists have argued on similar grounds that one cannot have duties to oneself, since the very notion of duty or obligation

suggests that a duty or obligation is not something from which one can release oneself; whereas if a duty were a duty to oneself, one would be able to release oneself.

24 Though even in such a world there might still be states of affairs that Aquinas would have called 'bad'; for instance, if there were change in such a world, then some things would simply cease to be.

25 The phrase 'however finite' occurs because, in the context of the dialogue as a whole, Philo, who is speaking here, has been asked to comment on the view that the problem of evil might be solved were it supposed that God were not infinite. Hume would take it that his point is all the stronger if it is assumed that God is infinite.

26 For a good discussion of these and related issues, see Rowe (1986) and the references given there. Rowe accepts that there is a difference between arguments designed to show that the existence of God *cannot* be reconciled with the existence of evil, and arguments which aim to show that the existence of evil makes the existence of God less likely. He himself proposes an argument of this latter kind.

27 Hume is somewhat grudging in admitting even the consistency of such a position. Some writers have argued, to my mind mistakenly, that such a view is not even consistent. See, for instance, Mackie (1955: 200). For an attempt to refute the charge of sheer inconsistency, see Plantinga (1974a: ch. 5).

28 Hume offers specific reasons in suppose of *ii)* which will be considered below.

29 Even on the assumption that there is a God, it still remains opaque to us what God's standards for worlds might be. Christian religious tradition rather oscillates between admiration for God's creation, in which 'man alone is vile', and saying that the entire world is somehow 'fallen', and is unclear about what an ideal or restored world might be like. Some versions of the tradition hope merely for a better state for human beings; others speak of a 'new heaven and a new earth'.

30 I have abbreviated these passages, without, I hope, obscuring their force; but they need to be read in their full form to capture the wit and humour of Hume's writing here.

31 I am not, of course, assimilating free choice in every respect to the random decay of radioactive atoms. Free choices, as I see it, are made for reasons, not randomly. All I am saying is that they might also have the characteristic of being individually undetermined, but statistically predictable.

32 Alvin Plantinga (1974a: ch. 9; 1974b) has argued that God could not bring about a world in which all free choices were guaranteed to be morally good. While I do not dispute his conclusion, his reasons are to do with the impossibility of guaranteeing such an outcome. Plantinga believes that Molina's views are correct; I disagree, and hence my reasons for denying that God can ensure such an outcome have to do with his lack of knowledge of which world would contain that outcome.

Conclusion

1 A very useful collection of contemporary essays on these topics is to be found in Geivett and Sweetman (1992).
2 D.Z. Phillips, 'Faith, Skepticism, and Religious Understanding', in Geivett and Sweetman (1992): 81–91; Malcolm, 'The Groundlessness of Belief', *ibid.*: 92–103. Phillips, for example, writes (1992: 90),

> The assertion that to know God is to love Him is false if it is taken to imply that everyone who believes in God loves Him. What it stresses, quite correctly, is that there is no theoretical knowledge of God. As Malcolm said, 'belief in God involves some affective state or attitude'. . . . The man who construes religious belief as a theoretical affair distorts it.

Similarly, Malcolm says (1992: 100),

> I do not comprehend this notion of belief in *the existence of* God which is thought to be distinct from belief *in* God. It seems to me to be an artificial construction of philosophy, another illustration of the craving for justification.

3 Malcolm would not dispute this, indeed, would insist upon it:

> It is such a viewpoint or *Weltbild* (to use Wittgenstein's term), whether religious or scientific, that I am holding to be 'groundless.' I am not saying, of course, that these different ways of picturing the world do not have *causes*. Education, culture, family upbringing can foster a way of seeing the world. A personal disaster can destroy, or produce, religious belief. Religious people often think of their own belief as a result of God's intervention in their lives.
> My interest, however, is not in causes. What I am holding is that a religious viewpoint is not based on grounds or evidence, whether this is the Five Ways of Aquinas, the starry heavens, or whatever.

4 See McMullin (1984) for a defence of this position in science.

211

Bibliography

Ackrill, J.L. (1963) *Aristotle's Categories and De Interpretatione*, Oxford: Clarendon Press.

Adams, Marilyn McCord (1986) 'Redemptive Suffering', in Robert Audi and William Wainwright (eds) *Rationality, Religious Belief and Moral Commitment*, Ithaca, NY, and London: Cornell University Press.

—— (1987) *William Ockham*, Notre Dame, Ind.: University of Notre Dame Press.

Adams, Marilyn McCord and Kretzmann, N. (1969) *Ockham's 'Predestination, God's Foreknowledge and Future Contingents'*, New York: Meredith.

Adams, Robert M. (1971) 'Has it been Proved that All Existence is Contingent?', *American Philosophical Quarterly* 8: 284–91.

—— (1983) 'Divine Necessity', *Journal of Philosophy* 80: 741–52.

Alston, William P. (1985) 'Divine Foreknowledge and Human Freedom', *International Journal for Philosophy of Religion* 18: 19–32.

—— (1986) 'Does God Have Beliefs?', *Religious Studies* 22: 287–306.

Audi, Robert and Wainwright, William (eds) (1986) *Rationality, Religious Belief and Moral Commitment*, Ithaca, NY, and London: Cornell University Press.

Boyd, Richard (1985) 'Metaphor and Theory Change', in Andrew Ortony (ed.) (1985) *Metaphor and Thought*, Cambridge: Cambridge University Press.

Brody, Baruch A. (ed.) (1974) *Readings in Philosophy of Religion*, Englewood Cliffs, NY: Prentice-Hall.

Burns, Robert (1989) 'The Divine Simplicity', *Religious Studies* 25: 271–93.

Burrell, David B. (1979) *Aquinas, God, and Action*, London: Routledge & Kegan Paul.

—— (1984) 'God's Eternity', *Faith and Philosophy* 1: 389–406.

Catan, J.R. (ed.) (1980) *St Thomas Aquinas on the Existence of God* (collected papers of J. Owens), Albany: New York State University Press.

Cottingham, John (1976) *Descartes' Conversation with Burman*, Oxford: Clarendon Press.

Curley, E.M. (1987) 'Descartes on the Creation of the Eternal Truths', in Willis Doney (ed.) *Eternal Truths and the Cartesian Circle*, New York and London: Garland.

D'Arcy, Eric (1963) *Human Acts*, Oxford: Clarendon Press.

Descartes, René (1984) *The Philosophical Writings of Descartes* (trans. J. Cottingham *et al.*), Cambridge: Cambridge University Press.

Doney, Willis (ed.) (1987) *Eternal Truths and the Cartesian Circle*, New York and London: Garland.

Duff, Anthony (1982) 'Intention, Responsibility and Double Effect', *The Philosophical Quarterly* 32: 1–16.

Fischer, John Martin (ed.) (1989) *God, Foreknowledge and Freedom*, Stanford, Calif.: Stanford University Press.

Flint, Thomas (1983) 'The Problem of Divine Freedon', *American Philosophical Quarterly* 20: 255–64.

Frankfurt, H. (1987) 'Descartes on Eternal Truths', in Willis Doney (ed.) *Eternal Truths and the Cartesian Circle*, New York and London: Garland.

Freddoso, Alfred J. (ed.)(1983), *The Existence and Nature of God*, Notre Dame, Ind.: University of Notre Dame Press.

—— (1988) *Molina 'On Divine Foreknowledge'*, Ithaca, NY: Cornell University Press.

Freeland, Cynthia A. (1991) 'Accidental Causes and Real Explanations', in Lindsay Judson (ed.) *Aristotle's Physics: A Collection of Essays*, Oxford: Clarendon Press.

Garber, Daniel (1986) 'Semel in Vita; The Scientific Background to Descartes' Meditations', in Amélie Oksenberg Rorty (ed.) *Essays on Descartes' Meditations*, Berkeley: University of California Press.

Gaskin, G.C.A. (1978) *Hume's Philosophy of Religion*, London: Macmillan.

Geach, Peter (1969) *God and the Soul*, London: Routledge & Kegan Paul.

—— (1977a) *Providence and Evil*, Cambridge: Cambridge University Press.

—— (1977b) *God, Good and Evil*, Cambridge: Cambridge University Press.

—— (1987) 'Omnipotence', in Willis Doney (ed.) *Eternal Truths and the Cartesian Circle*, New York and London: Garland.

Geivett, R. Douglas and Sweetman, Brendan (eds) (1992) *Contemporary Perspectives on Religious Epistemology*, Oxford and New York: Oxford University Press.

Hamlyn, D.W. (1968) *Aristotle's* De Anima *Books II and III*, Oxford: Clarendon Press.

Hankey, W.J. (1987) *God in Himself: Aquinas's Doctrine of God*, Oxford: Oxford University Press.

Harré, R. and Madden, E.H. (1975) *Causal Powers: A Theory of Natural Necessity*, Oxford: Blackwell.

Hick, John (1990) 'An Irenaean Theodicy', in his *Classical and Contemporary Readings in the Philosophy of Religion*, Englewood Cliffs, NJ: Prentice-Hall.

Hughes, Christopher (1989) *On a Complex Theory of a Simple God*, Ithaca, NY: Cornell University Press.

Hughes, Gerard J. (ed.) (1987a) *The Philosophical Assessment of Theology*, London: Search Press.

—— (1987b) Aquinas and the Limits of Agnosticism', in Gerard J. Hughes (ed.) *The Philosophical Assessment of Theology*, London: Search Press.

Irwin, T.H. (1982) 'Aristotle's Concept of Signification', in Malcolm Schofield and Martha Nussbaum (eds) *Language and Logos*, Cambridge: Cambridge University Press.

Ishiguro, Hide (1987) 'The Status of Necessity and Impossibility in Descartes', in Willis Doney (ed.) *Eternal Truths and the Cartesian Circle*, New York and London: Garland.

Judson, Lindsay (ed.)(1991) *Aristotle's Physics: A Collection of Essays*, Oxford: Clarendon Press.

Kenny, Anthony (1979) *The God of the Philosophers*, Oxford: Clarendon Press.

Kirwan, Christopher (1971) *Aristotle's Metaphysics, IV–VI*, Oxford: Clarendon Press.

Kripke, Saul (1972) 'Naming and Necessity', in D. Davidson and G. Harman (eds) *The Semantics of Natural Language*, Dordrecht: Reidel.

Kuhn, T.S. (1985) 'Metaphor in Science', in Andrew Ortony (ed.) *Metaphor and Thought*, Cambridge: Cambridge University Press.

Leff, Gordon (1975) *William of Ockham*, Manchester: Manchester University Press.

Leplin, J. (ed.) (1984) *Scientific Realism*, Berkeley: University of California Press.

Lewis, David (1973) *Counterfactuals*, Cambridge: Cambridge University Press.

—— (1979) 'Counterfactual Dependence and Time's Arrow', *Nous* 13: 455–77.

Mackie, J.L. (1955) 'Evil and Omnipotence', *Mind* 64: 200.

McMullin, Ernan (1984), 'A Case for Scientific Realism', in J. Leplin (ed.) *Scientific Realism*, Berkeley: University of California Press.

Malcolm, Norman (1977) 'The Groundlessness of Belief', in Stuart C. Brown (ed.) *Reason and Religion*, Ithaca, NY: Cornell University Press, reprinted with additions in R. Douglas Geivett and Brendan Sweetman (eds) (1992) *Contemporary Perspectives on Religious Epistemology*, Oxford and New York: Oxford University Press.

Mann, W.E. (1975) 'The Divine Attributes', *American Philosophical Quarterly* 12: 151–9.

—— (1982) 'Divine Simplicity', *Religious Studies* 18: 451–71.

—— (1983) 'Simplicity and Immutability in God', *International Philosophical Quarterly* 23: 267–76.

Mavrodes, George (1984), 'Is the Past Unpreventable?', *Faith and Philosophy* 1: 131–46

Miller, Barry (1992) *From Existence to God*, London: Routledge.

Ortony, Andrew (ed.) (1985) *Metaphor and Thought*, Cambridge: Cambridge University Press.

Phillips, D.Z. (1970) *Faith and Philosophical Enquiry*, London: Routledge & Kegan Paul. Part reprinted as 'Faith, Skepticism, and Religious Understanding' in R. Douglas Geivett and Brendan Sweetman (eds) (1992) *Contemporary Perspectives on Religious Epistemology*, Oxford and New York: Oxford University Press.

Pike, Nelson (1965) 'Divine Omniscience and Voluntary Action', *Philosophical Review* 74: 27–46.

214

—— (1970) *God and Timelessness*, London: Routledge & Kegan Paul.

Plantinga, Alvin (1973) 'Which Worlds Could God have Created?', *Journal of Philosophy* 70: 539–55.

—— (1974a) *God, Freedom and Evil*, London: Harper & Row.

—— (1974b) *The Nature of Necessity*, Oxford: Clarendon Press.

—— (1980) *Does God Have a Nature?*, Milwaukee, Wis.: Marquette University Press.

—— (1981) 'Is Belief in God Properly Basic?', *Nous* 15; reprinted in R. Douglas Geivett and Brendan Sweetman (eds) (1992) *Contemporary Perspectives on Religious Epistemology*, Oxford and New York: Oxford University Press.

—— (1986) 'On Ockham's Way Out', *Faith and Philosophy* 3: 235–69.

—— (1990) *God and Other Minds*, Ithaca, NY: Cornell University Press.

Prior, Arthur (1968) 'The Formalities of Omniscience', in his *Papers on Time and Tense*, Oxford: Oxford University Press.

Pylyshyn, Z.W. (1985) 'Metaphorical Imprecision and the "Top Down" Research Strategy', in Andrew Ortony (ed.) *Metaphor and Thought*, Cambridge: Cambridge University Press.

Quine, W.V.O. (1961) *From a Logical Point of View*, Cambridge, Mass.: Harvard University Press.

Quinn, Philip L. (1978) *Divine Commands and Moral Requirements*, Oxford: Clarendon Press.

Rorty, Amélie Oksenberg (ed.) (1986) *Essays on Descartes' Meditations*, Berkeley: University of California Press.

Rowe, William L. (1986) 'The Empirical Argument from Evil', in Robert Audi and William Wainwright (eds) *Rationality, Religious Belief and Moral Commitment*, Ithaca, NY, and London: Cornell University Press.

Schofield, Malcolm and Nussbaum, Martha (eds) (1982) *Language and Logos*, Cambridge: Cambridge University Press.

Sorabji, Richard R. (1980) *Necessity, Cause and Blame*, Oxford: Clarendon Press.

Soskice, Janet Martin (1985) *Metaphor and Religious Language*, Oxford: Clarendon Press.

Sprigge, Timothy (1988) *The Rational Foundations of Ethics*, London: Routledge.

Stalnaker, Robert C. (1976) 'Possible Worlds', in *Nous* 13: 65–75.

Stump, E. and Kretzmann, N. (1985) 'Absolute Simplicity', *Faith and Philosophy* 2: 353–82.

Swinburne, Richard (1977) *The Coherence of Theism*, Oxford: Oxford University Press.

Wierenga, Edward R. (1989 *The Nature of God*, Ithaca, NY, and London: Cornell University Press.

Wilson, Margaret Dauler (1978) *Descartes*, London: Routledge & Kegan Paul.

Zagzebski, Linda Trinkaus (1991) *The Dilemma of Freedom and Foreknowledge*, Oxford: Oxford University Press.

Index

accident 38–40, 128, 191n8, 195n19, 207n24 (*see also* necessity, accidental; and cause, accidental)
accountability 165–71
Ackrill, J. L. 204
action, relevant description of 154–6
actuality 13, 26, 27–9
Adams, Marilyn McCord 126, 199n14, 200n20, 202nn31–2, 205n14, 207n2
Adams, Robert Merrihew 193n1
Alston, William P. 203n44
annihilation 31–3, 195n22
Anselm 14–17, 26, 192n16
Aquinas 19, 54–5, 60, 133, 173, 178, 184, 188, 193n6, 195n19, 198n14; 'accident' 7; applied to existence 11–13; accidental causation 163–71; cosmological arguments 35–7, 193n4, 195n22; definition 13–17; eternity 69–70, 75–7; 'evident', meaning of 14–17; evil 159–61; existence 11–17; first principles 185, 191n12, 205n6; free-will 117–19, 194nn9–10; future contingents 73–8, 199–200nn16–19; God as causal explanation 108–9, 193n3; identity of attributes in God 42–6, 115, 194n16, 195n17; immutability of God 88, 120, 193n8, 200n22; knowledge in

God 66–78, 83, 88–90, 92–3, 198n12, 199n18, 199n19;necessary being 16–17, 57; ontological argument, criticism of 14–17, 20; possibility 115–21, 145, 194n11
Aristotle 15, 16, 17, 19, 27, 44, 60, 118, 126, 191n11, 192n20, 193n3, 194n11; accidental causation 47, 166–8, 208n14, 209n21; categories 5–6, 13, 15, 127, 190n2, 195n21, 196n25, 208n15; first principles 15, 36, 118, 205n6; future contingents 79–80, 83, 111, 201n23; knowlege, nature of 65–6, 100–1, 197n1, 197n6; necessity/ possibility 115–16; Prime Mover 100–1, 152
Augustine 65, 67, 159–61, 178

blameworthiness 153–5, 161
Boethius 65, 69
Boyd, Richard 197n30
Burns, Robert 193n1
Burrell, David 194n13

Cambridge change 38–9, 193n6
cause 31, 191n12, 205n18, 206n19; accidental 47, 163–71, 208n14, 209n21; contingency, relation to 31–3, 49–50, 60–2; casual explanation 30, 46–8, 108–10, 149, 170, 182, 192nn20–1, 193n3; 'existence',

216

Index

'Reformed Epistemology' 185
Rowe, William L. 210n26

Scotus, Duns 65, 79, 91, 142–3
Sorabji, Richard 203n44
Sprigge, T. L. S. 209n22
statistical explanation 108–11, 182
Stump, Eleonore 193n1
Suarez, Francisco 205n15
sufficient reason 171, 192n21

time's arrow 82, 104, 117, 127,
148, 201n27

transfer of necessity argument
75–6, 106–7
truth conditions of counterfactuals
of freedom 111–12

unmoved mover 31

Wittgenstein, Ludwig 185, 204n4,
211n2

Zagzebski, Linda T. 196n29,
199n15, 203n44